Keeping the Rabble in Line

Noam Chomsky

Interviews
with David Barsamian

Common Courage Press   Monroe, Maine

Library of Congress Cataloging in Publication Data
Chomsky, Noam.
Keeping the rabble in line: interviews with David
Barsamian / Noam Chomsky.
p. cm.
ISBN 1-56751-033-7. --ISBN 1-56751032-9 (pbk.)
1. Chomsky, Noam--Political and social views. 2.
Chomsky, Noam--Interviews. I. Barsamian, David. II Title.
P85.C47A3 1994
410'.92--dc20   94-13221
CIP

Common Courage Press
P.O. Box 702
Monroe, ME 04951
207-525-0900 fax: 207-525-3068

Fourth Printing

Contents

Introduction   3

World Bank, Gatt and Free Trade   5

They Don't Even Know That They Don't Know   33

Race   61

Class   105

Media, Knowledge, and Objectivity   147

Crime and Gun Control   175

The Emerging Global Economic Order   203

Reflections on Democracy   241

Health Care   271

Index   309

Introduction

Keeping the Rabble in Line is a sequel as well as a departure from *Chronicles of Dissent*. In this latest collection Noam Chomsky focuses on economic and trade issues and the emerging global economic order. While an increasingly spectacle-driven media wine and dine us on a menu of O.J. Simpson, Tonya Harding, or whatever the current diversion is, major shifts in the international scene are occurring. As Chomsky points out, nation-states are becoming increasingly challenged by the power and reach of transnational corporations. The latter may be the defining feature of the coming era. Our response will be crucial. Again and again in these interviews and elsewhere Chomsky suggests the need to organize and become active. Passive consumption of information is not enough. *Rabble* will hopefully get people moving in a practical direction, be it direct action protests, getting involved with or establishing a community radio station, producing and distributing a video, starting a bookstore, publishing a newsletter or having discussions in your living room with a few friends.

I think Chomsky's contribution lies in the fact that he constantly stresses not just the need to be informed and act but that we are all capable of doing so. His own commitment, involvement and accessibility is a concrete example. He is a cartographer. He provides a detailed road map to assist in figuring out where things are and in charting out routes. And in another sense he is a memory bank. So while the punditocracy engineer history

3

Chomsky is there as a constant corrective to remind us about the concerted U.S. effort to destroy popular organizations in post-war Europe or the monstrous crimes of the Indochina War or the real accomplishments of the Nixons, Kissingers, Clintons and other luminaries who direct the global pillage.

The interviews in this collection were recorded in Chomsky's office at MIT or by phone. "Crime and Gun Control" was a live radio call-in on KGNU in Boulder. Titles reflect the core theme of the interviews but each discussion covers several topics. Many people from all over ask me to ask him certain questions. It would be impossible to acknowledge everyone's contribution but Carlos Otero in particular has been most helpful with his criticisms, suggestions and encouragement. My thanks to Sandy Adler for her transcriptions. Much appreciation to Noam Chomsky for his time and effort.

—David Barsamian
August 1, 1994

The World Bank, GATT and Free Trade

April 20, 1992

DB *In 1944 at the Bretton Woods conference in New Hampshire the World Bank and the International Monetary Fund (IMF) were both created. What function do these two major financial entities play?*

Their early role was in helping to carry through the reconstruction of the state capitalist industrial societies that had been wrecked by the Second World War. After that they shifted to what is called "development," which is often a form of controlled underdevelopment in the Third World, which means designing and supporting particular kinds of programs for the Third World. At this point we move into controversy. Their effect, and you can argue about their intention, is overwhelmingly to integrate the South, the old colonial areas, into the global society dominated by concentrated sectors of wealth within the North, the rich society.

DB *You know that old song, "Where Have All The Flowers Gone"? Well, where have all the billions gone?*

5

KEEPING THE RABBLE IN LINE

The World Bank has lent tens of billions of dollars. Who lent what to whom exactly? What did it do there?

You can't answer that simply. In the advanced industrial societies [that money] helped carry out a reconstruction from postwar damage. In the Third World [lending has] had mixed effects. It's had effects in changing the nature of agriculture, developing infrastructure, steering projects towards particular areas and away from other areas. It's been part of the long process of trying to undercut import substitution and move toward export oriented agriculture. By and large [World Bank loans have] been a subsidiary to the policies of those who control it. The United States has an overwhelming role in the financial institution because of its wealth and power. And the United States and its immediate allies have designed programs of what they called development throughout the world. The money may have gone into anything from dams to agro-export producers to occasionally some peasant project.

DB *The International Monetary Fund has been vilified in the Third World for the draconian measures that it has imposed on those developing countries.*

Take a Latin American country today. There is a huge debt crisis. Remember that the Bretton Woods system basically broke down in the early 1970s. The Bretton Woods system involved regulation of currencies, convertibility of the dollar for gold, all sorts of other rules which essentially made the United States an international banker. By 1970 or so the U.S. could no longer sustain that. It was very advantageous to the United States in the 1950s and 1960s. It allowed enormous overseas investment by American corporations. But by 1970 the U.S. was unable to sustain [the role of international banker]. President Nixon dismantled the system in 1971. That led to an enormous amount of unregulated currency floating around in international channels. The world was awash with unregulated capital, particularly after the rise in the oil prices. Bankers wanted to lend that capital, and they did. They lent it primarily to Third World countries, which means to elite elements. For example, Latin American dictatorships would go on huge borrowing binges. The results were praised in the West as "economic miracles," like the Brazilian "miracle" under the generals which left that country saddled with huge indebtedness. When the 1980s came along, U.S. interest rates went up and started pulling money toward the United States and increasing interest payments on the debt. The Latin American economies started going into free fall. Capital flowed out of them at a rapid rate. They were unable to control their own internal wealthy classes. The capital export from Latin America may not have been at the level of the debt, but it probably wasn't very far below it. There was a flow of hundreds of billions of dollars from south to north, partly debt service, which far outweighs new aid by the late 1980s—payment of interest on the debt, and so on, and other forms of capital flight. By now, deeply impoverished African countries are even exporting capital to the international lending institutions.

The net effect of this is what some people jokingly call a program in which the poor in the rich countries pay the rich in the poor countries. That's approximately the way it comes out. Then the IMF comes along, run by the wealthy countries, which have certain rules for the weak. They are that if you have a high level of inflation and the currency isn't stable and various other economic indicators aren't satisfied, then you impose extreme forms of austerity: balance the budget, cut back services, control the currency, etc. That's neoliberal free market economics. That's typically disastrous for the general mass of the population. That's why the rich countries themselves will never accept those rules unless they're forced to. For example, there was a time in the late 1970s when Britain was forced to adopt certain IMF rules because of its weakness. But no country rich or powerful enough would ever do it, like the U.S., for example, which has incredible debt but doesn't accept IMF "suggestions". We're too powerful to follow those rules. Third World countries, which are much weaker, especially those which are under the control of Western-oriented elites anyway, who often benefit by it, do follow the rules and there's disaster for the population. That's why you get vilification. The same thing is happening in Eastern Europe now. The whole neoliberal free market story is basically designed for the benefit of the people who are going to win the game. Nobody else follows those rules. The West doesn't follow them either when it's not going to win. For example, the World Bank estimates that right now protectionist measures imposed by the rich countries cost the Third World more than twice as much as total aid going from the North to the South—and that "aid" is mostly a disguised form of export promotion.

World Bank, Free Trade, GATT

DB *To whom are the World Bank and the IMF accountable?*

To the people who put the money in, which means a bunch of rich countries, primarily the United States, which is the dominant element there. It's mainly funded by the wealthy states, and the U.S. has the largest vote, so that's who they're beholden to.

DB *Where does the General Agreement on Tariffs and Trade, GATT, fit into this economic picture? One commentator has called it the "economic teeth of the new world order."*

GATT is the international trading system, also set up in the 1940s. It's in the news now because for the last several years the Uruguay Round of GATT negotiations has been going on with an effort to achieve some new form of freeing up international trade. Freeing up international trade in itself, in a general sense, is not a bad thing. It's often a good thing. The point is, nobody goes into that game, if they have the power, without ample protection for their own internal needs. So for example every one of the Western powers, including the United States, is entering the GATT negotiations with a certain agenda, a mixture of liberalization and protectionism geared to the particular strengths and weaknesses of that economy. When we speak of "that economy" we mean the people in the dominant positions in it. So the European Community wants high level protection for the aerospace industry and agricultural production. The United States has a mixture of poli-

9

cies. It's calling for liberalization and free trade in many areas. On the other hand, it's also calling for enhanced protection in areas where the U.S. is strong. Take so-called services like banking. The U.S. is calling for a liberalization of services in the Third World, which would have the instantaneous effect of swamping and overwhelming all Third World banks and financial institutions by western ones, since they're so much richer and more powerful. That would eliminate the possibility of any national industrial development programs within the Third World. That's the kind of liberalization that the U.S. is in favor of. It means that Third World economies would be managed by western banks and those who run them and the governments that are tied to them.

On the other hand, the U.S. is calling for more protection in other areas, particularly intellectual property rights, which includes anything from pop music to cinema to software to patents. Right now the U.S. is racing ahead in patenting what may turn out to be parts of genes. The idea is to patent the genes of corn, or for that matter humans, so that future biotechnology, which will involve various kinds of genetic engineering, will be in the hands of mainly U.S. private firms. They will control that field, and they want to make sure it's protected. So they want long patent rights and so on. That means that drugs, software, new technology, new agricultural forms, any form of biotechnology that may involve health will be in the hands of Merck Corporation and others like them who will make tens of billions of dollars in profits. It means that India, which could duplicate a lot of this much cheaper, duplicate Merck drugs at a fraction of the cost, will not be permitted to do it. The U.S. also demands product rather than only process patents, to insure, say, that India's pharmaceutical industry doesn't invent a cheaper way to produce some drug—a barrier to efficiency and innovation, but a boon for profits. That's understandable on the part of the rich. They want to control the future, naturally, and that means control technology. The biotechnology aspect, the patenting of genes, has been causing an international furor in the scientific world. It can have a huge impact in the future. One shouldn't minimize it.

The U.S. (like others) also insists on a high level of protection for U.S. shipping. Shipping between U.S. ports has to be in U.S. ships. If Alaskan oil comes down to California, it has to be in U.S. ships. The U.S. insists that anything involving U.S. goods be done to a very high percentage in U.S. ships, which benefits the U.S. maritime industry.

Similarly, "defense" expenditures are not considered subsidies under GATT rules. That's enormously important for the U.S., which spends more on its military system than the rest of the world combined, as has always used that as a cover for massive public subsidy to high-tech industry. The point is that there is a mixture of protectionism and liberalization geared to the interests of those who are designing the policies, which are the powerful economic forces within the state in question. That's not a great surprise, after all, but that's what GATT is all about, and that's what the negotiations are about.

If the current GATT programs succeed, it's clear that they're tending towards a world government ruled by a club of rich men who meet in their organizations, like the G-7 meetings, the meetings of the seven richest industrial countries, which have their own institutions, like the IMF and the World Bank, which have a network of arrangements established in GATT and which administer a system of what's sometimes been called "corporate mercantilism." Remember that although this is called "liberalization" and "free trade," there's a tremendous amount of managed trade internal to it. So huge corporations which are often more powerful than many states carry out controlled, managed trade internally. This means trade across borders, too, because they're internationalized. They do planning of investments, of production, of commercial interactions, manipulation of prices, and so on, and they naturally manage it for their own interests. Corporate mercantilism is fine. It's governments that are not allowed to get into the game. The rich western powers don't have any objection at all to managed trade. They just don't want it to be done by governments, because governments have a dangerous feature that corporations don't have: governments may to some extent fall under the influence of popular forces, usually to a limited extent. But to some extent there's always that fear. There's no such fear in corporations. They are immune from any form of public control or even surveillance. Therefore they are much more acceptable management agents for this mercantilist system being designed globally in the interests of the rich. GATT plays its role in this.

DB *You mentioned the powerful economic forces. Increasingly those forces transcend frontiers. There has been a massive internationalization of capital and finance over the last few years. What are the implica-*

tions of that?

First of all, there's nothing novel about it. Back in the 1930s there were, for example, notorious interconnections between, say, I.G. Farben in Germany and Du Pont. In fact, big U.S. corporations were essentially producing for the German war machine right up until the war and some even claim afterwards in various devious ways. But there was a big change after the Second World War. There was a big upsurge in the creation of multinational firms, even beyond the traditional multinationals, for example, the energy corporations, which always were highly internationalized. But it extended much beyond. The Marshall Plan, for example, gave a big shot in the arm to the internationalization of capital. It would designate some project in Belgium where you could build a steel complex. It would then encourage bids from American corporations, which would naturally win the bidding most of the time. Marshall Plan funds were then used, as intended, to underlie the expansion of U.S. investment through the rich areas, primarily in Europe. That led to an explosion of international corporations. U.S. foreign investment exploded in the 1950s and 1960s. Not long after came European international capital. Britain had always been substantially involved in the internationalization of capital. In recent years Japan has joined the game and done plenty of foreign investing. This has increased through the 1980s.

There are a lot of reasons for this in the recent period. One is the one I mentioned before, the break-down of the Bretton Woods system, which led to an enormous amount of unregulated internationalized wealth. Another was a revolution in telecommunications, which makes it extremely easy to control international operations in which production is done in one place and the financing comes from somewhere else and you shift the dollars around. That means you can have executive offices in a skyscraper in New York and production facilities in Papua, New Guinea and fake banks in the Cayman Islands which may be nothing more than a fax machine set up to evade regulation. You can transfer funds around. You can control and manage importing and exporting within the corporate empire through management decisions. It can be scattered all over the world, with branch offices in Zurich. That's had a lot of effect. Everyone knows that the U.S. share in international trade has been declining in the last ten years. But in fact if you look at the share in international trade of U.S.-based corporations, it has not been declining. It may have been either stable or slightly increasing. Everyone knows the U.S. is supposed to have a big trade deficit. On the other hand, if you take into account the operations of overseas producers that are part of U.S.-based corporations, and imports into the United States that are actually transfers from U.S. corporations operating abroad to the same U.S. corporations operating internally, if they import parts for their own production, it probably levels out the trade deficit, maybe even gives the U.S. a trade surplus.

The functioning institutions in the world system are increasingly corporate empires. I say "increasingly" because national states, the rich states, at least, retain substantial importance. They are instruments of integrated corporate systems. And also increasing because it's an old phenomenon. It goes back to the origins of capitalism. It is true that it has grown by leaps and bounds in recent years.

DB *To continue with GATT: The Environmental News Network has said that GATT will "open borders for businesses seeking lower labor costs and less rigorous environmental regulation, thus blackmailing U.S workers to accept deteriorating working conditions and lower wages or lose their jobs." Do you think that's a fair assessment?*

It's not even controversial. Of course it will have that effect. It's already having that effect. Take the free-trade agreement with Canada. It's actually working both ways. Canada has just objected to U.S. environmental regulations on use of asbestos, claiming that that's interference with free trade. Canada is an asbestos exporter, and they want the barriers lowered. Perhaps they've already won on that, meaning that U.S. environmental regulations on asbestos will have to decline. Sooner or later the U.S. is probably going to object to the Canadian Health Service as an interference with free trade because it means that Canadian-based corporations are freed from the burden of paying parts of health costs that U.S. corporations have to bear because of the grotesquely incompetent and highly bureaucratized health system. Threats from U.S. insurance companies were enough to cause Ontario to drop plans for a provincial auto insurance program that would have reduced costs, but cut out the highly inefficient private corporations—an interference with free trade, they claimed, and won. Canada has lost several hun-

15

dred thousand jobs. There are various estimates, but none are less than a quarter of a million jobs, to the United States, manufacturing and similar type labor, because Canadian corporations would much prefer to produce in the southeastern United States, where the government enforces what are called "right-to-work laws," which means state policy coerces labor to ensure that there will be no unionization. As a result, working conditions are far inferior. Wages are less. Naturally, corporations will move to such places. Even the threat to move serves to discipline labor. In general, the effect of the free-trade agreements will be to move to the lowest common denominator with regard to wages, and environmental protection.

DB *So do you think that under the rubric of free trade that the Canadian health care system would be seen as an unfair advantage that Canadians have?*

It hasn't yet happened, but I would expect it. I expect that American corporations sooner or later may decide that it would be a good idea to undermine the Canadian Health Service by an argument of that sort. There are a lot of calculations involved in that. One problem is that production is so internationalized that Canadian corporations are often U.S. corporations.

DB *What did you make of the spectacle of the President of the United States going to Japan with about a score of CEOs of major U.S. corporations and essentially demanding a kind of "international affirmative action," as Jesse Jackson has called it?*

16

First of all, remember that the propaganda phrase was, "I'm going for jobs, jobs, jobs." How much Bush cares about jobs you can see by looking at U.S. policy towards American workers. So while he's talking about jobs, jobs, jobs, the U.S. government is trying to set up the basis for *maquiladora* industries in Central America to take away American jobs. The phrase means "profits, profits, profits." That's what he was there for. It was kind of stupid for the CEOs to come along. It left the United States as an object of ridicule. But whether they were along or not, that's what the trip was for. Everybody should have known that. The trip was to coerce Japan into accepting managed trade, meaning what's called here "fair-trade practices," which means mercantilist arrangements between powerful states to violate free-trade arrangements and ensure that their own powerful economic forces get benefits. There's nothing novel about that. The Reagan administration combined free-trade bombast with a highly protectionist record. Take control over imports. Various kinds of control over imports amount to duties. They practically doubled, from about twelve percent to about twenty-three percent, during the Reagan years, through what are sometimes called "voluntary arrangements," meaning "you do what we say or we'll close off your market." The latest effort to get Japan to buy American auto parts is just another part of the state-managed trade system that the rich always insist upon while of course beating their breasts about free trade when you can use it as a weapon against someone else.

DB *Is Japan powerful enough to resist?*

17

That's an interesting question. No one really has answers to these questions. The domestic and international economies are only very dimly understood by anyone. So anything we say will sound a lot more confident than it ought to be. My own suspicion has always been that the strength of the Japanese economy has been overestimated, that it's much flimsier than is alleged. For objective reasons. Japan is a resource-poor country, highly dependent upon export for survival. In particular it depends very heavily on the U.S. market. It's expanding into Asian markets, but that doesn't compare with the U.S. market. The U.S. remains the richest country in the world. Also, it's dependent, unlike the United States—which has plenty of internal resources and enough military power to control other sources of raw materials—on trade for resources and raw materials as well. Also, the Japanese, when you look at the numbers, look very rich. But if you look at the way people live, they don't look very rich. People are crammed into tiny apartments. They live a highly coerced and submissive existence. If you develop any reasonable quality of life standards, Japan would not rank very high by many measures, although it ranks quite high in others, like health, for example. So it's a mixed story. It think there are serious weaknesses in that economy. I'm not all that surprised by the current recession and financial crisis in Japan. They have such resources and capital. They'll doubtless pull out of this one.

DB *Along with the Arab oil producing states and some portions of Europe, Japan seems to be the only other area where there is excess capital formation for* *investment.*

There is a lot of excess capital, but it's not clear what it's going to look like after this crisis has passed. A lot of it was based on very chancy investments and a huge bubble in real estate which was highly inflated. But it's still true. They have plenty of excess capital. In my opinion, German-based Europe is a more likely prospect for a world economic leader in the long term.

DB *You just said "crisis," which reminds me of something I've been hearing as long as I can remember, and I am certain you have as well, the "current crisis in capitalism." It seems to be an ongoing story. Is this particular crisis any different?*

There has been a global stagnation for about twenty years now. The growth rates and the rise in productivity of the 1950s and 1960s are things of the past. It leveled off around the early 1970s. Things like the breakdown of the Bretton Woods system were symptomatic. Since then there has been a kind of stagnation. It's not level across the globe. For example, for Africa it's been a catastrophe. For Latin America it's been a catastrophe. In fact, for most of the domains of the capitalist world it has been absolutely catastrophic, including internally. Large parts of American and British society have suffered severely, too. On the other hand, other sectors have done quite well. The so-called newly industrializing countries of East Asia, the ones in the Japanese orbit, like South Korea and Taiwan, didn't succumb in the 1980s to the international crisis of capitalism as Latin America did. Up until then their growth rates had been pretty comparable. But they separated sharply in the 1980s, with the East Asian ones doing much better. Again, nobody really knows the reasons for this, but one factor appears to have been that, unlike Latin America, the East Asian countries don't make any pretense of following free-market rules. Capital flight was a huge problem in Latin America. The wealthy just sent their capital elsewhere, or else it was just payment on debt. East Asian countries didn't do that. South Korea has no capital flight problem because the state is powerful enough not only to control labor, which is the norm, but also to control capital. You can get the death penalty for capital flight. Other forms of state-corporate managed industrial and financial development did protect them from this global crisis of capitalism. Within the rich countries there were various reactions. The United States and Britain are probably the ones that suffered most from it, thanks to Reaganite and Thatcherite measures.

Whether you call this a crisis or not, it's not a well enough defined term so you can answer the question. For a very large part, probably a considerable majority, of the American work force, real wages have either stagnated or maybe even declined for about a twenty-year period.

DB *The decline of major U.S. industries, such as auto, textiles, electronics, etc., is well documented. It's not even a matter of discussion. The fastest area of growth in jobs in the U.S. is in such areas as janitors, waiters, truck drivers.*

Actually, the fastest growing white collar profession is security guard.

DB *What does that tell you?*

It means that there is a large superfluous population that has to be controlled and a large number of rich people who have to be protected from them.

DB *Is there any economic strategy or planning to create real jobs with decent wages?*

For U.S. workers? Why should there be?

DB *It would seem that elites would want to protect their position.*

But their position does not rely primarily on U.S. labor. They do want to have a domestic work force for services, but production is a different matter.

DB *But if there's major economic dislocation in this country, unrest would surely result and their position of power and strength would be threatened.*

That depends on whether you can keep the public under control. For example, the *Washington Post* reported on a study about black males in Washington, D.C.

DB *Forty-six percent of all black males between 18 and 35 are incarcerated in the District of Columbia.*

21

I think they say at any particular moment about seventy percent of them are somehow within the control of the justice system, on probation, etc. That's a way of keeping people from bothering us: keep them in jail. If they're not useful for wealth production they have to be controlled somehow. But it's not clear that that's a threat to the elites in the Washington area. Or take New York City, which is an absolute disaster. But you can walk around wealthy sectors of downtown Manhattan that look very glitzy and cheery.

DB *Prison construction in the U.S. is one of the fastest growing industries.*

Yes. The U.S. has by far the highest per capita prison population in the world. Even things like the drug epidemic are functional in a way. I'm not claiming that the government starts it for this purpose. Things go on because they have certain functions for elite groups that set policy. One effect of the so-called "drug war," which has very little to do with controlling drugs and a lot to do with controlling people, has been to create a huge explosion in the prison population. Anybody who works with prisons will tell you that a very substantial part of the prison population is people who are in there for possession, not for harming anyone. That's a technique of control. Whether it's an economical technique of control you could argue. Look how much it costs to control people by putting them in prison and having them on drugs and therefore not bothering you or having them shooting and robbing each other in inner cities. How that compares with other techniques of social control would be a hard question to answer.

However, to go back to your original question. If you were a wealthy professional or corporate executive living in Westchester County, there are certain things you want. You want a comfortable environment, a golf course, to be able to go to the theater in downtown Manhattan. You want your executive offices to be in good shape. You want fancy restaurants around. You want to be able to leave your limousine somewhere without having it broken into. You want good schools for your children. You want a powerful army to protect your interests. You want a skilled work force insofar as you need it. But much of what happens in this country is of no interest to you. If most of the country goes down the tube, that's no big problem.

DB *I love your comment " 'Ultimately' is a notion that does not occur in capitalist planning." Why not?*

First of all, there are no capitalist systems. If there were a capitalist system it couldn't survive for more than a couple of weeks. The only capitalist systems are the ones that are imposed on Third World countries for the purpose of weakening them so that they'll collapse and be taken over by the rich. But there are systems that are more or less capitalist. The more capitalist they are, that is, the more competitive, and less planned and integrated, the more they will tend towards short-term gains. That's inherent in the system. To the extent that a system is competitive and unplanned, those participating in it will be devoting their resources, both intellectual and capital, to short-term gain, short-term profit, short-term increase in market share. The reasons for that are pretty straightforward. Let's imagine that there are three car companies: Ford, General Motors, and Chrysler. Let's say they're really competitive. Then suppose that General Motors decided to put its resources into dealing with problems of global pollution or even trying to produce better cars ten years from now that would be better than those of Ford and Chrysler. At the same time its competitors Ford and Chrysler would be putting their resources into increasing profits and market share tomorrow, next month, next year. During that period, General Motors would be out of luck. They wouldn't have the capital and the profits to carry out their plans. That's exactly why in countries like Japan in the 1950s, the ministry that directed and organized the Japanese economy, together with the big corporate conglomerates, explicitly and openly decided to abandon free-market illusions and to carry out national industrial planning aimed at Japanese development in "strategic sectors" with high long-term potential. In newly developing industries, the industries of the future, the startup costs can be quite considerable. Profit doesn't come for some time. In a competitive, more capitalist society, you're out of luck. But in a more managed society you can deal with that. There are many well-known free-market inadequacies that typically lead capitalist entrepreneurs to call upon the state to intervene for their benefit. In Japan this led to a conscious decision to carry out substantial, organized, planned interference with the market mechanism so that the economy could prosper. Questions of pollution are perfect examples. If one company tries to devote resources to effects on the environment, they will simply be undercut by other companies which are not doing it. Therefore they will not be in a position to compete in the market. These are matters which are inherent in our capitalist systems. There were experiments with *laissez faire* in Britain in the nineteenth century, when people actually took their own rhetoric seriously. But they pretty quickly called it off. It's too destructive.

DB *So you're saying that this class of managers is impervious to the bridges literally collapsing on the homeless and tunnels bursting under the city of Chicago?*

Not because they're bad people, but because if they stopped being impervious to it they wouldn't be managers any more. Suppose that the CEO of some big corporation decides he's going to be a nice guy and devote his resources from that corporation to the homeless people under the bridges that are falling down or to global pollution.

DB *He's out of a job.*

He's out of a job. That's inherent in the system. These are institutional facts. If you want to watch this at its more extreme limits, you should take a look at the World Bank plans on pollution. These recently surfaced. One of my favorite issues of the *New York Times* must have been February 7, back in the business section. There was a report called something like "Can Capitalism Save the Ozone Layer?" Ozone being a metaphor for saving the environment. The question was whether capitalism could save the environment. That was a story by their financial correspondent Sylvia Nasser. The World Bank had come out with a consensus report for the rich countries on a position to take at the Rio conference in June on the global environment. It was written by Lawrence Summers, the chief liberal economist from Harvard. The idea is that the rich countries should take the position, led by the World Bank, that the problem of pollution is that the poor countries, the Third World, don't follow rational policies. "Rational" means market policies. Many of them are resource and raw material producers, energy producers, and they sometimes try to use their own resources for their own development. That's irrational. That means that they're using resources for themselves, often at below market rates, when there are more efficient producers in the West who would use those resources more efficiently. That's interference with the market. Also, these Third World countries often introduce some measures to protect their own population from total devastation and starvation, and that's an interference with the market. It's an interference with rational market policies. The effect of this Third World irrationality is to increase production in places where it shouldn't be taking place, to increase development in places where it shouldn't be going on, and that causes pollution. So if we could only convince those Third World countries to behave rationally, that is, to give all their resources to us and stop protecting their own populations, that would reduce the pollution problem.

This document was produced with a straight face. It happened that on the same day on the same page of the *New York Times* there was a little article, unrelated, about a World Bank memo, an internal memo, that had leaked. It had been published by the London *Economist*, a right-wing British *Wall Street Journal*, but weekly. It was written by the same Lawrence Summers. The *Times* had a brief, slightly apologetic summary of it, including an interview with Summers in which he claimed it was intended to be sarcastic. The World Bank memo added to what I have just said about Third World irrationality. It said that any kind of production is going to involve pollution. So what you have to do is to do it as rationally as possible, meaning with minimal cost. So suppose we have a chemical factory producing carcinogenic gases that are going into the environment. If we put that factory in Los Angeles, we can calculate the number of people who will die of cancer in the next forty years. We can even calculate the value of their lives in terms of income or whatever. Suppose we put that factory in Sao Paulo or some even poorer area. Many fewer people will die of cancer because they'll die anyway of something else, and besides, their lives aren't worth as much by any rational measure. So it makes sense to move all the polluting industries to places where poor people die, not where rich people die. That's on simple economic grounds.

Combine that with the other document. What it says is that the Third World should stop producing and protecting its own population because that's irrational. We should send our polluting industries to them because that is rational. Summers in this memo points out that you might have counterarguments to this based on human rights and the right of people to a certain quality of life. But he points out that if we allowed those arguments to enter into our calculations, then just about everything the World

Bank does would be undermined. That's quite accurate. That's supposed to be a *reductio ad absurdum*. Obviously we can't undermine everything the World Bank does, so obviously we can't allow such considerations to enter. We consider only economic rationality, of course geared to the interests of the World Bank. That's what you do with pollution. Try to convince the Third World to stop producing and to stop protecting their own population and to accept our pollution. It's all perfectly explicable on rational economic grounds. Any graduate student in economics can prove it to you.

DB *Apropos of this blindness of the planners: you have a fantasy ...*

It's not blindness. I think it's very reasonable on their part.

DB *Within their framework.*

Yes.

DB *You tell of a fantasy that involves the* Wall Street Journal *and the greenhouse effect.*

Someone asked me once and I simply said that if I had the talent, which I don't, I would write a short story about the *Wall Street Journal*. I suppose their offices are on the seventeenth floor of some New York skyscraper. They're sitting there in that office putting out an issue of the *Wall Street Journal* claiming once again that the greenhouse effect is just a fraud invented by left fanatics. As the issue goes to press the water level would have risen to that point and you could hear them gurgling as they start the printer running. That's about what it's like.

DB *Let's talk about organized labor unions in the United States. Only fifteen or sixteen percent of the total U.S. work force is now unionized, far below, perhaps by half or even more, what it was decades ago. This is the era of givebacks, benefits reductions, skipping, deferring or eliminating raises. Does organized labor really have a positive, progressive role to play?*

It should, but it's in a very weakened state. It's been weak for a long time, but it was smashed during the 1980s. It started with Reagan's success in breaking the air-traffic controllers' strike, and it's continuing until today. The UAW just lost a serious strike at Caterpillar. Their strategy has been so overcome by class collaboration—We nice guys work together with management—that when the crisis came at Caterpillar they were probably unprepared. They were simply wiped out. At this point Caterpillar probably won't even live up to the terms of the latest agreement. It seems to be continuing to lock them out. These are serious blows to the labor movement, and that means to American democracy, but they're much to the benefit of the small sectors that are enriching themselves. Does labor have a part to play? It depends on whether working people can get their act together and rebuild the labor movement and turn it into a powerful force for both people's rights and democracy as it once was. It's going to have to be rebuilt from the bottom up. Labor's role has declined significantly since the 1940s. They're not unaware of it. Doug Fraser, the former head of the UAW, pointed out almost fifteen years ago that there has been a bitter, one-sided class war led by American capitalists fighting against labor, while labor, meaning labor bureaucrats, have been seduced by class-collaboration slogans. They're not fighting a class war. The effect of a bitter, one-sided class war is very evident.

DB *The* New York Times, *in talking about the economic woes, says "There is little mystery about what caused the economic problems. The country is suffering a hangover from the mergers, rampant speculation, overbuilding, heavy borrowing and irresponsible government fiscal policy in the 1980s." How well did the* Times *and its brethren in the media during this period of economic dislocation and decline actually cover the events and give the American people information that they could act upon?*

The *Times* isn't in the business of giving the American people information they can act upon. They hailed the Reagan revolution and its achievements. There were sectors of the population that profited marvelously, including the corporate sectors, of which the *Times* is a part. They couldn't fail to see that there are social costs. You can't walk around New York City and not see that there are severe social costs, so they probably saw it too. But this was considered as a glorious period of success. There were people who were upset about it. Take a look at, say, Mondale's funding in 1984: a lot of it was from fiscal conservatives who were worried about the long-term effects to their own interests of this kind of mad-dog Keynesianism, wild crazed spending, and government stimulation of the economy through borrowing that was going on through the Reagan years. People could see that that was going to be very problematic for the economy. Take what's just happened in Chicago. The estimates of the costs of fixing those leaks in the underground tunnels might have been at the level of $10,000. They didn't fix them because they wanted to save the $10,000 as part of the cutback in civic services. The net effect will be a loss of maybe over a billion dollars or more. That's a loss to private capital, too.

DB *But compared to the S&L bailout that's peanuts.*

Yes, the S&L bailout is much bigger than that. Chicago is just one piece of a growing disaster. Spending on infrastructure has declined radically in the last ten years, and that's going to have its costs. What happened in Chicago is going to happen all over the place.

DB *It can't help but affect even the elites. The area that was flooded ...*

And it's hurting them in Chicago. Chicago businesses are suffering. Insurance companies are going to suffer.

DB *They're not going to like that.*

No, but there's not a lot that they can do about it except to accept more long-term, integrated state corporate planning. There are other possibilities, like democracy, but nobody's going to talk about that.

DB *Yeah, right. And maybe there will just be more slogans like "belt-tightening" and "austerity" and "biting the bullet" as opposed to genuine economic policy.*

There *is* genuine economic policy, but it's geared to the short term economic interests of the rich. It's very genuine. And there's plenty of state intervention for that purpose. Take the Pentagon budget. That's massive state intervention in the economy for the benefit of the rich. That's what keeps the electronics industry going, for example.

They Don't Even Know That They Don't Know

December 16, 1992

DB *'Tis the season of fantasies and fairy tales, and in that holiday spirit, today's* New York Times *editorial offers the following history lesson: "America became rich by tapping its natural resources and building large manufacturing plants that imposed rigid work rules." What an inspiring story!*

Actually, it's a good year to mention that. This year is sort of historic in this respect. For one thing, it's the centenary of the destruction of the largest union in the United States, the American Steelworkers Union, by Andrew Carnegie, who had just in 1892 established the Carnegie Steel Works, which became the first billion dollar U.S. corporation. His most advanced plant was in Homestead, Pennsylvania, a working-class city with a working-class mayor and a lively cultural scene and a commitment to workers' rights and a union base. He locked the workers out. They took over control of the plant and the town. He sent Pinkerton guards, who were driven away. He then got the National Guard sent in, which took over. It was exactly as the *New*

33

York Times described. In fact, they described it at the time. He was able not only to destroy the union, but to institute twelve-hour work days, and miserable labor standards. The company history published not too long after described this as the basis for the enormous profits that they made. Although he was a pacifist, he succeeded in overcoming his pacifist principles to take on a huge contract for steel for naval vessels. The U.S. was then building up a big navy for purposes of international intervention. He also succeeded crucially, and this is important, in destroying utterly the democratic structure of the town and the region. Scholars who went in to investigate Homestead afterwards found that people were afraid to talk to them. They wouldn't even talk in their homes because they were too terrified of blacklisting and other retaliation. When Mother Jones, the eighty-nine-year-old labor organizer, came to Homestead in 1919 to try to help organize the union again, she was carted off by the cops when she tried to make a public statement. As late as the 1930s, when Roosevelt's Secretary of Labor, Frances Perkins, came to Homestead, she had to be under police protection. It wasn't until the mid-1930s, in the course of union organizing and great public activism, that the elements of democracy were restored to Homestead, and they didn't last very long. The attack on the union started right away. Nineteen-ninety-two is a historic year in that respect, too. This is the first time in sixty years that a major corporation has dared to use the ultimate weapon against a major union. Caterpillar broke a UAW strike by hiring scabs, just as Carnegie and Frick had done a century earlier. So the *Times* has a point to make. If you impose harsh enough working standards, you can create profits. As the *Times* well knows, it turns out to be much easier than before to move production to high-repression, low-wage areas like Mexico or increasingly, Eastern Europe or Indonesia. There you can really impose iron work rules and extract a lot of profit and meanwhile leave the United States with the inner cities that we see. So all that's accurate. I'm glad to see the *Times* saying something true. They could have added a little background but you can't ask for everything.

DB *"America became rich by tapping its inner resources." The brave and enterprising European settlers came to these shores and found this vast, empty, fertile land with abundant flora and fauna and developed it, like some natural process.*

That's partly true. They first had to exterminate the native population and drive them off the lands. "Exterminate" is the word they used, and it's what they did. After exterminating the population and bringing in huge numbers of slaves to work for them, they developed the resources.

DB *At the Little Rock economic conference and elsewhere there is much talk of economic recovery and restoring competitiveness. Gar Alperovitz takes a dim view that federal policy can reverse basic problems. He writes in today's* New York Times *that what is being proposed is "not likely to make a dent in our deeper economic problems. We may simply be in for a long, painful era of unresolved economic decay." Would you agree?*

I didn't see that piece but I did read this morning's *Financial Times* from London, and they talk with some pleasure of the fiscal conservatism shown by Clinton and his advisors. There are some real issues here. First of all, as regards Gar Alperovitz's comment, it's accurate, but we have to be careful in the use of terms. When he says America is in for a long period of decline, we have to decide what we mean by "America." If by the United States we mean the geographical area, he is, I'm sure, right. There has been decline, and there will be further decline, and the country is picking up many of the aspects of a Third World society. That's an automatic consequence of sending productive labor elsewhere. GM, as the press constantly reports, is closing some twenty-four factories in North America. But what you only read about in the small print is that it's opening new factories, including for example a $700 million high-tech factory in former East Germany, an area of huge unemployment where they can pay forty percent of the wages of Western Europe and none of the benefits. Or, as the *Financial Times*, the leading world business journal, puts it, they don't have to worry about the "pampered West European workers" any longer, they can just get highly exploited Third World workers now that Eastern Europe is being pushed back to its traditional Third World status. It's the same in Mexico, Thailand, etc.

There is a consequence to that. We become a Third World country in some respects. So if by the United States we mean the geographical area, he's right. If by the United States we mean U.S.-based corporations, then he's not right. In fact, the indications are to the contrary. Profits are doing fine, and a small sector is enriching itself. Even production by U.S.-based corporations is doing well, if we view the matter globally, as they do. I think Gar is right in saying that the policies now being discussed will have only a cosmetic effect on the United States as a geographical area. But I think they will probably be beneficial to the United States as a system of U.S.-based finance and industry, which is why the business community tended to give Clinton a good deal of support.

These last couple of days, the conference, and the elections, too, did deal with a significant issue. As usual, the issue had to do with a tactical disagreement within business circles. They are facing an objective problem, there's no doubt about it. The core of it has to do with what's called "industrial policy." We have to put aside a lot of nonsense before we can talk about this. The United States has always had an active state industrial policy, just like every other industrial country. Outside of ideologues, the academy, and the press, no one thinks that capitalism is a viable system, and nobody has thought that for sixty or seventy years, if ever. It has been understood certainly since the Great Depression and the Second World War, if not long before, that the only way a system of private enterprise can survive is if there is extensive government intervention to regulate disorderly markets and protect private capital from the destructive effects of the market system, to organize a public subsidy for targeting advanced sectors of industry, etc. So every advanced country, whether it's Germany or Japan or by now South Korea or certainly the United States, France, etc., has always had an active industrial policy. You can trace this back to the first industrializing country, England, and it's always been true of U.S. history, increasingly consciously so, since the Depression and the Second World War. Nobody called it industrial policy. It was always masked within the Pentagon system, which was, internationally, an intervention force, though domestically the Pentagon always was, and was understood to be from the late 1940s, a method by which the government can coordinate the private economy, can provide welfare to it, can subsidize it, can arrange the flow of taxpayer money to research and development, provide a state-guaranteed market for excess production, and target advanced industries for development, etc. Just about every successful and flourishing aspect of the U.S. economy has always relied on this kind of government involvement. Much of it has been masked by the Pentagon system.

Why are people now talking about industrial policy? The reason is that the mask is dropping. That's an objective problem. It is very difficult now to get people to be willing to lower their consumption, their aspirations in order to divert investment funds to high-technology industry on the pretext that the Russians are coming. There are various efforts to continue this. In fact, the current public relations stunt in Somalia, in my opinion, is an effort which I don't think is going to work to try to reinvigorate this system. But the system is in trouble. Economists and bankers have been pointing out openly for some time that one of the main reasons why the current recovery is so sluggish is that the government has not been able to resort to the traditional pump priming mechanism, the traditional mechanism of economic stimulation, namely increased military spending with all of its multiplier effects. That's just not as readily available.

There's another fact that goes right along side it, which is independent of this. The cutting edge of technology and industry has for some time visibly been shifting in another direction, away from the electronics-based advanced industry of the postwar period and towards biology-based industry and commerce. Biotechnology, genetic engineering, design of seeds and drugs, even animal species, etc. is expected to be a huge growth industry with enormous profits. It's vastly more important than electronics. In comparison, electronics is a sort of frill. This has to do with the means of life and existence, which the government and U.S. corporations hope that U.S. commercial enterprises will dominate and if possible even monopolize. But it's very hard to disguise government involvement in that behind the Pentagon cover. Even if the Russians were still there you couldn't do that. So there are some real problems. That's why you have open discussion now of industrial policy. It was pretty openly proposed and discussed in the Little Rock meetings, and in fact throughout the campaign. There are differences between the two political parties on this. The Clinton people are more up front about these needs. The Reagan-Bush types, who are more fanatically ideological, still to some extent have their heads in the sand about it, although the Reagan administration was highly protectionist and did set up a government corporation to try to get the computer-chip industry back into operation. That succeeded. They were a bit more dogmatic on this issue. I think that's one of the main reasons why Clinton had substantial business support.

Those are real phenomena. They will have to be dealt with. Or take the question of "infrastructure" or "human capital," a kind of vulgar way of saying keep people alive and allow them to have an education. By now the business community is well aware that they've got problems with that. Take, for example, the *Wall Street Journal*, which has been the most extreme advocate of Reaganite lunacies for the past ten years. They're now publishing articles in which they're bemoaning the consequences—without, of course, conceding that those are the consequences. They had a big news article a couple of weeks ago on the state of California and the collapse of the educational system, which they are very upset about. It was about San Diego. Businessmen in the San Diego area have relied on the state system, on a public subsidy, to provide them with skilled workers, junior managers, applied research, etc. The system is in collapse. The reason is obvious: the large cutbacks in social spending in the federal budget and the huge federal deficit, all of which the *Wall Street Journal* supported, simply transferred the burden of keeping people alive and functioning to the states. The states are unable to support that burden. They are in serious trouble. They tried to hand it down to the municipalities, which are also in serious trouble. One of the consequences is that the very fine educational system in the state of California is in serious difficulty, and now businessmen are complaining about it. They want the government to get back into the business of providing them with what they need: skilled workers and research. That's going to mean a reversal of the fanaticism that the *Wall Street Journal* and others like it have been applauding for all these years.

DB *At the Little Rock conference I heard Clinton talking about structural problems and rebuilding the infrastructure. One attendee, Ann Markusen, a Rutgers economist and co-author of the book* Dismantling the Cold War Economy, *talked about the excesses of the Pentagon system and the distortions and damages that it has caused to the U.S. economy. So it seems that there is at least some discussion of these issues that I don't recall ever coming up before.*

The reason is that they simply can't fully maintain the Pentagon based system with the propaganda pretexts gone. So you've got to start talking about it.

DB *Talking about it is one thing, but do they really have a clue about what do to? Can they have a clue?*

I think they have a clue about what to do. They know perfectly well what they can do. If you listen to smart economists like Bob Solow, who started the thing off, they have some pretty reasonable ideas about what to do. What they want to do is openly done by Japan and Germany and every functioning economy, namely rely on government initiatives to provide the basis for private profit, and do it openly. The U.S. has been doing it indirectly through the Pentagon system, which is in fact kind of inefficient. It won't work anymore anyway, for the most part. So they would like to do it openly. The question is whether that can be done. One problem is that the enormous debt created during the Reagan years, at all levels—federal, state, corporate, local, even household—makes it extremely difficult to launch constructive programs. That's why they're faced with this contradiction.

DB *There is no capital available.*

Yes. In fact, that was probably part of the purpose of the Reaganite borrow and spend program.

DB *To eliminate capital?*

You recall about ten years ago, when David Stockman was kicked out, he had some interviews with William Greider which he pretty much said that the idea was to try to put a cap on social spending simply by debt. There will always be plenty to subsidize the rich, but you won't be able to pay aid to mothers with dependent children, only aid to dependent corporate executives. They may have overdone it. Furthermore, there is another problem, a cultural and ideological problem. They have for years relied on propaganda based on denial of these truths. It's other countries that have government involvement and social services. We're rugged individualists. So IBM doesn't get anything from the government. In fact, they get plenty, but it's through the Pentagon, among many other ways, for example, regressive fiscal measures. Propaganda aside, the population is pretty individualistic and kind of dissident and doesn't take orders very well, by comparative standards, and it's not going to be easy to sell people on subsidizing advanced sectors of the economy. These cultural factors are significant. In Europe there has been a kind of social contract. It's now declining, for exactly the reasons that I mentioned, but it has been largely imposed by the strength of the unions, in my opinion, the organized work force, and the relative weakness of the business community, which is not as dominant in Europe as it has been here for historical reasons. That led to a kind of social contract, if you like, in which the government does see primarily to the needs of private wealth, but it also creates a not insubstantial safety net for the rest of the population. So they have general health care, reasonable services, etc. We haven't had that, in part because we don't have the same organized work force and we have a much more class conscious and dominant business community. In Japan, pretty much the same results were achieved, but the reasons were largely the highly authoritarian culture. People just do what they're told. So you tell them to cut back consumption, they have a very low standard of living, considering their wealth, work hard, etc. and people just do it. That's not going to be so easy to do here. There are going to be many problems.

DB *You mentioned the GM plant moving to Mexico. There's also Smith Corona in Cortland, New York, the last U.S.-based typewriter company. That, too, is moving to Mexico. There's a whole* maquiladora *corridor along the border, with incredible levels of lead in the water, high levels of pollution and toxic waste, and workers working for five dollars a day.*

43

Actually, the case that I mentioned was GM moving to Eastern Europe, which is in a way more interesting. It tells you what the Cold War was all about. But you're right about Mexico. One of the major issues before the country right now, right through the whole electoral period, is NAFTA, the North American Free Trade Agreement. It's quite interesting to see how that's been handled. You learn a lot about the country and the future from looking closely at that. There is no doubt that NAFTA is going to have a very large scale effect on the life of Americans, and Mexicans, too. You can debate what the effect will be, but nobody doubts that it will be significant. Quite likely the effect will be to accelerate just what you've been describing, the flow of productive labor to Mexico, which is a totalitarian dictatorship, very brutal and repressive. Therefore you can guarantee low wages. During what's been called the "Mexican economic miracle" of the last decade, wages have dropped sixty percent. Union organizers get killed. If the Ford Motor Company wants to toss out its work force and hire slave labor, they just do it. Nobody stops them. Pollution goes on unregulated. It's a great place for investors. One might think that NAFTA, which includes sending productive labor down to Mexico, might improve their real wages, maybe level the two countries. But that's most unlikely. One reason is the repression, which prevents organization that could lead to raising wages. Another consequence of NAFTA will be flooding Mexico with capital-intensive agricultural products from the United States, all based ultimately on big public subsidies, which will undercut Mexican agriculture. So they will be flooded with American crops, which will drive millions of people off the land

44

to urban areas or into the *maquiladora* areas. This means another major factor driving down wages. It's not at all clear that NAFTA will lead to raising wages. It will almost certainly be a big bonanza for investors in the United States and for the wealthy sectors in Mexico which are their counterparts, the ones applauding the agreement, and the professional classes who work for them. It will very likely be quite harmful for American workers. The overall effect on jobs is uncertain, but it's very likely that wages and work conditions will suffer. Hispanic and black workers are the ones who are going to be hurt most.

DB *While those jobs are being lost, U.S. corporate profits are increasing. Is that what you're saying?*

Corporations are doing very well. This is one of the best years for corporate profits.

DB *Will NAFTA and GATT, the General Agreement on Tariffs and Trade, essentially formalize on an institutional level North-South relations?*

That's the idea, in fact. It will also almost certainly degrade environmental standards. For example, corporations will be able to argue that EPA standards are violations of free trade agreements. This is already happening in the Canada-U.S. part of the mislabeled free trade agreement. Its general effect will be to drive life down to the lowest level while keeping profits high. One can debate this, but there's no doubt that the consequences are significant, and it's interesting to see how it's been handled. It didn't even arise in the campaign. The public hasn't the

45

foggiest idea what's going on. In fact, they can't know. One reason is that NAFTA is a secret. It's an executive agreement which is not publically available. To give you an indication of the extent to which this is true, in 1974 the Congressional Trade Act was passed. One of its provisions was that on any trade-related issue there has to be an analysis and input by the Labor Advisory Committee based in the unions. Obviously they have to have an analysis and report on NAFTA. NAFTA was signed by the President. It's an executive agreement. That was mid-August of this year. The Labor Advisory Committee was notified. They were informed that their report was due on September 9 of this year. However, they were only given the text about twenty-four hours before the report was due, ensuring that they couldn't even convene and obviously couldn't write a serious report. These are conservative labor leaders, not the kind of guys who criticize the government much. They nevertheless wrote a very acid report. They said, to the extent that we can look at this thing in the few hours given to us, it looks like it's going to be a total disaster for working people, for the environment, for Mexicans, and a great boon for investors. They pointed out that property rights are being protected all over the place but working rights are never mentioned. They also bitterly condemned the utter contempt for democracy that was demonstrated by not even allowing them to look at it. They said parts of it are still being kept secret. GATT is the same. Nobody knows what's going on there unless they're some kind of specialist.

DB *Have you seen details of these treaties?*

You can see details in the secondary comment on them, like the Labor Advisory Committee report. Theoretically, by now it's possible to get a text. But the crucial point is that, even if you and I could get a text, what does that mean for American democracy? How many people even know that this is going on? The Labor Advisory Committee report was never reported by the press. People not only don't know what's happening to them, they don't even know that they don't know. GATT is even more far reaching. I just came back from a couple of weeks in Europe, where this is a pretty big issue in the European Community context. One of the big public concerns in the European Community is described as nationalism, but what it really has to do with, I think, is what's called in EC parlance the "democratic deficit," meaning the gap that is developing between executive decisions, which are secret, and democratic, or at least partially democratic institutions, like parliaments, which are less and less able to influence decisions made at the Community level. All of this is a marvelous device for rendering democratic forums meaningless. It means crucial decisions with enormous impact are being raised to a level where the population can't influence them even indirectly through parliaments and furthermore doesn't know about them. And as in this case, doesn't even know that it doesn't know. That leads us towards a goal that has long been sought, namely maintaining democratic forms but ensuring that there's no interference with private power. This is a reflection of the globalization of the economy.

Over history, governmental institutions have, to a considerable extent, tended to reflect the form that's being taken by economic power and its organization. It's not one hundred percent, but there is a strong tendency in that direction. That's what we're now seeing. The economy is being internationalized, meaning that the geographical industrial countries are being deindustrialized but the corporations are doing fine. This internationalized economy, run largely by transnational corporations and supernational banks are creating their own governmental structures, like GATT and NAFTA and the IMF and the World Bank and the G-7 meetings, etc. The international business press is pretty up front about it. They call it a "de facto world government" which is going to reflect these interests.

DB *It seems that the Clinton-Gore administration is going to be in a major conflict over its support for NAFTA and GATT at the same time, at least on a rhetorical level, talking about its commitment to environmental protection and creating jobs for Americans.*

I would be very surprised if there's a big conflict over that. I think your word "rhetorical" is accurate. Their commitment is to U.S.-based corporations, which means transnational corporations. They very much like this special form that NAFTA is taking with special protection for property rights but no protection for workers' rights. And with the methods being developed to undercut environmental protection. That's in their interests. I doubt that there will be a conflict in the administration about this unless there is a lot of public pressure.

DB *There's been almost a domino effect, in terms*

of Canada, the United States, and Mexico. Canadian businesses are moving to states in the deep South and U.S. businesses moving to Mexico.

And remember that Canadian and U.S. businesses are pretty closely interlinked. Again, we have to be very careful when we use words like "Canada" and "United States" or "Mexico." These always were propaganda terms which covered up a lot. You just have to look at some of the figures. About ten years ago, when the latest U.N. figures were made available, about forty percent of world trade was internal, intrafirm transfers, transfers internal to a particular corporation. That is, it was centrally managed trade. It's not really trade, just interchanges between branches of a big transnational corporation. That's forty percent of world trade. Undoubtedly the figure's higher now.

Take a look at neo-classical economics, the kind of stuff you're supposed to bow before. It has a theory about this, i.e., ideally there's a free-market sea and within it are little islands which are little individual firms. Of course, everybody understood that a particular business, say a grocery store down the street, internally doesn't work by free trade. Internally it's centrally managed. So you have centrally managed islands in the free-market sea. The free-market sea was always more of less of a joke. But by now the islands are about the scale of the sea. This is increasingly centrally managed trade by major corporate structures. It's been called "corporate mercantilism" with its own governmental structures developing and the public increasingly marginalized to a pretty remarkable extent.

KEEPING THE RABBLE IN LINE

DB *Talk about the political economy of food, its production and distribution, particularly within the framework of IMF and World Bank policies. These institutions extend loans under very strict conditions to the South. They must promote the market economy, and they need to pay back the loans in hard currency. They have to increase exports, like coffee, so that we can drink cappucino, or beef so that we can eat hamburgers, all at the expense of indigenous agriculture.*

Basically the picture's the way you have described. The individual cases are quite interesting. Take the great economic miracle in Latin America, which is now being used as the basis for applying the same medicine in Eastern Europe. In fact, the same people are going. Jeffrey Sachs, a leading Harvard expert, who carried through what's considered the highly successful economic miracle in Bolivia, then went off to Poland and Russia to teach them the same rules. It's interesting to have a close look. Take Bolivia. It was in trouble. It had had brutal dictators, highly repressive, huge debt, the whole business. The West went in, Sachs was the advisor, with the IMF rules: stabilize the currency, increase agro-export, cut down production for domestic needs, subsistence agriculture, etc. It worked. The figures, the macroeconomic statistics looked quite good. The currency has been stabilized. The debt has been reduced. The GNP is increasing. There are a few little flaws in the ointment: poverty has rapidly increased. Malnutrition has increased. The educational system has collapsed. But most interesting is what has in fact stabilized the economy: agricultural exports—but not coffee. Coca. Some specialists on

Latin American economies estimate that it now accounts for probably about two-thirds of Bolivian exports. The reason is obvious. Take a peasant farmer somewhere, flood his area with U.S.-subsidized agriculture, maybe through a Food for Peace program, so he can't produce or compete. Set up a situation in which the only way he can function is as an agricultural exporter. He's not an idiot. He's going to turn to the most profitable crop, which happens to be coca.

The peasants of course don't get much out of this. They also get the guns and the DEA helicopters. But they get something. At least they can survive. And you get a flood of coca exports. The profits mostly go to the big syndicates, or, for that matter, to New York banks. Nobody knows how many billions of dollars of this pass through New York banks or their offshore affiliates, but it's undoubtedly plenty. Plenty of it goes to U.S. based chemical companies which, as is well known, are exporting chemicals to Latin America far beyond any industrial needs, mainly the chemicals that are used in cocaine production, which is an industrial activity. So there's plenty of profit. It's probably giving a shot in the arm to the U.S. economy as well. And it's contributing nicely to the international drug epidemic, including here. That's the economic miracle in Bolivia. And that's not the only case. But yes, these are the kinds of consequences that will follow from what has properly been called "IMF fundamentalism." It's having a disastrous effect everywhere it's applied, except that it's regarded as successful. From the point of view of the perpetrators, it is quite successful. So Latin America is supposed to be undergoing a dramatic recovery, and in a sense it is. As you sell off public assets, there's lots of money to be made, so much of the capital that fled Latin America is now back. The stock markets are doing nicely.

Take a look at Chile. There's another big economic miracle. The poverty level has increased from about twenty percent during the Allende years up to about forty-four percent now, after the great miracle. Similarly in country after country. But the elite sectors, the professionals, the businessmen, are very happy with it. And they're the ones who make the plans, write the articles, etc. So there's a lot of praise for the economic miracle here, too. It's just a far more exaggerated version of what we see here. Here we see it in a relatively mild way as compared with the Third World, but the structural properties are the same. The wealthy sector is doing fine. The general public is in deep trouble.

DB *Between 1985 and 1992, for example, in the United States, Americans suffering from hunger rose from twenty to thirty million, this while novelist Tom Wolfe, a great admirer of yours (Not!), described the 1980s as one of the "great golden moments that humanity has ever experienced."*

Take a look at last Sunday's *New York Times Magazine*. There was an article which was properly apolitical, but if you just add the background politics you can explain it. It was about the Boston City Hospital, the hospital for the poor, the general public in Boston, not the fancy Harvard teaching hospital. They didn't say so in the article, but a couple of years ago they had to institute a malnutrition clinic because they were getting Third World levels of malnutrition and their funds are so slight that they had to institute triage, take the cases that you can save more easily. That's something that has never happened before. Most of the deep starvation and malnutrition in the country had pretty well been eliminated by the Great Society programs in the 1960s. But by the early 1980s it was beginning to creep up again, and now the latest estimates are thirty million or so in deep hunger. It gets much worse over the winter because parents have to make this agonizing decision between heat and food. The effect is the kind of things described in that article: children dying because they're not getting water with some rice in it.

DB *The group Worldwatch says that one of the solutions to the shortage of food is control of population. Do you support efforts to limit population?*

First of all, there is no shortage of food. There are problems of distribution, serious problems. However, that aside, I think undoubtedly there should be efforts to control population. There are well-known ways to control population: increase the economic level. Population is very sharply declining in industrial societies. Many of them are barely reproducing their own population. Take Italy, which is a late industrializing country but has been industrializing. The birth rate now doesn't reproduce the population. That's a standard phenomenon. The reasons are pretty well understood. Economic development is the best method of population reduction.

DB *Coupled with education?*

Coupled with education and, of course, the means for birth control. The United States has had a terrible role. It will not help fund international efforts to even provide education about birth control.

DB *The globe is burning while various Neroes are fiddling. A study reported in the current issue of the British journal* Nature *indicates with greater precision and certainty than ever before that global warming is increasing. It predicts anywhere from a four to six degree increase in temperature. The resulting change in the earth's climate would have disruptive and possible catastrophic consequences for both human society and natural ecosystems.*

This has been pretty well known to scientists for over twenty years. I remember when I first heard it from the head of the Meteorology and Earth Sciences Department at MIT, a very distinguished scientist and incidentally a big skeptic about catastrophism. But by about 1970 he was convinced that there was a very serious problem ahead. There has been much debate about the timing, but the course of developments is not really in doubt. There are some hold-outs, like the editors of the *Wall Street Journal*, but it's pretty clear. This new study seems to sharpen up the estimates. It narrows the range that had already been assumed and adds more evidence to it.

Nobody can be certain about these things, of course. There's always going to be a margin of error, and a lot is simply not understood. But to play games with these possibilities is just insane. You have to take seriously a worst-case analysis.

DB *Carl Sagan spoke in Boulder a few months ago and talked about the environmental crises transcending narrow state interests and state abilities to address them, thus opening the way to global cooperation. This is something you've talked about as well.*

The question is: Who's going to do the global cooperation? There's plenty of cooperation going on.

DB *The global enforcer.*

There's that, and there's also this de facto world government, reflecting the needs and interests of the global corporations and banks. That's global cooperation. What is lacking, however, is global cooperation arising out of popular democratic structures. That's not only lacking, it's declining, because the democratic structures are declining. So to talk about global cooperation is not helpful. Global cooperation among the transnational corporations is just going to make the problem worse.

DB *There is a burst, a surge of tribalism all over the world: nationalism, religious fanaticism, racism, from L.A. to the Balkans to the Caucasus to India. Why now?*

First of all, let's remember that it's always been going on.

DB *I grant you that, but it seems more pro-*

nounced.

In parts of the world it's more pronounced. Take Eastern Europe. Up until a couple of years ago it was under the control of a very harsh tyranny. A tyranny like the Soviet system basically immobilizes the civil society, which means that you eliminate what's good, but you also eliminate what's bad. One of the things that was bad in that civil society traditionally was very bitter ethnic hatreds. Europe altogether is a very racist place, even worse than we are. But Eastern Europe was particularly ugly. One of the reasons why I'm here is that a lot of my parents and grandparents fled from that. It was held down by the general repression of civil society, which repressed democratic forces but also ethnic hatreds and hostilities. Now that the tyranny is gone, the civil society is coming back up, including its warts, of which there are plenty. Elsewhere in the world, say in Africa, yes, there are all kinds of atrocities. They were always there. One of the worst atrocities was in the 1980s. South African atrocities, meaning U.S.-backed atrocities, from 1980 to 1988, were responsible for about a million-and-a-half killings, plus about $60 billion of damage, only in the region surrounding South Africa. Nobody here batted an eyelash about that, because the U.S. was backing it. If you go back to the 1970s in Burundi, there was a huge massacre, hundreds of thousands of people killed. Nobody cared.

In Western Europe, you are getting an increase in localism. This is in part a reflection of the decline in the representative character of the democratic institutions. So as the European Community slowly consolidates towards executive power, reflecting big economic concentrations, people are trying to find other ways to preserve their identity, and that leads to a lot of localism. That's not the whole factor, but it's a lot of it. You should be careful with what's called "racism" in the United States. Take Los Angeles. There's plenty of racism. But remember that there's an unpronounceable five letter word in the United States, namely "class." And a lot of the conflict is in fact class. There are tremendous disparities between black and white populations in health, infant mortality, etc. But a substantial factor of that is actually a class factor. At every class level, from homeless up to executive, blacks are worse off than whites. Nevertheless, a lot of the disparity between blacks and whites is class-based—poor whites are not much better off than poor blacks. Race and class are pretty well correlated, so you get confusions. As the population moves towards a kind of a Third World character, people get bitter and desperate. And as the democratic institutions become more and more evacuated of content, people look for other things. They may look for a savior, like a guy from Mars like Ross Perot. Or they may turn to religious fanaticism, or other things.

DB *Or resurrect the Kennedy myth.*

That's another case, in my opinion.

DB *Germany is the country everyone loves to hate. It's a very convenient target. It's interesting to see what the German government response has been to the incidents in that country to restrict immigration—they* *had the most liberal asylum policies in the world—limit civil liberties, and ban political parties.*

When anything happens in Germany, people get pretty upset. And they're right. There is a history, after all. Nevertheless, we should remember a few things. As you said, Germany had the most liberal policy. Furthermore, they had by far the largest number of refugees. Europe is an extremely racist place. The localism is way beyond anything that we're used to. To an extent that you rarely find here, people tend to live near where they were raised and hate the person in the next village. There's a lot of talk about German racism, and it's bad enough. For example, kicking out the Gypsies and sending them off to Romania is such a scandal you can't even describe it. The Gypsies were treated just like the Jews in the Holocaust, and nobody's batting an eyelash about that because nobody gives a damn about the Gypsies. But we should remember that there are other things going on, too, which are getting less publicity. Take Spain. It was admitted into the European Community with some conditions, one of which was that it is to be what is pretty openly called a "barrier" to these hordes of North Africans who the Europeans are afraid are going to flock up to Europe. It's a narrow distance. There are plenty of boat people trying to get across from North Africa to Spain, kind of like Haiti and the Dominican Republic. The boats are sinking in the Mediterranean, or if people happen to make it, they are expelled by the Spanish police and navy. It's very ugly. There are of course reasons why people are going from Africa to Europe and not the other direction. There are five hundred years of reasons for that. But it's happening, and Europe doesn't want it. They want to preserve their wealth and keep the poor people out.

The same problem is happening in Italy. There was a recent electoral victory by the Lombard League, a group that seems to have a kind of neo-fascist element. It reflects northern Italian interests. Part of their concern is the same thing: North Africans drifting up through Sicily and into Italy and coming up from the south. They don't want them. They want rich white people. Europe has not been a heterogenous society to anything like the extent that the United States has. Nor has it been as mobile a society as the United States. These matters have been a bit under the cover, but they're harder to keep under the cover.

DB *What are your two new books?*

One is called *Year 501*. As the title indicates, it's an effort to look back over and rethink the major themes of the past five hundred years, the period of the European conquest of the world, and to look at the forms that it's taken, the principles and themes that underlay it and ask what they suggest about year 501, meaning the future. In my opinion it's basically more of the same adapted to current contingencies with elements of the kind we've been discussing. The second book is called *Rethinking Camelot*. The main focus is on two years, 1963-64, the presidential transition and the planning for the Vietnam War. That's a fascinating period that we probably know more about than almost anything in American history. There's huge documentation. It's extremely important. It led to one of the largest atrocities of the whole five-hundred-year era, namely the Indochina War, which had enormous consequences. Major decisions were being made at that time. It takes on added interest because of the fact that there was a presidential transition and an assassination which has led to a lot of, in my view, fantasies, but at least beliefs that something crucial happened, that some major change in American history took place at the time of the Kennedy assassination which cast a pall on everything that followed. This has been fostered in large part by Kennedy intellectuals. After the Tet Offensive in 1968, when corporate America basically called off the war, they completely changed their story as to what had happened. If you take a look at the people who had written memoirs, Kennedy's associates, they came out with new versions totally different from the old ones, in which it turned out that Kennedy was a secret dove and was trying to withdraw. There was no hint of that in the earlier versions or, for that matter, in the secret record or anywhere else. But they have an obvious stake in trying to recover the image of Camelot and make it look beautiful. Arthur Schlesinger is the most remarkable example. Also, large sectors of the popular movements have been involved in this, to a certain extent even immobilized by these ideas, especially in the last year or two.

Race

January 14, 1993

DB *The latest news bulletins report that Allied bombers are currently attacking Ankara, Jakarta, Tel Aviv, and even Washington, D.C., because of their defiance of UN resolutions. Would you care to comment?*

Not Port-au-Prince?

DB *You just wrote a book called* Year 501, *and it's beginning the same way that Year 499 began, with the bombing of Iraq, which is very much what you anticipated.*

Although this bombing is of a very different character. This one is a matter of George Bush and Saddam Hussein playing to their respective audiences and each giving the other appropriate assistance in the action. It's difficult to conceal. I noticed Bob Simon on CBS the other night just after the bombing, reporting from Baghdad, saying, This is the best gift that Bush can give to Saddam Hussein. Conversely, although for a short time only, Saddam Hussein will now again, even more, be able to appeal not only to his own population but to a considerable part of the Arab world and a lot of the Third World as someone who is defying imperialist violence. The bombing was immediately denounced by the Arab League as an act of aggression against an Arab coun-

61

try. The Arab countries wouldn't take part. Certainly at home he's guaranteed a worshipful reception on the part of those who transmit pictures of the world to the public. The same with Bush: worshipful reception at home, easy action, overwhelming force against people who can't shoot back. You can strut around the stage and strike heroic poses. It emphasizes what he wants to go down in history as his one achievement, namely killing a lot of people without getting shot at.

DB *There was Libya in the 1980s and now Iraq in the 1990s, convenient punching bags. But Muammar Qaddafi and Saddam Hussein also play their part. They're great villains. They're easy to hate, too.*

Qaddafi is sort of a small time thug, but Saddam Hussein is a major one. On the other hand you have to bear in mind that the villainy is totally irrelevant. He was as much a villain before August 2, 1990. His worst crimes by far are during the period when he was a highly admired ally who was being strongly supported by the United States, so strongly that he even almost approached the level of Israel. Israel, I had thought, would be the only country in the world that could bomb an American ship (the *Liberty*), kill a couple of dozen American sailors and get away with it completely. But I was wrong. Iraq was able to do it, too. Iraq was able to bomb the U.S.S. *Stark* in the Gulf, killing Americans, and get away with it because they were such close allies. That was in 1987, the period when the U.S. was tilting strongly toward Iraq to try to make sure that they won the Iraq-Iran war. It continued until the one crime for which Saddam

Hussein cannot be forgiven: he disobeyed orders on August 2. Immediately after, within a few months, the U.S. was supporting him again. There was no secret about it. In March, right after the fighting stopped, when Saddam Hussein turned to crushing the Shiites in the South and then the Kurds in the North, the U.S. stood by quietly and assisted him. The Kurds finally got some publicity. They're blue-eyed and Aryan. But the Shiites got no publicity. They were much harder hit. That was right under the nose of American forces. Iraqi generals were appealing to the American forces to let them have some arms so they could fight off Saddam Hussein's troops. Stormin' Norman was just sitting there and watching, maybe writing his memoirs at the time. This was reported. It received sober approval in the press: Yes, we don't like Saddam Hussein, but we have to support him in the interests of stability, meaning retaining our power in the region. In fact, at that time, the government was actually kind enough to explain for once exactly what they were doing. It's worth paying attention to the words, passed through the government spokesman at the *New York Times*, chief diplomatic correspondent Thomas Friedman, who described U.S. policy as handed to him, which is that the U.S. is seeking the "best of all worlds": an iron-fisted Iraqi junta which could wield the iron fist in Iraq just the way Saddam Hussein did before the invasion of Kuwait, much to the satisfaction of the U.S. allies Turkey and Saudi Arabia and obviously the boss in Washington. That's what they want. This makes it extremely clear. You can't miss the message. It's explicit and clear and lucid. They want a Saddam Hussein, and since he's now an embarrassment, they want a clone, somebody equivalent to

Saddam Hussein who will be able to wield the iron fist again just like he did. So the crimes are irrelevant. Yes, he's a demon, but that's irrelevant. What's relevant is the obedience. That's a pattern that goes way back in history. We supported Mussolini and Hitler for similar reasons.

DB *No noise from the servants' quarters.*

Yes.

DB *What do you think of this new concept in statecraft, the "no-fly zone"?*

Anyone's going to try to lead with their strength, and the U.S. strength is in high-technology military capacity. The U.S. government recognizes that classical intervention is no longer an option. This is one of the major changes since the 1960s; in fact it's a change in world history. I think they well understand that the population will not tolerate the classical forms of intervention. We should remember what that means. Classical intervention is, for example, when Woodrow Wilson sent the Marines to attack Haiti and the Dominican Republic and conquer them, killing thousands of people, tearing apart the constitutional system and reinstating virtual slavery, turning the countries over to western investors, turning them both into plantations. Neither country has recovered. In the case of Haiti we stayed there for almost twenty years. Or marauding around Nicaragua searching for Sandino. Or another form of classical intervention, actually one that set some new precedents, was Kennedy thirty years ago, when he sent the U.S. Air Force to start bombing villages, authorized napalm and defoliation, and sent U.S. military forces in as combat advisors. All of that's classical intervention. That's finished. Nobody assumes that that's even possible any longer. They can only carry out what an early Bush administration high-level planning document stated: only rapid and decisive intervention against much weaker enemies which will lead to very quick victory without any fighting. Anything else will undercut political support. There is no longer any political support.

That gets back to no-fly zones. No-fly zones nobody knows about. It's clean. The only people who get killed are other people. There's never any interaction between the military forces. So what was called a "combat" between U.S. and Iraqi jets wasn't a combat. It wouldn't be a combat if I sat here pushing a button and a bomb went off halfway around the world. The Iraqi jets are only "in combat" when U.S. planes are out of their range. So there are cheap wars. We can attack, but we never get shot at. That the public will still tolerate. That's what no-fly zones are about.

DB *What about the role of the UN in these various interventions now, giving its approval?*

First of all, the UN doesn't really give its approval. It just stays back. So during the Gulf War, the UN did not give its approval. The UN was neutralized. There was a series of resolutions. When Iraq invaded Kuwait, the Security Council passed resolution 660, which is the usual kind of resolution that's introduced after some act of aggression. It called for

Iraq to withdraw. It had a second part, which was immediately forgotten, because the U.S. wouldn't tolerate it. The second part was that Iraq and Kuwait should immediately undertake negotiations to settle issues between them. The U.S. wasn't having that. They didn't want negotiations. The second part dropped out of history. But the first part stayed. Iraq should withdraw. The only difference between that and any other UN resolution was that this time it wasn't vetoed. A similar resolution had been introduced just a few months earlier, when the U.S. invaded Panama. Of course that time it was vetoed. The U.S. has vetoed dozens of such resolutions. Same thing when Israel invaded Lebanon.

Then came a series of resolutions leading ultimately to the final one, 678, in which the UN simply washed its hands of the matter. In late November 1990 the UN simply said, Look, it's out of our hands. Any state can do anything they feel like. That's one of the most destructive attacks on the UN that has ever taken place. The UN simply said, We cannot carry out our function. The UN charter is very explicit that no state can use violence unless explicitly authorized by the Security Council. The UN didn't do that, but simply said, We have to wash our hands of the matter. The reason is the U.S. is going to do what it feels like.

DB *So yesterday's bombing was illegal?*

It had no authorization at all. Nobody even pretends that it did. Furthermore, whatever the Iraqis were doing with the missiles, whatever games they were playing, right or wrong, you can discuss it at some other level, but as far as the UN resolutions are concerned, it's conceded in the small print that they did not violate any resolution. As to the other things, impeding access of UN inspectors and moving into Umm Qasr port to pick up their equipment, that's arguably in violation of resolutions in a technical sense, but the UN simply made a comment—didn't condemn them as they condemn lots of things— authorizing no actions. The bombing was completely unilateral, a unilateral decision by the United States, which apparently was made even before the UN meeting. The aircraft carrier *Kitty Hawk* was already preparing. The only reason they didn't attack a day earlier was because the weather was bad, meaning it would have occurred even before the UN meeting. It was independent of it. The UN never authorized any such action.

Independently of all of this the UN has been neutralized in another respect. For a long time, many decades, from about the late 1960s through the end of the 1980s, the United States was intent on essentially destroying the United Nations, because it simply was not a pliable instrument of U.S. policy. Under Reagan, the U.S. didn't pay its dues. It was way in the lead in vetoing Security Council resolutions in the past quarter-century. It was doing everything it could to undermine and eliminate the organization, especially those parts of it that were concerned with Third World affairs, like UNESCO. However, by about 1989 or 1990, the situation changed. The UN came back into favor. During the Gulf War there was a long series of awed articles about the "wondrous sea change" in the United Nations. What happened is that it fell back into line.

The UN is essentially the five permanent members of the Security Council. They run the Security Council. The General Assembly you can dismiss. The great power doesn't pay any attention to it. The United States always had two automatic votes in the Security Council, usually three. Britain is a kind of colony. France will make a couple of noises, but they go along. So they had three votes out of the five. With the collapse of the Soviet Union they had four. Russia became even a more loyal client than Britain, which is hard to imagine. That gives four automatic votes. China is very dependent on U.S. trade. It will at most abstain. That means the U.S. essentially has the Security Council in its pocket.

The disappearance of the Soviet Union is one of a number of factors that had the effect of essentially eliminating Third World voices. As long as the Soviet Union was there, two big gangsters parading around, there was some space for independent forces, there was room for non-alignment. You could play one power against the other, or they'd squabble between themselves. With the Soviet Union gone and only one gangster left, that's finished. Furthermore, it's very important to remember that there was a tremendous crisis of capitalism that swept most of the capitalist world in the 1980s. Especially the former colonial world, which was devastated. The only areas that escaped were those in the region around Japan which didn't submit to the neoliberal orthodoxy and standard economic principles that had a devastating impact on Africa, Latin America, and parts of Asia that weren't in the Japanese orbit, like the Philippines.

That also undermines very strongly any form of

Third World independence. There are other factors, but the net effect is that the UN is pretty much back in the pocket of the United States, which means that it's getting a much more favorable press at this point. Of course, not when it does things that the U.S. doesn't want. For example, there was a condemnation of Iraq, although it didn't authorize bombing. There was a simultaneous condemnation of Israel for deporting 415 alleged Hamas members from Gaza. They deported mostly the intellectuals, the professional class. At one university virtually the whole staff was kicked out. There was condemnation of that. Of course the U.S. doesn't mind that, so therefore it doesn't matter. So it's the usual story: insofar as the United Nations will be an instrument of U.S. power or can at least be made to look it, it is a useful organization. When it isn't doing what the U.S. wants, then it can disappear.

DB *Does Operation Restore Hope in Somalia represent a new pattern of intervention?*

I think it represents another try. I don't think that really should be classified as an intervention. It should be classified as a PR operation for the Pentagon. The U.S. has some interests in Somalia, but I don't think they're major. The U.S. was, of course, deeply involved in Somalia. This has to be finessed by the press at the moment, because it's not a pretty story. From 1978 through 1990—it's not ancient history—the U.S. was the main support for Siad Barre, who was a kind of Saddam Hussein clone, tearing the country apart. He probably killed fifty or sixty thousand people, according to Africa

Watch. He destroyed the civil and social structure, in fact, laid the basis for what's happening now. The U.S. was supporting and may well be still supporting him. We don't know exactly. We know that the forces, mostly loyal to him, are being supported through Kenya, which is very much under U.S. influence. It's possible that that support continues. Anyhow we certainly did through the end of 1990.

The U.S. was there for a reason: there are military bases there which are part of the system aimed at the Gulf region. The main U.S. intervention forces, overwhelmingly, have always been aimed at the Middle East. This was part of the system of bases surrounding that. However, I doubt that that's much of a concern at this point. They are much more secure bases and more stable areas. What is needed now, desperately needed, is some way to prevent the Pentagon budget from declining. In fact, it's kind of intriguing that it was almost openly stated this time. So Colin Powell, the Chairman of the Joint Chiefs, made a statement about how this was a great public relations job for the military. The *Washington Post* had an editorial describing it as a bonanza for the Pentagon. The reporters could scarcely fail to see what was happening. After all, when the Pentagon calls up all the news bureaus and major television networks and says, Look, be at such-and-such a beach at such-and-such an hour with your cameras aiming in this direction because you're going to watch Navy Seals climbing out of the water and it will be real exciting, nobody can fail to see that this is a PR job. There's a level of stupidity that's too much for anyone. So it was a big PR job. And it's needed. The best explanation for the intervention, in my opinion, was given in an article on the day of the intervention in the London *Financial Times* which didn't mention Somalia. It was about the U.S. recession and why the recovery is so sluggish. It quoted various economists from investment firms and banks and so on, the guys that don't just design models for mathematical journals but care about the economy. The consensus was that the problem with the recovery from the recession was that the standard methods of government stimulation of the economy weren't available. The pump priming through the Pentagon system, one of the major government devices for management of the economy, simply was not available to the extent that it had been in the past. The economy was therefore very sluggish, for that and other reasons.

That's a big problem. The Pentagon system has been the core of state industrial policy. It's declining. There have been various efforts through the 1980s to revitalize it. Bush put it pretty honestly in his farewell address when he explained why we intervened in Somalia and not Bosnia. What it comes down to is in Bosnia somebody might shoot at you. In Somalia it's just a bunch of teenaged kids. We figure 30,000 Marines can handle that. So it's just photo ops, basically. One hopes it will help the Somalis more than harm them, but they're more or less incidental. They're just props for photo opportunities for Pentagon public relations, which is a crucial thing. When the press and commentators say the U.S. has no interests there, that's taking a very narrow and misleading view. Maintaining the Pentagon system is a major interest for the masters of the U.S. economy.

DB *There was a Navy and Marine White Paper in September 1992 called "From the Sea." It discusses that the military focus shifts from global military threats to "regional challenges and opportunities" including "humanitarian assistance and nation building efforts in the Third World."*

But that's always been the focus, rhetoric aside. The military budget is mainly for intervention. In fact, even strategic nuclear forces were basically for intervention. It's not that we intended to use nuclear weapons against Grenada. But the point is that you have to think about the way strategy works. The U.S. is a global power. It wasn't like the Soviet Union. The Soviet Union carried out intervention right around its borders, where it had overwhelming conventional forces. The U.S. is a global power. It carries out intervention everywhere: in Southeast Asia, the Middle East, in places where it has no conventional advantage. Accordingly, it always had to have an extremely intimidating posture to make sure that nobody got in the way. That required what was called a "nuclear umbrella": powerful strategic weapons forces to intimidate everybody so that conventional forces could be an instrument of political power. In fact, virtually the entire military system—its military aspect, not its economic aspect—was geared for intervention, and that was usually covered as "nation building." In Vietnam, in Central America. We're always humanitarian. So when the Marine Corps documents say we now have a new mission, humanitarian nation building, that's just the old mission. We now have to emphasize it more than before because traditional pretext is gone. There was always an ideological framework in which you could place this, namely the conflict with the Russians. If you had to carry out nation building, humanitarian efforts by attacking and destroying South Vietnam, that was to block Soviet expansion. That part's gone. You can't any longer be blocking Soviet expansion. So we're now just focusing on what was left, the humanitarian nation building. But it's the same as it's always been. It's just the current form of imperialist concern.

DB *What kind of impact will the injection of U.S. armed forces into Somalia have on the civil society? Somalia has been described by one U.S. military official as "Dodge City" and the Marines as "Wyatt Earp." What happens when the marshall leaves town?*

First of all, that description has nothing to do with Somalia. One crucial striking aspect of this intervention is that there's no concern for Somalia. No one who knew anything about Somalia was involved in planning it, and there is no interaction with Somalis as far as we know. Since the Marines have gotten in the only people they have been dealing with are the so-called "warlords," and they're the biggest gangsters in the country. They're dealing with them. But Somalia is a country. There are people who know and care about it. They've described it. They don't have much of a voice here. One of the most knowledgeable is a Somali woman named Rakiya Omaar, who was the Executive Director of Africa Watch. She did most of the human rights work, writing, etc., up until the intervention, which she strongly opposed and was then fired from Africa

Watch. She knows Somalia well. Another is her co-director, Alex de Waal, who resigned from Africa Watch in protest after she was fired. Apart from his human rights work, he is also an academic specialist on the region. He has published a major book with Oxford University Press on the Sudan famine and has written many articles on this. He knows not only Somalia but the region very well. And there are others. Their picture is typically quite different. In fact, many things are not controversial. Most of Somalia recovered from the U.S.-backed Siad Barre attack. Siad Barre's main atrocities were in the northern part of Somalia, what formerly had been a British colony. It was recovering. It's pretty well organized. It has its own civil society emerging, a rather traditional one, with traditional elders and lots of new groups, womens' groups, have come up in this crisis. They could use aid, doubtless, but it's kind of recovering.

The area of real crisis was one region in the south, in part because of the forces of General Mohammed Hersi, known as Morgan, Siad Barre's son-in-law, which are supported from Kenya. They were carrying out some of the worst atrocities. The forces of General Mohammad Farah Aidid and Ali Mahdi were also rampaging. It led to a serious breakdown in which people just grabbed guns in order to survive. There was a lot of looting. That's when you get these teenaged gangsters. That's a description of a certain region. It was at its worst in the early part of 1992. By September-October it was already being overcome and this part of Somalia was also recovering. If you look at the serious aid groups, not U.S. Care, and not the UN, which are extremely incompetent, as everyone agreed, but the ones who are doing most of the work, like the International Red Cross, Save The Children, the smaller groups that were carrying out development projects, like the American Friends Service Committee, which had been there for many years, or Australian Care, which was a major provider—they were getting most of aid through. They were giving figures of about eighty or ninety percent of the aid getting through by early November. The reason was that they were working with the reconstituting Somalian society. In this corner of real violence and starvation, things were already recovering, rather on the pattern of what had already taken place in the north. There were plenty of problems, but it was recovering.

A lot of this had been under the initiative of a UN negotiator, Mohammed Sahnoun, of Algeria, who was extremely successful and highly respected on all sides. He was working with traditional elders, with the newly emerging civic groups, especially women's groups. They were coming back together under his guidance, or at least initiative. He had good contacts everywhere. He was kicked out by Boutrous Ghali in October because he publicly criticized the incompetence and corruption of the UN effort. They put in an Iraqi replacement who maybe would have achieved something, maybe not. It was over because of the Marine intervention. A U.S. intervention was apparently planned from shortly after the election. The official story is that it was decided upon at the end of November, when George Bush saw heartrending pictures on television. But in fact U.S. reporters in Baidoa in early November saw Marine officers in civilian clothes walking around and scouting out the area, planning for where they were going to set up their base. This was rational timing. The worst crisis was over. The society was reconstituting. You could be pretty well guaranteed a fair success at getting food in, since it was getting in anyway. Thirty thousand troops would only expedite it in the short term. Not too much fighting, because that was subsiding. Good timing for Bush, too, because it means you get the photo opportunities and then you leave and somebody else faces the problems later on, which are bound to arise.

So it wasn't Dodge City. There was an area which was horrible and was recovering. What this massive intervention will do to that is very hard to predict. It could make it worse, could make it better. It's like hitting a seriously ill patient with a sledge hammer. Maybe it will help. Maybe it won't. But that comment about Dodge City simply reflects what is true: nobody cared. They didn't try to find out what Somalia was, because they didn't care. Somalis are props. What happens to them is incidental. If it works, great, we'll applaud and cheer ourselves and bask in self-acclaim. If it turns into a disaster, we'll treat it the same way we do with other interventions that turn into disasters. After all, there's a long series of them. Take Grenada. That was a humanitarian intervention. We were going to save the people from tragedy and turn it into what Reagan called a "showplace for democracy" or a "showplace for capitalism." In fact, they poured aid in. It had the highest per capita aid in the world the following year, next to Israel, which is in another category. And it turned into a complete disaster. The society is in total collapse. About the only thing that's functioning there is money laundering for drugs. But nobody hears about it. The television cameras were told to look somewhere else. So if the Marine intervention turns out to be a success, which is conceivable, then there will be plenty of focus on it and how marvelous we are and have to do it again. If it turns into a disaster it's off the map. Forget about it. So either way you can't lose.

DB *There's another factor at work here I'd like you to comment on: the notion of intervention on humanitarian grounds is a claim that's always made by the powerful against the weak. You don't have Bangladesh sending troops to help quell the situation in South Central L.A.*

Not only that, but it is so routine that it's just like saying "hello" when you walk into a room. Take, say, American history. When the U.S. was expelling or exterminating the native population back right from the Revolution on, it was always described as "humanitarian." We're their benefactors. When Andrew Jackson proclaimed his Indian Removal Act, which set off virtual genocide, he described it to Congress with great self-acclaim, describing in a teary voice what a great benefactor he was to the Indians. He said that white people wished that they were getting such benefits from us. After all, the white settlers, when they go out to the West, they don't get huge government grants, they don't have the U.S. military lead the way for them. But when the Cherokees are being sent out there on what was called the "Trail of Tears," on which about half of them died, they were being accompanied by the U.S.

Army and even given a couple of cents to get started. It was a tremendous gift. We were so benevolent. In fact, right after the American Revolution, in 1783, there was a commission established to try to determine what to do with the Indians. The question was: How do we kick them out of their land now that we've won? They decided to expel them, remove them from one area to another, rob their lands. It's worth reading what they wrote: They said we shouldn't go overboard in generosity. Our natural generosity should have certain limits, because if generosity goes too far, it becomes harmful to everybody. So we should be generous as always, but not too generous, while we're robbing them of their lands.

This is a refrain which is such a deep element of the national culture that to refer to it in this case is misleading. There's no atrocity that's been carried out that hasn't been described as humanitarian and beneficial to the victims.

DB *Comment on the events in the former Yugoslavia. This constitutes the greatest outburst of violence in Europe in fifty years—tens of thousands killed, hundreds of thousands of refugees. This isn't remote East Timor we're talking about—this is Europe. It's a living room war on the news every night.*

In a certain sense what's happening is that the British and American right wings are essentially getting what they asked for. Since the 1940s they've been quite bitter about the fact that Western support for a short time turned to Tito and the partisans and against Mikhailovich and his Chetniks and the Croatian anti-Communists, including the Ustasha, who were outright Nazis. The Chetniks were also playing with the Nazis and were mainly trying to overcome the partisans. They won. The partisan victory imposed a communist dictatorship, but it also federated the country. It suppressed ethnic violence, and created the basis of some sort of functioning society in which the parts had their role. That collapsed for a variety of reasons, and now we're essentially back to the 1940s, but without the partisans. Serbia now has inherited the ideology of the Chetniks. Croatia has inherited something of the ideology of the Ustasha, far less ferocious than the Nazi original, but similar in some ways. They are now doing pretty much what they would have done if it hadn't been for the partisan victory.

Of course, the leadership of Serbia and Croatia come from the Communist Party, but that's because every thug in the region was part of the ruling apparatus. (Yeltsin, for example, was a tough CP boss.) It's interesting that the right wing, at least its more honest elements, approve. For example, Nora Beloff, a right wing British commentator on Yugoslavia, had a letter in the London *Economist* condemning the people who are denouncing the Serbs in Bosnia. She's saying it's the fault of the Muslims. They are refusing to accommodate the Serbs who are just defending themselves. She's been a supporter of the Chetniks from way back, no reason why she shouldn't continue to support Chetnik violence, which is what this amounts to. Of course there's another factor. She's a super fanatic Zionist, and the fact that the Muslims are involved already makes them guilty in her eyes.

KEEPING THE RABBLE IN LINE

DB *Some say that just as the Allies should have bombed the rail lines to Auschwitz to prevent the deaths of many people in concentration camps, so we should now bomb Serbian gun positions surrounding Sarajevo that have kept that city under siege. Would you advocate the use of force?*

First of all, there's a good deal of debate about the Second World War, and how much of an effect bombing would have had. Putting that aside, it seems to me that a judicious threat of force, not by the Western powers but by some international, multinational group could have, at an earlier stage, suppressed a good deal of the violence and maybe blocked it. Whether that would mean bombing gun positions or not is a question that you can't make a decision about lightly. For one thing, you have to ask not only about the morality of it, but also about the consequences. The consequences could be quite complex. For example, conservative military forces within Russia might move in. They already are there, in fact, to support their Slavic brothers in Serbia, and they might decide to move in en masse. (That's traditional, incidentally. Go back to Tolstoy's novels and you can read about how the Russians saved their Slavic brothers from attacks. That's now being reenacted.) At that point you're getting fingers on nuclear weapons. It's also entirely possible that an attack on the Serbs, who feel that they're the aggrieved party, could inspire them to move more aggressively in Kosovo, the Albanian area, which could very well set off a large-scale war, with Greece and Turkey involved. So it's not so simple.

Or what if Bosnian Serbs, with the backing of

both the Serbian and maybe even other Slavic regions, started a guerrilla war? Western military "experts" have suggested it would take maybe a hundred thousand troops just to hold the area. So bombing Serbian gun emplacements sounds simple, but one has to ask about the consequences. That's not so simple.

If it were possible to stop the bombardment of Sarajevo by threatening to and maybe even actually bombing some emplacements, I think you could give an argument for it. But that's a very big if.

DB *Zeljko Raznjatovic, known as Arkan, a fugitive bank robber wanted in Sweden, was elected to the Serb Parliament in December 1992. His Tiger's Militia is accused of killing civilians in Bosnia. He's among ten people listed by the U.S. State Department as a possible war criminal. Arkan dismissed the charges and said, "There are a lot of people in the United States I could list as war criminals."*

That's quite correct. By the standards of Nuremberg, there are plenty of people who could be listed as war criminals in the West. It doesn't absolve him in any respect, of course.

DB *Christmas came early in 1992 for at least six former Reagan administration officials implicated in the Iran-Contra scandal. There was a presidential pardon on Christmas Eve. Bush said of the pardonees, "The common denominator of their motivation, whether their actions were right or wrong, was patriotism." That doesn't sound like the position of German defense lawyers at Nuremberg.*

No. They couldn't have gotten away with it, but it was quite accurate. Probably Himmler and Goering were acting as patriotic Germans. I frankly didn't take the pardons all that seriously. It was a highly selective prosecution. They didn't go after top people or the important issues. What they were being charged with is minor issues. Lying to Congress is bad, it's a serious violation of law which carries a five-year jail sentence. But as compared with carrying out huge international terrorist operations, it's pretty small potatoes. Nobody was charged with conducting an illegal war against Nicaragua. They were only charged with lying to Congress about it. It indicates the values that lie behind the prosecution. In other words, kill and torture whoever you like, but be sure to tell us. We want to take part too. If you think about it, that's exactly what happened in Watergate. The charges against Nixon never included bombing Cambodia. It did come up in the hearings, but the only respect in which it came up was that Nixon had lied to Congress about it. There was no charge ever that he had sent U.S. bombers to devastate Cambodian peasant society, killing tens of thousands of people. That was never even considered a crime. So to pardon people for lying to Congress makes a certain amount of sense if we understand it as meaning, Look, the major crimes are never even being discussed. It's kind of like catching Al Capone on his income tax.

DB *I've never heard you talk about Gandhi. Orwell wrote of him that "...compared to other leading political figures of our times, how clean a smell he has managed to leave behind." What are your views on the*

Mahatma?

I'd hesitate to say without undertaking a much closer analysis of what he did and what he achieved. There were some positive things there. For example, his emphasis on village development and self-help and communal projects. That would have been very healthy for India. Implicit in what he was suggesting was a model of development for India that could well have been a much more successful and humane one than the Stalinist model that was adopted, the development of heavy industry, etc. The talk about nonviolence you really have to think through. Sure, everybody's in favor of nonviolence rather than violence, but under what conditions and when? Is it an absolute principle?

DB *You know what he said to Louis Fischer in 1938 about the Jews in Germany. He said that German Jews ought to commit collective suicide which would "have aroused the world and the people of Germany to Hitler's violence."*

That is a tactical proposal, not a principled one. He's not saying they should have walked cheerfully into the gas chambers because that's what nonviolence dictates. He's saying, If you do it you may be better off. So that's a tactical proposal. It reflects no moral principle. It has to be evaluated on its merits. If you evaluate it on its merits, from that point of view, divorcing it from any principled concern other than how many people's lives can you save by doing this, it's conceivable that it was true. I don't think it's likely, but it's conceivable, not out of the question, that that would have aroused world concern in a way in which the Nazi slaughter surely did not. I think that the argument for it is very slight. On the other hand, there's nothing much that the Jews could have done anyway.

DB *Orwell adds that after the war Gandhi justified his position, saying, "The Jews had been killed anyway and might as well have died significantly."*

Again, he's making a tactical, not a principled statement. One has to ask the question what the consequences would have been of the actions he recommended. That's speculation based on little evidence. For him to have directed that recommendation at the time is kind of grotesque. What he should have been emphasizing was: Let's do something to prevent them from being massacred. The right position to take at the time was, Look, they can't do anything. Powerless people who are being led to slaughter can't do anything. Therefore it's up to others to do something for them. To give them advice on how they should be slaughtered is not very uplifting, to put it mildly. You can say the same about other things all the time. Take people being tortured and murdered in Haiti. You want to tell them, The way you ought to do it is to walk up to the killers and put your neck in front of their knife and maybe people on the outside will notice. Could be. But a little more significant would be to tell the people who are giving the murderers the knives that they should do something different.

DB *India today is torn asunder by various sepa-*

*ratist movements, Kashmir is an incredible mess, occu-
pied by the Indian army, and there are killings, deten-
tions, and massive human rights violations, in the
Punjab and elsewhere. I'd like you to comment on a
tendency in the Third World to blame the colonial masters for all the problems that are besetting the countries
today. They seem to say, "Yes, India has problems but
it's the fault of the British," as if India was once a great
big happy place.*

How to assess blame for historical disasters is a
difficult matter. You could ask the same thing about
the health of a starving and diseased person. There
are a lot of different factors that enter into it. If there
was a torturer around who was torturing them, that
certainly had a role. But maybe after the torture is
over, the person eats the wrong diet and lives a dis-
solute life and dies from the effects of that. That's
what we're talking about here. It's not easy to sort
out the proportion of blame. There's no doubt that
imperial rule was a complete disaster. Take India.
Bengal was one of the richest places in the world
when the first British merchant warriors arrived
there. They described it as a paradise. Today this
area is Bangladesh and Calcutta, the very symbols of
despair and hopelessness. These rich agricultural
areas produced unusually fine cotton, the major
commodity of that period. They had, by the standards of the day, advanced manufacture. Dacca,
which is the capital of Bangladesh, was compared by
Clive, the British conqueror, to London.

About a century later, in debates in the House of
Lords, Sir Charles Trevelyan described how Dacca
had collapsed from a major manufacturing center

and thriving city to a marginal slum under the impact of British rule. In Bengal, and throughout the parts of India that they controlled, the British undermined and tried to destroy the existing manufacturing system, which was comparable to their own in many respects. As the industrial revolution was urbanizing and modernizing England, India was becoming ruralized, a poor, agrarian country. Adam Smith, over two hundred years ago, deplored the depredations that the British carryied out in Bengal, which, as he puts it, first of all destroyed the agricultural economy, and then turned "dearth into a famine." The British overseers even took agricultural lands and turned them over to poppy production for the opium trade to China. The only thing that the British could sell to China was opium, and Bengal was one of the places where they produced it. There was huge starvation.

Indian manufacturing in other areas was considerable. For example, an Indian firm built one of the flagships for the English fleet during the Napoleonic Wars. Britain imposed harsh tariff regulations, starting in about 1700, to prevent Indian manufacturers from undercutting British textiles. That's the beginning of the industrial revolution, beginning with textile production and extending to other things. They had to undercut and destroy Indian textiles because India had a comparative advantage. They were using better cotton and had, by the standards of the day, a relatively advanced industry. It wasn't until 1846 that Britain suddenly discovered the merits of free trade. By that time their competitors had been destroyed and they were way ahead. They were very well aware of it. The British liberal historians, the big advocates of free trade in that period they say: "Look, what we're doing to India is not pretty, but there's no other way for the mills of Lancaster to survive. We have to destroy the competition."

And it continued. Nehru, in 1944 in a British prison, wrote an interesting book (*The Discovery of India*) in which he pointed out the correlation between how long the British have influenced and controlled each region, and the level of poverty. The longer the British have been in a region the poorer it is. The worst, of course, was Bengal, where the British arrived first.

In Canada and North America, they just wiped out the population. You don't have to get to current, "politically correct" commentators to describe this. You can go right back to the founding fathers. The first Secretary of Defense, General Henry Knox, who was in charge of Indian removal from 1784 on, said that what we're doing to the native population is worse than what the Conquistadors did in Peru and Mexico. He said future historians will look at these actions, what would be called in modern terminology "genocide," and paint them with "sable colors." They weren't going to look good to history.

John Quincy Adams, the intellectual father of Manifest Destiny, became an opponent of both slavery and the policy toward the Indians long after he left power. He felt that he himself had been involved in a crime of extermination of such enormity that he believed God would punish the country for this monstrous deed. So in North America we just essentially exterminated and expelled the population.

Latin America was more complex, but the initial

population was virtually destroyed within a hundred and fifty years. What was left was a mixture. Meanwhile, Africans were brought over as slaves, which had a major effect on devastating Africa even before the colonial period. The conquest of Africa drove it back even further. After the West had robbed the colonies—as they did, no question about that, and there's also no question that it contributed to their own development—they changed the relationships to so-called "neo-colonial", domination without direct administration, which was also generally a disaster.

How do you sort the guilt at this point? If Israel is committing crimes against the Palestinians, does that justify the Holocaust? I suppose some unreconstructed Nazi could say, look at what those guys do as soon as you let them go. Just means we didn't do anything. It's all their fault.

DB *To continue with India: talk about the divide-and-rule policy of the British Raj, playing Hindus off against Muslims. You see the results of that today.*

Which is not to say that it was pretty before, because it wasn't. The Marathi invasions were ugly and brutal. But the fact is that the level of brutality introduced by the Europeans was novel almost everywhere in the world. Naturally, any conqueror is going to play one group against another. In India, for example, I think about ninety percent of the forces that the British used to control India were Indians.

DB *There's that astonishing statistic that at the height of British power in India, they never had more* *than 150,000 people there.*

That was true everywhere. It was true when the American forces conquered the Philippines, killing a couple hundred thousand people. They were helped by Philippine tribes. They exploited conflicts among local groups. There are always plenty who will side with the conquerors. Just take a look at the Nazi conquest of Europe. Take Western Europe; let's forget the Third World. Nice, civilized Western Europe. Places like Belgium and Holland and France. Who was rounding up the Jews? The local people. In fact, in France they turned them over faster than the Nazis could handle them. If the United States was conquered by the Russians, George Bush, Elliott Abrams, and the rest of them would all be working for the invaders and sending people off to concentration camps. Ronald Reagan would be reading their ads on TV. That's the traditional pattern. Invaders very naturally play upon any kind of rivalries and hostilities that they find to get one group to work for them against others

You can see it right now with the Kurds. The West is trying to mobilize Iraqi Kurds to destroy Turkish Kurds. Turkish Kurds are by far the largest number, and historically, they were the ones who were the most repressed. It's not covered much in the West because Turkey is an ally, so you don't cover the atrocities they carry out. But right into the Gulf War they were bombing in Kurdish areas. Tens of thousands of people were driven out. But now the western goal is to use the Iraqi Kurds as a weapon to try to restore what they call "stability" in Iraq, meaning their own kind of system.

Last October there was a very ugly incident in which there was a kind of pincer movement between the Turkish army and Iraqi Kurdish forces to expel and destroy Kurdish guerrillas from Turkey. Independently of what we might think of those guerrillas, there's no doubt that they had substantial popular support in southeastern Turkey. But the Iraqi Kurdish leaders and some sectors of Kurdish population were going to cooperate because they thought they could gain something by it. You could understand their position. Not necessarily approve of it—that's another question. These are people who are being crushed and destroyed from every direction. If they grasp at some straw for survival, it's not surprising, even if grasping at that straw means helping to kill their cousins across the border. That's the way conquerors work. They've always worked that way. They worked that way in India.

India wasn't a peaceful place before the British, no, nor was the western hemisphere a pacifist utopia. But that aside, everywhere the Europeans went they raised the level of violence to an extraordinary degree. On that serious military historians have no doubts. As the most recent historian of the East India Company puts it, "warfare in India was still a sport, in Europe it had become a science."

Europe had been fighting vicious, murderous wars internally and it had developed a culture of violence, as well as the means of violence, which were unsurpassed. The culture of violence was extraordinary. European wars were wars of extermination. Everywhere the Europeans went, whether it was the Portuguese or the Spanish or the English or the Dutch, they fought with a level of violence which appalled the natives. They had never seen anything like it. That was true virtually over the entire world, with very few exceptions. In fact, from Europe's viewpoint, these colonial wars were what we call today small wars. It didn't take very many forces to destroy huge numbers of natives, not so much because the technology was better, but because the Europeans fought differently. If we were to be honest about the history, we would describe European colonialism simply as a barbarian invasion.

The British and Dutch merchants who moved into Asia broke into relatively free trading areas which had been functioning for long, long periods with pretty well established rules. More or less free, fairly pacific. Sort of like free trade areas. The description of what they did is just monstrous. They introduced a level of violence which had never been felt before. They destroyed what was in their way.

The only ones who were able to fend it off for a while were Japan and China. Japan did manage to fend it off almost entirely. That's why Japan is the one area of the Third World that developed. That's striking. The one part of the Third World that wasn't colonized is the one part that's part of the industrial world. That's not by accident. To strengthen the point, you need only look at the parts of Europe that were colonized. Parts of western Europe were colonized, like Ireland, which is very much like the Third World, for similar reasons. The patterns are striking. China sort of made the rules and had the technology and was powerful, so they were able to fend off Western intervention for a long time. But when its defense finally broke down in the nineteenth century, the country collapsed.

So it's completely correct that the post-colonial period had seen many brutal monsters develop. But when people in the Third World blame the history of imperialism for their plight, they have a very strong case to make. It's interesting to see how this is treated in the West these days. On January 7, 1993 there was an amazing article in the *Wall Street Journal* by Angelo Codevilla, a so-called scholar at the Hoover Institute at Stanford, criticizing the intervention in Somalia. He says, Look, the problem in the world is that Western intellectuals hate their culture and therefore they terminated colonialism. Only civilizations of great generosity can undertake tasks as noble as colonialism to try to rescue these barbarians all over the world from their miserable fate. The Europeans did it and of course gave them enormous gifts and benefits. But then these western intellectuals who hate their own cultures forced them to withdraw. The result is what you now see. You really have to go to the Nazi archives to find anything comparable to that. Apart from the stupendous ignorance that is so colossal that it can only appear among respected intellectuals, the moral level is— you have to go back to the Nazi archives. But it's an op ed in the *Wall Street Journal*. It probably won't get much criticism.

There are counterparts in England, the *Sunday Telegraph*, the *Daily Telegraph*. It's interesting to read the right-wing British press after Rigoberta Menchú won the Nobel Prize. They were infuriated, especially their Central America correspondent. Their view is, true, there were atrocities in Guatemala. But either they were carried out by the left wing guerrillas or they were an understandable response on the part of the respectable sectors of the society to the violence and atrocities of these Marxist priests. So to give a Nobel Prize to the person who's been torturing the Indians all these years, Rigoberta Menchú ... it's hard for me to reproduce this. You have to read the original. Again, at it's worst, it's straight out of the Stalinist and Nazi archives. It's very typical of British and American culture.

DB *That brings in the whole question of race and racism and how that factored into the relationship between what I'll call the "North" and the "South."*

There has always been racism. But it developed as a leading principle of thought and perception very much in the context of colonialism. It's not that it wasn't there before. It obviously was. But it gained entirely new dimensions and new significance in the imperialist context. That's understandable. When you have your boot on someone's neck, you have to have a justification for it. The justification has to be their depravity. If you can find anything to hang their depravity on, like the color of their eyes, it's that. It's very striking to see this in the case of people who are not very different from one another. Take a look at the British conquest of Ireland, which was the earliest of the western colonial conquests. It was described in the same kind of terms as the conquest of Africa. The Irish were a different race. They weren't human. They were a depraved race of people who had to be crushed and destroyed.

DB *Some Marxists connect racism as a product of the economic system, of capitalism. Would you accept* *that?*

No. It has to do with conquest. It's oppression. If you're oppressing somebody, maybe you're robbing them, it doesn't have to be torture. If you're robbing somebody, oppressing them, controlling them, dictating their lives, it's a very rare person who can say, Look, I'm a monster. I'm doing this for my own good. Even Himmler didn't say that. There's a standard technique of belief formation that goes along with oppression, whether it's throwing them in the gas chambers or charging them too much at a corner store or anything between those. There's a standard mode of reaction, and that is to say that it's their depravity. That's why I'm doing it. Maybe I'm even doing them good. If it's their depravity, there's got to be something about them that makes them different from me. What's different about them will be whatever you can find.

DB *And that's the justification.*

Then it becomes racism. You can always find something, like a different color hair or eyes, they're too fat, they're gay. Whatever it might be. You find something that's different enough. Of course you lie about it, so it's easier to find more.

DB *Do you know the scorpion and camel story? There's a scorpion who wants to cross the river. He needs the camel to help him across. He asks the camel, "Hey, come on. Give me a lift." The camel says, "What are you, crazy? I know who you are. You're going to sting me." The scorpion says, "No, no, no. I'm a* *reformed scorpion. I'm a good guy. I wouldn't do some-thing like that."* So after much persuasion the camel finally relents and says, "OK. Hop on." So the scorpion gets on the camel's back. In the middle of the river, the camel feels a sting in his back and realizes that the scorpion has just stung him. He starts howling and cursing and says, "You promised me you wouldn't do this! We're both going to die now. We're going to drown. You're insane." The scorpion says, "Well, it's in my nature." This leads to human nature. Is racism some-thing that's acquired or learned, or is it innately endowed?*

I don't think either of those is the right answer. There's no doubt that there's a rich human nature. We're not rocks. Anybody sane knows that an awful lot about us is genetically determined, in our behav-ior, our attitudes. That's not even a question among sane people. When you go beyond that and ask what it is, you're entering into near-total ignorance. We know there's something about human nature that forces you to grow arms, not wings, and to undergo puberty at roughly a certain age. And by now we know that things like acquisition of language are part of human nature even in its very specific forms, things about the visual system and so on. When you get to cultural patterns, belief systems, etc., the guess of the next guy you meet at the bus stop is as good as the best scientist. People can rant about it if they like, but they basically know virtually nothing.

In this particular area we can make some kind of reasonable speculation. I think most reasonable is the one I've just outlined. It's not so much that racism is in our genes. What is in our genes is the need for improving your own self-image.

DB *For domination.*

No. For justifying what you do. I can't believe that everybody doesn't know this from their own lives. If any person thinks about their own life honestly for a minute, they'll think of plenty of things that they did that they shouldn't have done. Maybe they stole something from their brother when they were ten. If you look back honestly and ask yourself, Did I say to myself at the time, I'm a rotten bastard but I'm going to do this because I want it? Or did you say, Look, I'm right to do this for this and that reason? The answer almost invariably is the second. It doesn't matter whether it was a minor or major thing. That's probably in our nature. It's probably in our nature to find a way to recast anything that we do in some way that makes it possible for us to live with it.

If we move into the social sphere, the sphere of human interactions, where there are institutions and systems of oppression and domination, people who are in those positions of authority and domination, who are in control, who are doing things to others, who are harming them, are going to pursue this course of constructing justifications for themselves. They may do it in sophisticated ways or non-sophisticated ways, but they're going to do it. That much is in human nature. One of the consequences of that can turn out to be racism. It can turn out to be other things, too.

Take the sophisticated ones. One of the intellectual gurus of the modern period in the United States is Reinhold Niebuhr, who was called the "theologian of the establishment." He was revered by the Kennedy liberal types, by people like George Kennan. He was considered a moral teacher of the contemporary generation. It's interesting to look at why he was so revered. I actually went through his writings once. The intellectual level is depressingly low. But there's something in there that made him appealing. It was what he called the "paradox of grace." What it comes down to is, no matter how much you try to do good, you're always going to do harm. Of course, he's an intellectual, so they have to dress it up with big words and big volumes. But that's what it comes down to.

That's very appealing advice for people who are planning to enter into a life of crime. To say, no matter how much I try to do good I'm always going to harm people. That's the paradox of grace. You can't get out of it. A wonderful idea for a Mafia don. Then he can go ahead and do whatever he feels like, and if he harms people, Oh my God, the paradox of grace. That, I think, explains why he was so appealing to American intellectuals in the post-World War II period. They were preparing to enter into a life of major crime, major criminal actions. They were going to be either the managers or else the commissars for a period of global conquest, running the world, which is obviously going to entail enormous crimes. Isn't it nice to have this doctrine before us? Of course we're superbenevolent and humane, but the paradox of grace! Again, if you're an intellectual you dress it up and write articles about it.

The mechanisms, however, are quite simple and elementary. I think all of that is, if you like, part of our nature, but in such a transparent way that you don't even call it a theory. Everybody knows this from their own experience, if they stop to think about it. Like just about everything that's understood about human beings, everybody knows it if they stop to think about it. It's not quantum physics. Mostly what's known is on the surface. Think about yourself and you can see it right there. Forget the big words and the polysyllables and the intellectual apparatus and just think about it. It's easy to see how that transmutes itself into racism.

Take the Serbs and the Croats. All they want to do right now is murder each other. They're indistinguishable. They use a different alphabet, but they speak the same language. They belong to different branches of the Catholic Church. That's about it. But they're perfectly ready to murder and destroy each other. They can imagine no higher task in life.

DB *What about the so-called "competitive ethic" of competition? Is there any evidence that we are naturally competitive? Proponents of the free market theory and the advocates of market capitalism say that you've got to give people the ability to compete—it's a natural thing.*

There are certainly conditions under which people will compete. There are conditions under which people will cooperate. For example, take a family. Suppose that whoever is providing the money for the family loses his or her job, so they don't have enough food to eat. The father is probably the strongest one in the family. Does he steal all the food and eat it, so all the kids starve? I guess there are people who do that, but then you lock them up. They're pathological. There's a defect there somewhere. No, what you do is share. Does that mean they're not competitive? No. It means that in that circumstance you share. Those circumstances can extend quite broadly. For example, they can extend to the whole working class. When you have periods of working class solidarity, people struggling together to create unions and decent working conditions, a republic of labor in which people would control their work and not have to suffer wage slavery. That's the United States, after all. Take a look at the Homestead lockout a century ago, when Andrew Carnegie established the world's first billion-dollar corporation by destroying the biggest union in the country.

He destroyed it right in Homestead, which was a working-class town with working-class solidarity. That was a period of enormous ethnic hatred and rivalry and racism, at that time directed mostly against the Eastern European immigrants, the Huns and the Slovaks. But during that conflict they worked together. It's one of the few periods of real ethnic harmony. They worked with Anglo-Saxon Americans and Germans and the rest of them. There are circumstances in which competition shows up and in which cooperation does. Again, I doubt that any person can fail to see this in their own life.

Let me tell you a personal story. I'm not particularly violent. But when I was in college, I had to take boxing. The way you did it was to spar with a friend, but we all found, and we were amazed, that pretty soon we wanted to kill each other. After doing this pushing around for a while, you really wanted to hurt that guy, your best friend. You could feel it coming out. It's horrifying to look at, and again I doubt that people have failed to see this in themselves and something about their lives. Does that mean that the desire to hurt people is innate? In certain circumstances, this aspect of our personality will dominate. There are other circumstances in which other aspects will dominate. You want to create a humane world, you change the circumstances.

DB *How crucial is social conditioning in all of this? Let's say you're a child growing up in Somalia today.*

How about a child growing up in Boston, just down the street? Or even here, in Cambridge. Just last summer a foreign student at MIT was killed, knifed, just a few blocks from here, by a couple of teenagers from the local high school. They were engaged in a sport that works like this: high-school kids are supposed to walk around and find somebody walking the street. One of the kids is picked, and he's supposed to knock the person down with one blow. If he fails to do it, the other kids beat up the kid who failed. So that's the sport. So they were walking along and saw this MIT kid. One of them was chosen and knocked him down with one blow. For unexplained reasons they also knifed him and killed him. They didn't see anything especially wrong with it. They walked off and went to a bar somewhere. Somebody had seen them, and they were later picked up by the police. They hadn't even tried to get away. They didn't see anything wrong with it. They're growing up in Cambridge, not on Brattle Street, but probably in the slums, which are not Somali slums by any means, not even Dorchester slums. But surely kids in the western suburbs wouldn't act like that. Are they different genetically? No. There's something about the social conditions in which they grew up that makes this an acceptable form of behavior, even a natural form of behavior. Anyone who has grown up in an urban area must be aware of this. I can remember from childhood, there were neighborhoods where if you went in you'd be beaten up. You were not supposed to be there. The people who were doing it, kids, felt justified and righteous about it. They were defending their turf. What else do they have to defend?

DB *Speaking of Brattle Street, just last night I was there. Panhandlers, people asking for money, people sleeping in the doorways of buildings. This morning at Harvard Square in the T station it was more of the same. The spectre of poverty and despair has increasingly come into the vision or the sightlines of the middle- and upper-class. You just can't avoid it as you could years ago when it was limited to a certain section of town. This has a lot to do with the pauperization, the internal Third Worldization, I think you call it, of the United States.*

There are several factors, which we've discussed before. In part it's an immediate corollary to what's called the globalization of the economy. Furthermore, there is a tremendous expansion of unregulated capital in the world seeking stable currencies and low growth. These factors have immediate, obvious consequences, namely extension of the Third World model to industrial countries. The Third World model is a sector of extreme wealth and privilege amidst huge misery and despair among useless, superfluous people. The model is extending to the entire world.

Take a look at the NAFTA discussions. The argument for NAFTA, the North American Free Trade Agreement, is that it's not going to hurt many American workers, just unskilled workers, defined to mean about seventy percent of the work force. That's one of the things you're seeing.

Look at South Central Los Angeles. That's an area where there were factories, but not any more. They moved to Eastern Europe, Mexico, and Indonesia, where you can get peasant women off the land. That's the part of free trade the elites advocate. They don't advocate the other parts of it. But the parts they can benefit from they advocate. That internationalization of production will have the effect, over the long term, of giving the industrial countries a sort of Third World aspect themselves.

There are other things happening everywhere in the industrial world, but most strikingly in four major English speaking countries—England, the United States, Australia and New Zealand. I think the reason for that is pretty obvious. These are the countries that in the 1980s took at least minimally seriously some of the rhetoric that they preached. In most of the world, the free market rhetoric is not taken seriously. But England under Thatcher and the United States under the Reaganites and Australia and New Zealand under Labor governments to a limited extent adopted some of the doctrines they preached for the Third World. Naturally, the population suffered for it.

DB *Deregulation?*

Deregulation, something a little bit like structural adjustment, which in the Third World means eliminate welfare, eliminate subsidies, stop building roads, give everything to the investors and something will trickle down by some magic, some time after the Messiah comes. The western countries of course would never really play this game completely. It would be too harmful to the rich. But they flirted with it in these English-speaking countries. And they suffered. When you say "they" suffered, you've got to be careful. The population suffered. The rich did fine, just as they do in the Third World. When I say there's a catastrophe of capitalism in the Third World, that doesn't mean for the rich people. They're doing just great.

DB *That's the paradox of 1992.*

The *New York Times* did have a headline in the business pages: "Paradox of 92: Weak Economy, Strong Profits." Big paradox. That's the story of the Third World. It's the story now of Eastern Europe. And it's also the story in Thatcherite England, Reaganite America, and Labor party Australia and New Zealand. Most of the population suffered as the societies moved more towards the Third World pattern than is the case, say, in continental Europe or Japan. In the periphery of Japan what you're getting is a move out of the Third World pattern into an industrial pattern, as in South Korea and Taiwan, who dismiss neoliberal economics as a joke, are able to develop internally.

DB *Thank you.*

Class

January 21, 1993

DB *It's a given that ideology and propaganda are phenomena of other cultures. They don't exist in the United States. Class is in the same category. You've called it the "unmentionable five-letter word."*

It's kind of interesting the way it works. For example, there was quite an interesting study done by Vicente Navarro, a professor at Johns Hopkins, who works on public health issues. There are lots of statistics about things like quality of life, infant mortality, life expectancy, etc., usually broken down by race. It always turns out that blacks have horrible statistics as compared with whites; there's a huge gap. He decided to reanalyze the statistics, separating out the factors of race and class. So, let's look at white workers and black workers versus white executives and black executives. He discovered that a considerable part of the distinction between blacks and whites was actually a class difference. That's natural because there's a correlation between race and class. If you look at poor white people, white workers, and white executives, the gap between them is enormous. He did the study, obviously of relevance to epidemiology and public health. He submitted it to the major American medical journals. They all rejected it. He then sent it to the world's leading medical journal, *Lancet*, in Britain. They accepted it right away.

KEEPING THE RABBLE IN LINE

In the United States you're not allowed to talk about class differences. In fact, only two groups are allowed to be class conscious in the United States. One of them is the business community, which is rabidly class conscious. When you read their literature, it's all full of the danger of the masses and their rising power and how we have to defeat them. It's kind of vulgar Marxist, except inverted. The other is the high planning sector of the government. So they're full of it, too. How we have to worry about the rising aspirations of the common man and the impoverished masses who are seeking to improve standards and harming the business climate. So they can be class conscious. They have a job to do. But it's extremely important to make other people, the rest of the population, believe that there is no such thing as class. We're all just equal. We're all Americans. We live in harmony. We all work together. Everything is great.

There's a book, *Mandate for Change*, put out by the Progressive Policy Institute, the Clinton think tank. It's a description of the program for the Clinton administration. It was part of the campaign literature, a book you can buy at an airport newsstand. It has a section on "entrepreneurial economics," which is going to avoid the pitfalls of the right and the left. It gives up these old fashioned liberal ideas about entitlement, welfare mothers have a right to feed their children, that's all passé. We're not going to have any more of that stuff. We now have "enterprise economics," in which we improve investment and growth. The only people we want to help are workers and the firms in which they work. There are workers, there are the enterprises in which they work, and that's who we're interested in benefitting. We're going to help them.

There's somebody missing from this story. There are no managers, no bosses, no investors. They don't exist. It's just workers and the firms in which they work. We're going to help them. The word "entrepreneurs" shows up. Entrepreneurs are people who assist the workers and the firms in which they work. The word "profits" appears once. I don't know how that sneaked in, that's another dirty word, like "class." But the picture is, all of us are workers. There are firms in which we work. We would like to improve the firms in which we work, like you'd like to improve your kitchen. Get a new refrigerator. Improve the firm in which you work. That's all they're interested in, just helping us folks out there.

Another mechanism used to achieve the same result is a kind of interesting innovation in the language in the last couple of years. That's the word "jobs." It's now used to mean "profits." So when, say, George Bush took off to Japan with Lee Iacocca and the rest of the auto executives, you remember his slogan was "Jobs, jobs, jobs." That's what he was going for. We know exactly how much George Bush cares about jobs. All you have to do is look at what happened during his tenure in office, when the number of unemployed and underemployed has now reached about seventeen million or so officially. I don't know what is unofficially, about another eight million, a million of them during his term. He was trying to create conditions for exporting jobs overseas. He continued to help out with the undermining of unions and the lowering of real wages. So what does he mean when he says and the media shout,

"Jobs, jobs, jobs"? It's obvious: "Profits, profits, profits." Figure out a way to increase profits. So it goes down the line.

The idea is to create a picture among the population that we're all one happy family. We're America. We have a national interest. We're working together. There's us nice workers, the firms in which we work, the media that labor to tell us the truth about the things that matter to us, the government that works for us. We pick them. They're our servants. And that's all there is in the world, no other conflicts, no other categories of people, no further structure to the system beyond that. Certainly nothing like class. Unless you happen to be in the ruling class, in which case you're very well aware of it.

DB *So then issues like class oppression and class warfare, equally exotic, occur only in obscure books and on Mars?*

Or in the business press, where it's written about all the time, and the business literature, or in internal government documents. It exists there because they have to worry about it.

DB *You use the term "elite." Samir Amin says it confers too much dignity upon them. He prefers "ruling class." Incidentally, a more recent invention is "the ruling crass."*

The only reason I don't use the word "class" is that the terminology of political discourse is so debased it's hard to find any words at all. That's part of the point, to make it impossible to talk. For one thing, "class" has various associations. As soon as you say the word "class," everybody falls down dead. There's some Marxist raving again. But the other thing is that to do a really serious class analysis, you can't just talk about the ruling class. Are the professors at Harvard part of the ruling class? Are the editors of the *New York Times* part of the ruling class? Are the bureaucrats in the State Department? There are differentiations, a lot of different categories of people. So you can talk vaguely about the establishment or the elites or the people in the dominant sectors. But you can't get away from the fact that there are sharp differences in power which in fact are ultimately rooted in the economic system. You can talk about the masters, if you like. It's Adam Smith's word, you might as well go back to that. They are the masters, and they follow what he called their "vile maxim," namely "all for ourselves and nothing for other people." That's a good first approximation to it, since Adam Smith is now in fashion.

DB *You say that class transcends race, essentially.*

In an important sense, I think it does. For example, the United States *could* become a color-free society. It's possible. I don't think it's going to happen, but it's perfectly possible that it would happen, and it wouldn't change the political economy, hardly at all. Just as you could remove the "glass ceiling" for women and that wouldn't change the political economy at all. That's one of the reasons why you quite commonly find the business sector reasonably willing, often happy to support efforts to overcome racism and sexism. It basically doesn't matter that much. You lose a little white male privilege, but that's not all that important. On the other hand, basic changes in the core institutions would be bitterly resisted, if they ever became thinkable.

DB *And you can pay the women less.*

You can pay them the same amount. Take England. They just went through ten pleasant years with the Iron Lady running things. Even worse than Reaganism.

DB *So in this pyramid of control and domination, where there's class and race and gender bias, sexism, lingering in the shadows, certainly in the liberal democracies, is coercion, force.*

That comes from the fact that objective power is concentrated. Objective power lies in various places: in patriarchy, in race. Crucially it lies in ownership. It's very much worth overcoming the other forms of oppression. For people's lives, they may be much worse than the class oppression. When a kid was lynched in the South, that was worse than being paid low wages. So when we talk about what's at the core of the system of oppression and what isn't, that can't be spelled out in terms of suffering. Suffering is an independent dimension, and you want to overcome suffering.

On the other hand, if you think about the way the society works in general, it works pretty much the way the founding fathers said. The society should be governed by those who own it, and they intend to follow Adam Smith's vile maxim. That's at the core of things. Lots of other things can change and that can remain and we will have pretty much the same forms of domination.

DB *You've said the real drama since 1776 has been the "relentless attack of the prosperous few upon the rights of the restless many." I want to ask you about the "restless many." Do they hold any cards?*

Sure. They've won a lot of victories. The country's a lot more free than it was two hundred years ago. For one thing, we don't have slaves. That's a big change. You recall that Thomas Jefferson's goal, at the very left-liberal end, was to create a country without "blot or mixture," meaning no red Indians, no black people, good white, Anglo-Saxons. That's what the liberals wanted. They didn't succeed. They did pretty much get rid of the native population. But they couldn't get rid of the black population and they've had to incorporate them in some fashion into the society over time. Women finally received the franchise one hundred and fifty years after the Revolution. The right of freedom of speech was vastly extended. Workers finally won some rights in the 1930s, about fifty years after they did in Europe, after a very bloody struggle. They've been losing them ever since, but they won them to some extent. In many ways large parts of the general population were integrated into the system of relative prosperity, relative freedom, almost always as a result of popular struggle. The general population has lots of cards. That's something that David Hume pointed out a couple of centuries ago as a kind of paradox of government. In his work on political theory, he asks why the population submits to the rulers, since force is in the hands of the governed. Therefore, ultimately the governors, the rulers, can only rule if they control opinion. He says this is true of the most despotic societies and the most free. There is a constant battle between those who refuse to accept it and those who are trying to force them to accept it.

DB *How to break from the system of indoctrination and propaganda? You've said that it's nearly impossible for individuals to do anything, that's it's much easier and better to act collectively. What prevents people from getting associated?*

There's a big investment involved. Anybody lives within a cultural and social framework which has certain values and certain opportunities. It assigns cost to various kinds of action and benefits to others. You just live in that. You can't help it. We live in one that assigns benefits to efforts to achieve individual gain. Any individual can ask himself or herself, let's say I'm the father or mother of a family, what do I do with my time? I've got twenty four hours a day. If I've got children to take care of, a future to worry about, what do I do? One thing you can do is try to play up to the boss and see if you can get a dollar more an hour, or maybe kick somebody in the face when you walk past them. If not do it directly, do it indirectly, by the mechanisms that are set up for you within a capitalist society. That's one way. The other way you can do it is by spending your evenings going around trying to organize other people who will then spend their evenings at meetings, go out on a picket line, carry out a long struggle in which they'll be beaten up by the police and lose their jobs. Maybe they'll finally get enough people together so they'll ultimately achieve a gain, which may or may not be greater than the gain that you tried to achieve by following the individualist course. People have to make those choices. They make them within a framework of existing structures. Within the framework of existing structures, although it harms everyone in the long run, the choices for a particular individual are to maximize personal gain. In game theory it's called "prisoner's dilemma." You can set up things called "games," interactions, in which each participant will gain more if they work together, but you only gain if the other person works with you. If the other person is trying to maximize his or her own gain, you lose.

Let me take a simple case, driving to work. It would take me longer to take public transportation than to drive to work. As long as everybody else is driving, that's the way it's going to be. If we all took the subway and put the money into that instead of into roads, we'd all get there faster by the subway. But we all have to do it. It's only if we all do something a different way that we'll all benefit a lot more. The costs to you, to an individual, of working to try to create the possibilities to do things together can be severe. It's only if lots of people begin to do it, and do it seriously, that you get real benefits.

The same was true of every popular movement that ever existed. Suppose you were a twenty-year-old black kid in Atlanta in 1960, at Spelman College. You had two choices. One is: I'll try to get a job in a business somewhere. Maybe somebody will be willing to pick a black manager. I'll be properly humble and bow and scrape. Maybe I'll live in a middle-class home. That's one path. The other path was to join SNCC, in which case you might get killed. You were certainly going to get beaten and defamed. It would be a very tough life for a long time. Maybe in the long term you'll finally be able to create enough popular support that people like you and your family and your children will live better. It was hard to make that second choice, given the alternatives available. Fortunately, a lot of young people did, and it's a better world because of it. But society is very much structured to try to drive you toward the individualist alternative.

DB *You've noted polls that indicate that alienation from institutions keeps increasing. You've observed that the population is going in one way, toward Orlando, and the policy is going toward Santa Monica, in a completely different direction. Eighty-three percent regard the entire economic system as "inherently unfair." But it doesn't translate into anything.*

It can only translate into anything if people do something about it. That's true whether you're talking about general things, like the inherent unfairness of the economic system, which requires revolutionary change, or about small things. Take, say, health insurance. Even though in public very few articulate voices call for what's called a "Canadian style" system, the kind of system that they have more or less everywhere in the world, an efficient, nationally organized public health system that guarantees health services for everyone and if it were serious, as Canada isn't enough, would also do preventive care. But polls have shown for years that most of the population are in favor of it anyway, even though they've never heard anybody advocate it. Does it matter? No. There will be some kind of insurance company based, "managed" health care system which is designed to ensure that the insurance companies and the health corporations that they run will make plenty of money. The only way we could get what most of the population wants with regard to health care is either by a large-scale popular movement, which would mean moving towards democracy, and nobody in power is going to want that, or else if the business community decides that it's good for them. Which they might. Because this highly bureaucratized, extremely inefficient system designed for the benefit of one sector of the private enterprise system happens to harm other sectors. Auto companies pay more in health benefits here than they would across the border. They notice that. They may press for a more efficient system that breaks away from the extreme inefficiencies and irrationalities of the capitalist based system.

DB *Edward Herman wrote a book about elections in U.S. client states called* Demonstration Elections. *That might describe what happens in the United States. What functions do elections serve here?*

Today is the 21st of January. As anybody who bothered watching television for the last two or three days knows, it's supposed to make people feel good about themselves and that something wonderful is happening. We have a marvelous country. There's hope. There's a young man there with a pretty wife. They're baby boomers. Now everything's going to be great. So it's a way of overcoming the growing alienation, at least for a short period, without doing anything. It's like Roman circuses. I don't want to suggest it's of zero significance. There is some significance. How much, you can debate. But the hoopla about it, the big celebrations, is simply at the level of Roman circuses. You have to do something for the population.

DB *Talking about bread and circuses, the Romans would be in awe. Did you hear about the Elvis stamp? There were two choices. One showed the young Elvis in his prime, and the other a more mature Elvis. The Post Office ran an expensive publicity campaign and millions of people voted. They picked the younger Elvis and lined up in the middle of the night to buy the first stamps. Bread and circuses. Give them something really meaningful to vote on.*

Right. And get people excited about that and they won't worry too much about the fact that the economy is inherently unfair or their real wages are declining or their children are not going to live as well as they do. Let them worry about Elvis.

DB *You've called the function of the President of the United States the "CEO of corporate America."*

If you want to know how they feel about Bill Clinton, look at the stock market. It's doing rather nicely.

DB *Business right after the election was very positive.*

There was an article yesterday in the London *Financial Times*, the major international business journal, pointing out that the stock market was looking at Clinton and thinking he was doing the right things. Investors are happy.

DB *It's only in America that a billionaire can run for President and pose as a populist, as Ross Perot did. What was your take on his candidacy and the whole Perot phenomenon?*

The most interesting period, I thought, was when he just appeared, at the very beginning. He could have come from Mars, as far as anyone knew. Nobody knew what his program was. He probably didn't have one. He had nothing to say. He was just this guy who said, Look, I made a lot of money and I've got big ears and a big smile. Within about two weeks, he was running even with the two major candidates. I think what that indicates is pretty clear. It means the population is so desperate that if somebody lands from Mars, they'll try him.

DB *Calls for a third party assume that we have a two-party system. Is that off base?*

It's a question of definition. We certainly have two candidate-producing organizations. We don't have two parties that people participate in. We don't have two parties with different interests. They basically reflect one or another faction of the part of society that you're not allowed to mention in *Mandate for Change*, namely the owners and investors and managers. They both represent their interests. But they have different takes on it. And they also have different popular constituencies. That in fact has some effect. The popular constituencies have to be offered some crumbs, just to keep the system of bureaucratic and other power functioning. The main structure of decision making, which has to do with profit, with international affairs, with strategic issues, the popular constituency is allowed no role in that, no matter who's in office. But it can be given other things. For example, the Republicans tend to be somewhat more openly the party of the business classes and the rich. They hide it less than the Democrats. Therefore it's harder for them to appeal to the general public. Their appeal quite often is in terms of jingoism, violence, religious fundamentalism, and the so-called social issues. They've got to give some crumbs to their constituencies, so they give them those things. That's why you have the Supreme Court appointments that you've had in the last ten years. The big attack on civil rights, the racism, the attacks on welfare mothers. That's a gift to that sector of the population. It doesn't affect profits. It doesn't affect power, so you can give it to them. The Democrats have tried to appeal to a different constituency. They pretend to be the party of the people. So they have to do something for the working people, women, minorities. That means that they can be expected to get the crumbs, like the Supreme Court appointments. And when I say "crumbs," I don't mean to demean it. Those are things that can have an enormous effect on individual life. They just don't affect the structure of the political economy.

DB *"The phenomenal concentration of property and business under the control of monopolies known as 'corporations' is changing the commercial aspect of the world and also changing the social relations. At no time in history has combination succeeded combination in greater and greater aggregations like the present. The little fellow is no longer in it." August 31, 1895. J.A. Whalen's first editorial in the* Appeal to Reason.

The *Appeal to Reason* was an interesting left journal which about ten years after that appeared had about three-quarters of a million subscribers. One of the major journals in the country. It was part of a flourishing and lively labor press, all of which has disappeared, a big change over the last century. The comment is correct. Of course it has increased. The difference is that increasingly, especially in the last twenty years, the corporations have become much more international, with effects that we've discussed.

DB *Reagan comes to power in 1981 and the debt is one trillion dollars. Today it's four trillion dollars, and that's projected to grow by fifty percent over the next six years. Who owns the debt? Who's going to pay it?*

Debt just means people who buy government bonds and securities. They own the debt. Mostly the rich, naturally, at home and abroad. The people who pay it are taxpayers. The debt is just another mechanism for transferring wealth from the poor to the

119

rich, like most social policy. Of course, there's another form of payment. The debt takes away from the possibility of social spending that would benefit the general population. Incidentally, the debt itself, just the numbers, is not a huge problem. We've had bigger debts than that, not in numbers, but relative to GNP, in the past. What the debt is exactly is a bit of a statistical artifact. You can make it different things depending on how you count.

But whatever it is, it's not something that couldn't be dealt with. The question is, what was done with the borrowing? If the borrowing in the last ten years had been used for constructive purposes, say, for investment or infrastructure, we'd be quite well off. The fact is that the borrowing was used for enrichment of the rich, for consumption, which meant lots of imports, which built up the trade deficit; and for financial manipulation and speculation, which are very harmful to the economy.

DB *Given the economic situation, it would seem to be a propitious moment for the left, the progressive movement, to come forward with some concrete proposals. People are not unaware of what's going on: high rents, skyrocketing college tuition and medical costs, etc. Yet the left, if I can call it that, when not bogged down in internecine warfare, is seemingly in a reactive mode only. It's not proactive.*

What people call the "left," the peace and justice movements, whatever they are, in terms of numbers, I think they've expanded a lot over the years. On particular issues they focus on them and achieve things. They tend to be very localized. There's very little in the way of broader integration, of institutional structure. They can't coalesce around unions because the unions are essentially gone. To the extent that there's any structure it's usually something like the church. There is virtually no functioning left intelligentsia. Nobody's talking much about what should be done or is even available to give talks. So you have a very large number of people, an enormous constituency, with a local focus, both regionally and in terms of issues, and nothing much in the sense of a general vision or picture. That's the result of the success of the class warfare of the last decades in destroying, breaking up popular organizations and isolating people.

Also I should say that the policy issues that have to be faced are quite deep. It's always nice to have reforms. It would be nice to have more money for starving children. You can think of lots of reforms that should be carried out. But there are some objective problems which you and I would have to face if we ran the country. One objective problem, which was kindly pointed out to the Clinton administration by the *Wall Street Journal* in a front page article the other day is that if they get any funny ideas about taking some of their own rhetoric seriously—granted, that's not very likely, but just in case anybody has some funny ideas—spending money for social spending, the United States is so deeply in hock to the international financial community because of the debt and the sale of Treasury bonds, that they have a lock on U.S. policy. The lock is very simple. If something happens here, say, increasing workers' salaries, that the bondholders don't like, that's going to cut down their short-term profit, they'll just start withdrawing from the U.S. bond market, which will drive interest rates up, which will drive the economy down. They point out that Clinton's twenty-billion-dollar spending program can be turned into a twenty-billion-dollar additional cost to the government, to the debt, just by slight changes in the purchase and sale of bonds, with their automatic effects on increasing interest rates, etc. So social policy, even in a country as rich and powerful as the United States, which is the richest and most powerful of them all, is mortgaged to the international wealthy sectors here and abroad. Those are issues that have to be dealt with.

To deal with those issues means to face problems of revolutionary change. There's apparently a debate going on within the Clinton administration over whether there should be efforts to protect American workers no matter who owns an enterprise, or U.S.-based enterprises. All those debates are taking place within a framework of assumptions: the investors have the right to decide what happens. So we have to make things as attractive as possible to the investors. As long as the investors have the right to decide what happens, nothing much else is going to change. It's like saying in a totalitarian state, shall we change from proportional representation to some other kind in the state-run parliament. Maybe it will make a little change, but it's not going to matter much. Until you get to the source of power, which ultimately is investment decisions, other changes are cosmetic and can only take place in a limited way. If they go too far the investors will just make other decisions, and there's nothing you can do about it.

To challenge the right of investors to determine who lives, who dies, how they live and die, that would be to make a significant move toward Enlightenment ideals, actually the classical liberal ideal. That would be revolutionary.

DB *There's another factor at work here, and I'd like you to address it. That is the psychological one that it's a lot easier to criticize something than to promote something constructive. There's a completely different dynamic at work.*

You can see a lot of things wrong. Small changes you can propose. But to be realistic, substantial change, which will really change the large-scale direction of things and overcome major problems that we all see, will require profound democratization of the society and the economic system. If you take an enterprise, a business or a big corporation, internally it's a fascist structure. Power is at the top. Orders go from top to bottom. You either follow the orders or get out. There's very little else going on. Furthermore, the concentration of power in such structures means that virtually everything else, whether it's in the ideological or the political sphere, is sharply constrained, not totally controlled by any means, but sharply constrained. Those are just facts.

By now, the international economy imposes other kinds of constraints. You can't overlook those things. They're just true. If anybody bothered to read Adam Smith, instead of prating about him, they would see this pointed out very clearly. He pointed out that social policy is class-based. He took class analysis for granted. It wasn't even an issue. So, if you studied the canon properly at the University of Chicago, they taught you that Adam Smith denounced the mercantilist system and colonialism because he was in favor of free trade. That's half the truth. The other half of the truth is that he pointed out that the mercantilist system and colonialism were harmful to the people of England but very beneficial to the merchants and manufacturers who were the principal architects of policy. In short, it was a class-based policy which worked for the rich and powerful in England. The people of England paid the costs. He was opposed to that, because he was an enlightened intellectual, but he recognized it. Unless you recognize that you're just not in the real world.

DB *Huey Long once said that when fascism comes to this country it's going to be wrapped in an American flag. You have detected and commented on tendencies toward fascism in this country. You've even been quoting Hitler on the family and the role of women.*

It was kind of striking. After the Republican convention (fortunately I saved my self the pain of watching television, but I read about it) it struck such chords that I began to look up some literature from the 1930s, contemporary literature on fascism. I looked up Hitler's speeches in the late 1930s to women's groups and big rallies. The rhetoric was very similar to that of the "God and country" rally the first night of the Republican convention. I don't really take that too seriously. The reason is that the levers of power are firmly in the hands of the corporate sector. They will permit rabid fundamentalists to scream about God and country and family, but they're very far from having any influence over major power decisions, as you could see from the way the campaign developed. They were given the first night to scream and yell. They were even given the party platform. It's pre-Enlightenment. But then when the campaign started we were back to business as usual.

However, that can change. One of the consequences of the growing alienation and isolation of people is that they begin to develop highly irrational and self-destructive attitudes. You want to try to identify yourself somehow. You don't want to be just glued to the television set. You want something in your life. If most of the constructive ways are cut off, you turn to other ways. You can see that in the polls, too. I was just looking at a study published in England, done by an American sociologist, of comparative religious attitudes in various countries. The figures are shocking. Three-quarters of the American population literally believes in religious miracles. The numbers who believe in the devil, in resurrection, God does this and that—astonishing. These are numbers that you have nowhere in the industrial world. You've got to go to maybe mosques in Iran, or maybe do a poll among old ladies in Sicily. You might get numbers like this. This is the American population. Just a couple of years ago there was a study of what people thought of evolution. The percentage of the population that believed in Darwinian evolution at that point was nine percent. Like statistical error, basically. About half the population believed in divine guided evolution, Catholic church doctrine. About forty percent thought the world was created about six thousand years ago. Again, you've got to go back to pre-technological societies, or else devastated peasant societies, before you get numbers like that. Those are the kinds of belief systems that show up in things like the God and country rally. Religious fundamentalism can be a very scary phenomenon. That could be the mass base for popular movement of extreme danger. Also, these people are not stupid. They have huge amounts of money. They're organizing. They are moving the way they should, beginning to take over local offices where nobody notices them. There was a striking phenomenon in the last election, it even made the front pages of the national newspapers. It turned out that in many parts of the country ultraright fundamentalist fanatics had been running candidates without identifying them. It doesn't take a lot of work to get somebody elected to the school committee. Not too many people pay attention. You don't have to say who you are. You just appear with a friendly face and a smile and say, I'm going to help your kids, and people will vote for you. A lot of people got in as a result of organized campaigns to take over these local structures. That can build up and end up with a society that moves back to real pre-Enlightenment times. If that ties in with some charismatic power figure saying, "I'm your leader, follow me," that could be very ugly.

DB *There's also a huge increase in fundamentalist media, print, obviously in newspapers and magazines, but particularly in the electronic media. You can't drive across the country.*

That was true years ago. I remember driving

across the country in the 1950s, being bored out of my head and turning on the radio. Every station I could find was some ranting preacher. Now it's much worse, and of course now there's television.

DB *You talk about the standard techniques and devices that are used to control the population: construction of enemies, both internal and external, the creation of hatreds, religious enthusiasm, and then you say, "the techniques are constant for the same structural reasons." What are those structural reasons?*

The structural reason is that power is concentrated. The general policy is exactly the way that Adam Smith described it: it's designed for the benefit of its principal architects, the powerful. It serves the vile maxim of the masters: all for ourselves and nothing for anyone else. Those are the basic rules of the world. The way it works out depends on what the structures are. In our case it happens to be basically corporate structure. Much of the population is going to be harmed by that. Those policies are designed to turn state power into an instrument that works for the wealthy. Maybe there are some crumbs for the rest of the population, maybe not. But that's given.

Somehow you have to get the general public to accept this. Hume's paradox does hold: power is in the hands of the governed. If they refuse to accept it, you're in trouble, no matter how many guns you have. How do you do that? There are not a lot of ways. One way is to frighten people and make them cower in terror that only the great leader can save them. Saddam Hussein is coming. You'd better hide in the sand, and by a miracle I'll save you. Then you save them by a miracle. So the combination of fear and awe is a standard technique, used all the time. Diverting people to other things. Elvis stamps. That's a technique. Professional sports are another. Get people to go insane about somebody or other. It also has the effect of creating attitudes of subservience. Somebody else is doing it, and you're supposed to applaud them. They're doing something you could never dream of doing in your life. So there are many devices, but not a lot. You generally find one or another of them being employed.

DB *You're predicting that the next big target is going to be the schools.*

The schools are already a target. I think more generally what's going to happen is one or another move still further towards a two-tiered system designed for the two-tiered society. It's always been that, but more so than before. Better schools and more investment for relatively privileged sectors, what's called "choice." If you're in the slums, by some miracle you might be able to get in. Degradation or even elimination of the public education sector for large numbers of other people.

Increasingly, the assumption that it is not our responsibility as citizens to care for all of the citizens. What you have to do is work for yourself. That means try to create a system in which those with privilege, education and clout can get the education they want for their kids and the rest are out of luck.

DB *The conditions that form the U.S.-Israeli*

alliance have changed, but have there been any structural changes?

No significant structural changes. It's just that the need for the strategic alliance has intensified. Its viability has increased. The capacity of Israel to serve U.S. interests, at least in the short term, has probably increased. The Clinton administration has made it very clear that it's intending to go even beyond the extreme pro-Israeli bias of the Bush-Baker administration. Their appointment for the Middle East desk of the National Security Council is Martin Indyk, whose background is AIPAC, who has headed a fraudulent research institute, the Washington Institute for Near East Studies, which is basically there so that journalists who want to publish Israeli propaganda, but want to do it objectively, can quote somebody. The one hope that the United States has always had from the so-called peace negotiations is that the traditional tacit alliance between Israel and the family dictatorships that rule the Gulf states will somehow become a little more overt or solidified. And it's conceivable. There is a big problem, however.

The problem is that Israel's plans, which have never changed, to take over and integrate the occupied territories, are running into some objective problems. They have always hoped that in the long run they would be able to reduce the Palestinian population. Many moves were made to try to accelerate that. One of the reasons they instituted an educational system on the West Bank was in the conscious hope that more educated people would want to get out because there wouldn't be any job opportunities. For a long time it worked. They were able to get a lot of people to leave. They now may well be stuck with the population. This is going to cause some real problems, because they're intending to take the water and the land. That may not be so pretty and not so easy.

DB *What's Israel's record of compliance with the more than twenty Security Council resolutions condemning its policies?*

It's in a class by itself.

DB *No sanctions, no enforcement?*

None. Just to pick one at random: Security Council resolution 425, March 1978, called on Israel to withdraw immediately and unconditionally from Lebanon. They're still there. The request was renewed by the government of Lebanon in February of 1991, when everyone was going at Iraq. You can't do anything. The United States will block it. Many of the Security Council resolutions that the U.S. has vetoed have to do with Israeli aggression or atrocities. For example, take the invasion of Lebanon in 1982.

At first the United States went along with the Security Council condemnations, but within a few days the U.S. had vetoed the major Security Council resolution, which called on everyone to withdraw and stop fighting.

DB *The U.S. has gone along with the last few UN resolutions or deportations.*

The U.S. gone along, but refused to allow them to have any teeth. The crucial question is, do you do anything about it? For example, the United States went along with the Security Council resolution condemning the annexation of the Golan Heights. But when the time came to do something about it, that stopped.

DB *Lebanon is a dumping ground for deportees. Israel has taken and dropped by helicopter and bussed scores of deportees in the 1970s and 1980s. Why has that changed now? Why has Lebanon refused?*

It's not so much that it has refused. If Israel dropped some of them by helicopter into the outskirts of Sidon, Lebanon couldn't refuse. This time Israel, I think, made a tactical error. The deportation of 415 people is going to be very hard for them to deal with. It's an interesting background. I just read in *Ha'aretz*, the main Israeli journal, that the Shabak, the secret police, stated, which they rarely do, that they had only asked for seven people to be deported. The other four hundred or so were taken by the Labor government and added. Shabak announced that it wasn't on their initiative. They never said anything about deporting them.

But taking this big class of people, mostly intellectuals, clerics, etc., and putting them in the mountains of southern Lebanon, where it's freezing and they may start dying, that's not going to look pretty in front of the TV cameras, which is the only thing that matters. So they may have some problems, because they're not going to let them back in.

DB *International law transcends state law, but Israel says these resolutions are not applicable. How are they not applicable?*

Just like they're not applicable to the United States. The United States was condemned by the World Court. States do what they feel like. Of course, small states have to obey. Israel's not a small state. It's an appendage to the world superpower, so it does what the United States says it has to do. The United States tells it: You don't have to obey any of these resolutions, therefore they're null and void. As they are when the U.S. gets condemned. The U.S. never gets condemned by a Security Council resolution, because it vetoes them. But there are repeated Security Council resolutions condemning the United States which would have passed if it was any other country, and the General Assembly all the time. Take, say, the invasion of Panama. There were two resolutions in the Security Council condemning the United States for the invasion of Panama. We vetoed them both.

DB *I remember talking to Mona Rishmawi of Al Haq in Ramalla. She told me that when she would go to court, she wouldn't know whether the Israeli prosecutor would prosecute her clients under British mandate emergency law, Jordanian law, Israeli law, or Ottoman law.*

Or their own laws. There are administrative regulations, some of which are never published. The whole idea is a joke, as any Palestinian lawyer will tell you. There is no law in the occupied territories.

There's just pure authority. Even within Israel itself, the legal system is a joke when it comes to Arabs. It has to be covered up here. Arab defendants who come to the Supreme Court come after having been convicted. The convictions are in the high ninetieth percentile based on confessions. When people confess, everybody knows what that means. Finally, after about sixteen years, when one of the people who confessed and was tried turned out to be a Druse army veteran who was proven to have been innocent, it became a scandal. There was an investigation, and the Supreme Court stated that for sixteen years the secret services had been lying to them, had been torturing people and telling them that they hadn't. There was a big fuss in Israel about the fact that they had been lying to the Supreme Court. How could you have a democracy when they lie to the Supreme Court? Not the torture. Everyone knew it all along.

I recall once after an Amnesty International investigation of torture in Israel, one of the Supreme Court justices was in London and was interviewed by Amnesty International. They asked him, could he explain the extremely high percentage of confessions of Arabs. He said, "It's part of their nature" to confess. That's the Israeli legal system.

DB *About the deportations again: I heard Steven Solarz on the BBC a couple of weeks ago. He said the world has a double standard. Seven hundred thousand Yemenis were expelled from Saudi Arabia and no one said a word. Which is true. Four hundred and fifteen Palestinians get expelled from Gaza and the West Bank and everybody's screaming.*

Every Stalinist said the same thing. We sent Sakharov into exile and everyone is screaming. What about this other atrocity? There is always somebody who has committed a worse atrocity. For a Stalinist like Solarz—which is exactly what is he, the typical Stalinist hack—why not use the same line? In fact, as Solarz knows, Israel is treated with a very gentle hand, and the expulsion of Yemenis was part of the propaganda build-up for the war in the Gulf, hence acceptable.

DB *Israel's record and its attitude toward Hamas have evolved over the years. It once held it in favor, did it not?*

They not only held it in favor, they tried to organize and stimulate it. In the early days of the *intifada*, Israel was sponsoring Islamic fundamentalists. If there was a strike of students at some West Bank university, the Israel army would sometimes bus in Islamic fundamentalists to break up the strike. Sheikh Yaseen, an anti-Semitic maniac down in Gaza, who is the leader of the Islamic fundamentalists, was protected for a long time. They liked him. He was saying, Let's kill all the Jews. It's a standard thing, way back in history. Chaim Weizman, seventy years ago, was saying, Our danger is Arab moderates, not the Arab extremists. The invasion of Lebanon was the same thing. They invaded Lebanon openly in order to destroy the PLO, which was a threat because it was secular and nationalist and calling for negotiations and a diplomatic settlement. That was the threat. Not the terrorists. The facts are familiar in Israel, unmentionable here, as part of the general cover-up of crimes of an unusually favored ally. They've done the same thing again, and always make the same mistake.

In Lebanon they went in to destroy the threat of moderation and ended up with Hezbollah on their hands. In the West Bank, they wanted to destroy the threat of moderation, people who wanted to make a political settlement, and they're ending up with Hamas on their hands. The mistake was predictable. The result was predictable. But it's important to recognize how utterly incompetent secret services are. Intelligence agencies make the most astonishing mistakes. For the same reason that academics do. They've got the same kind of background, the same assumptions. Especially when they're in a situation of occupation or domination, the occupier, the dominant power, has to justify what they're doing. There is only one way to do it, that's to become a racist: you have to blame the victim. Once you become a racist in self-defense, you've lost your capacity to understand what's happening. This is a very standard procedure. The U.S. in Indochina was the same. They never could understand. The FBI right here is the same. They make the most astonishing mistakes, for similar reasons.

DB *Get us through these Orwellisms of "security zone" and "buffer zone."*

In southern Lebanon? That's what Israel calls it, and that's how it's referred to in the media. Israel invaded southern Lebanon in 1978. It was obvious at the time that the Camp David negotiations would have the consequence that they did, namely freeing

Israel up to attack Lebanon and integrate the occupied territories by eliminating Egypt as a deterrent. Any kindergarten child could have seen that, and by now it's even conceded. So Israel invaded Lebanon in 1978 and held on to it. That's when the resolution was passed. They usually held on to it through clients, at the time it was the Haddad militia.

When Israel invaded in 1982, the border had not been quiet. There had been a lot of violence across the border, all from Israel north. There was an American-brokered ceasefire which the PLO had held to scrupulously. But Israel carried out literally thousands of provocative actions, including heavy bombing of civilian targets in an effort to try to get the PLO to do something so that they'd have an excuse for the invasion that finally took place. It's interesting the way that period is portrayed in American journalism. Universally it is portrayed as the period when the PLO was bombarding Israeli settlements. What was happening in fact was that Israel was bombing and invading north of the border and the PLO wasn't responding. They were trying at that time to move towards a negotiated settlement. Israel invaded Lebanon. We know what happened then. They were driven out by what they call "terrorism," meaning resistance by people who weren't going to be cowed. Israel succeeded in awakening a fundamentalist resistance which they couldn't control. They were forced out. They held on to the southern zone, which they call a "security zone," but there's no reason to believe that it has the slightest thing to do with security. It's their foothold in Lebanon. It's run by a mercenary army, the South Lebanon Army, backed up by Israeli troops. They're very brutal. It's got horrible torture chambers. We don't know the full details, because they refuse to allow any inspections, by the Red Cross or anyone else. But there have been investigations by human rights groups, journalists and others who attest to overwhelming evidence from independent sources, people who got out, what goes on there, even Israeli sources. There was actually an Israeli soldier who committed suicide there because he couldn't stand what was going on. Some others have written about it in the Hebrew press. Ansar is the main one, which they very nicely put in the town of Khiyam which is a place where they carried out a massacre back in 1948. There was another massacre by the Haddad militia under Israeli eyes in 1982. That's mainly for Lebanese who refuse to cooperate with the South Lebanon Army. That's the security zone.

DB *Anti-Defamation League Director Abraham Foxman, in a January 11, 1993 letter to the* New York Times, *says that since assuming leadership the Rabin government has "unambiguously demonstrated its commitment to the peace process." "Israel is the last party that has to prove its desire to make peace." What's been the Rabin record?*

It's perfectly true that Israel wants peace. So did Hitler. Everybody wants peace. When you say somebody wants peace, that's a tautology. Everybody wants peace. The question is on what terms. The Rabin government, exactly as was predicted, harshened the repression in the territories. Just this afternoon I was speaking to a woman who has spent the last couple of years in Gaza doing human rights work. She reported what everyone reports, and what everybody with a brain knew: As soon as Rabin came it got tougher. He's the iron fist man. That's his record. Actually, Likud had a better record in the territories than Labor did. Torture and collective punishment stopped under Likud. There was one period when Sharon was there that it was bad, but under Begin it was generally better. When the Labor party came back into the government in 1984, torture started again, collective repression started again, the *intifada* came. Rabin stated publicly, it was published in February 1989 to a bunch of Peace Now leaders, that the negotiations with the PLO didn't mean anything. It was going to give him time to crush them by force, and they will be crushed, he said, they will be broken.

DB *It hasn't happened.*

It happened. The *intifada* was pretty dead. He has awakened it again. His own violence has succeeded in reawakening the *intifada*. Several things, including the recent expulsion. But the increased repression after Rabin came in did reawaken the rather dormant protests and resistance—possibly people just wanted to be left alone, they couldn't take any more. Rabin succeeded in reawakening it. He has increased settlement in the occupied territories, exactly as everyone predicted. There was a very highly publicized cutoff of settlement. It was obvious right away that it was a fraud. Foxman knows that. He reads the Israeli press, I'm sure. What Rabin stopped was some of the more extreme and crazy Sharon plans. Sharon was building houses all over

138

the place, in places where nobody was ever going to go, and the economy couldn't handle it. So he eased back to a more rational settlement program. I think the current number is eleven thousand new housing units going up. Labor tends to have a more rational policy than Likud, one of the reasons the U.S. has always preferred Labor. They do it more quietly, less brazenly. Also, it's more realistic. Instead of trying to make seven big areas of settlement, they're down to four. But the theory is the same: try to break up the West Bank in a way which will make full Jewish settlement everywhere that's worthwhile, but surrounding pockets of Arab population concentration. So big highways, a network of highways connecting Jewish settlements, avoiding some little Arab village way up in the hills. All of this is continuing. The goal is to arrange the settlements so that they separate the Palestinian areas, so that there's no connection between them. That's to make certain that any form of local autonomy will never turn into any meaningful form of self government. That's continuing, and the U.S. is of course funding it, because it's in favor of it, as it always was. But true, Rabin is delighted to have a peace process if it can be on his terms.

DB *Critics of the Palestinian movement point to what they call the "intrafada," the fact that Palestinians are killing other Palestinians, as if this justifies Israeli rule and delegitimizes any Palestinian national anspirations.*

You might look back at the Zionist movement. There was plenty of killing of Jews by other Jews. They killed collaborators, traitors, people they thought were traitors. And they were under nothing like the harsh conditions of the Israeli occupation. As plenty of Israelis have pointed out, the British weren't nice, but they were gentlemen compared with us. The first Haganah assassination, the Labor-based defense force, the first that's recorded, at least, was in 1921. I looked it up in the official Haganah history. It's described there straight. A Dutch Jew named Jacob de Haan, because he was trying to approach local Palestinians to see if things could be worked out between the new settlers and the Palestinians, had to be killed. One of the murderers is assumed to be the woman who later became the wife of the first President of Israel. They said in the history that another reason for assassinating him was that he was a homosexual. Don't want those guys around. There were Haganah torture chambers, assassins. Yitzhak Shamir became head of the Stern gang by killing the guy who was designated to be the head. Shamir was supposed to take a walk with him on a beach. He never came back. Everyone knows Shamir killed him. The American revolution was no different.

As the *intifada* began to self-destruct under tremendous repression, this killing got completely out of hand. It began to be a matter of settling old scores, gangsters killing anybody they disliked. Originally it was pretty disciplined. But when the repression got harsh enough and the leadership was taken away, thrown into concentration camps, the thing deteriorated. It ended up with a lot of random killing, which Israel loves. Then they can point out how rotten the Arabs are.

DB *It's a dangerous neighborhood.*

140

Yes, it is. They help make it dangerous.

DB *David Frum, a Canadian journalist, in the January 2, 1993* Financial Post, *calls you, among other things, the "great American crackpot." I think that ranks up there with the* New Republic's *Martin Peretz's comment placing you "outside the pale of intellectual responsibility." But Frum actually has some substantive things to say: "There was a time when the* New York Times *op ed page was your stomping ground." Have I missed something here?*

I guess I did too. I did once have an op ed, one. It was in 1971, I guess. I had testified before the Senate Foreign Relations Committee. This was the period when everybody in the *New York Times* was deciding we'd better get out of Vietnam because it was costing us too much. Senator Fulbright had in effect turned the Senate Foreign Relations Committee into a seminar. He was very turned off by the war at that time, by American foreign policy. He invited me to testify. That was respectable enough. So they ran a segment of ...

DB *Excerpts of your comments. There wasn't an original piece you had written for the* Times.

Maybe it was slightly edited, but it was essentially a piece of my testimony at the Senate Foreign Relations Committee. So it's true, the *Times* did publish a piece of testimony at the Foreign Relations Committee.

DB *And that was your "stomping grounds." What about letters? How many letters of yours have they printed?*

Occasionally, when something appeared there which was an outlandish slander and lie about me, I've written back to them. Usually they don't publish the letters. Sometimes I was angry enough that I contacted friends who were able to put enough pressure on so they would run a letter of response.

DB *I haven't seen one in years.*

Sometimes they just refuse. In the *Times Book Review* there were a bunch of vicious lies about me and the Khmer Rouge. I wrote back a short letter responding, and they just refused to publish it. I got annoyed and wrote back and I actually got a response, saying, we published a different letter that we thought was better.

DB *David Frum just can't stop lavishing praise upon you. He says, "Your views are exactly like the stuff peddled by Lyndon LaRouche and the Christic Institute." You had an incident involving the Larouchies that you've mentioned in several talks.*

It went as far as death threats. I had been following them pretty closely, partly because I knew some of the kids involved. They were children of personal friends. It grew out of the Columbia strike in 1968. Originally it was the National Caucus of Labor Committees. It was a Marxist group of serious young people who were going to live in working-class areas and organize people. You could like it or dislike it. It was perfectly rational. This guy Lyndon LaRouche, who had some other name then, was the guru. At first he looked like some sort of standard ex-Trotskyite. After a while you could see what was happening. These are hard things to do. You're giving up your life, your career, the only world you live in is your surroundings. He gradually began to introduce slightly crazy themes into the ideology. You could see him do it little by little. At each point everyone in the group, nineteen-year-old kids, had to make a decision: Am I going to go along with this or am I going to give up my life? A lot of people went along. After a while they were off in outer space. The positions were so insane you couldn't even talk about it.

They then got quite violent. They started something called Operation Mop-Up. They were going to take the hegemony of the left by going into some movement meeting with baseball bats and beating everyone over the head. At first nobody knew what to do about it. After a while they figured, OK, we'll come back with bigger baseball bats. The next thing they started was what amounted to an extortion racket against parents. A lot of the kids had middle-class parents. The idea was to go back to your parents and tell them that unless they sold the store and gave it to LaRouche, they were enemies of the human race, objective fascists, and you were never going to have anything to do with them again.

This went on for a while. I started getting approached at talks I was giving. Some old couple would come up. I remember once a couple came up, a guy who had a little grocery store somewhere. He told me this was what his kids were saying, what did I think he ought to do? Usually I didn't answer. This once I said, if you want me to tell you the truth, I'll tell you the truth. I told him what I thought. About a week later I got a message signed Labor Committee Intelligence Service: our Intelligence Service has learned that you're spreading rumors about the party. You have one week to clear yourself of these charges. I threw it into the waste basket. Shortly after their newspaper started coming out with crazed attacks. The funniest one was a pamphlet they put out for the Bicentennial, July 4, 1976. It was called "Terrorist Commanders." It had on the front a picture of me and Marc Raskin. It was quite amusing. It was about how the two of us run the KGB and the CIA and the PLO and the Queen of England and whoever else was in their conspiracy at the time. They said we were planning to put atom bombs in major U.S. cities at the time of the Bicentennial. I got it in August, a month after. Usually these end-of-the-world people, when it doesn't happen they have some reason. But they were still predicting it a month after it didn't happen. That was put on the windshield of my car with a death threat scribbled on it. I won't go into the details of what happened next. I didn't hear from them for a while. Since then it's similar things.

DB *Anyone who comes to visit your office at MIT will see a very large black and white photograph of Bertrand Russell in the hallway next to your door. What's the story behind that photograph?*

He's one of the very few people that I actually admire. I did have a big photograph of him. The office was vandalized during the Vietnam War years. A sauerkraut bomber. One of the things that was destroyed was that picture. Somebody succeeded in putting up another one.

DB *So does Russell exemplify the responsibility of intellectuals?*

Nobody is a hero, but he had a lot of very good characteristics and did a lot of things that I admire.

DB *You do endless rounds of interviews, and I certainly inflict a fair share of them on you, how do you keep awake, much less sustain interest? What constitutes a good interview? What engages you? The questions are interminable, and usually the same.*

They're not always quite the same. And I have to rethink things anyway. These are very important and interesting topics, and as long as people are interested in them, I'm going to keep talking about them.

DB *You can stay awake?*

Most of the time.

DB *Thank you.*

Media, Knowledge, and Objectivity

June 16, 1993

DB *It's about 7:00 a.m. here in Boulder, 9:00 where you are in Lexington. What is your morning routine like? Do you start off with reading the* Boston Globe *and the* New York Times?

Yes, and The *Wall Street Journal.* The *Financial Times.* Whatever.

DB *Is the morning a good time for you to work or are you interrupted with a lot of phone calls like this one?*

Usually, quite a lot.

DB *The* Boston Globe, *your daily newspaper, has just been acquired by the* New York Times. *The* Globe *is one of the last major papers in the country not owned by a chain. What are your thoughts on that?*

It's a natural continuation of a tendency that's been going on for a long time. Ben Bagdikian, for example, has been documenting it year after year. It's a natural phenomenon. Capital tends to concentrate. I frankly doubt that it would make much difference in the nature of the newspaper, at least for a few years. However, over time it probably will.

DB *There is a well-documented trend in the concentration of media ownership. Do you see any countertrends?*

What you are doing right now is a countertrend. It's just like everything that's going on in the world. There's a trend toward centralization of power in higher and higher levels, but there's also a countertrend towards regionalization, including what's called "devolution" in Europe, creation of grassroots movements, construction of alternatives. The new electronic technology, in fact, has given opportunities for lots of spreading of alternatives. Cable television offers alternatives. So things are going in both directions. Institutionally, the major tendency is centralization. The other tendency in the opposite direction, which is the only hopeful one, in my opinion, is much more diffuse and has nothing much in the way of organized institutional forms. But it's certainly going on at every level.

DB *There are also computer networks.*

They offer lots of possibilities. There are tens of thousands of people hooked up, maybe hundreds of thousands hooked into various networks on all kinds of topics and lots of discussion goes on and lots of information comes through. It's of varying quality, but a lot of it is alternative to the mainstream. That's still pretty much of an elite privilege at this point.

Media, Knowledge, and Objectivity

DB *I recently got a letter from a listener in Lafayette, Colorado, a few miles from Boulder. He heard your talk "Manufacturing Consent," which you gave at the Harvard Trade Union Program in January. I thought the listener's comments were telling. He said after hearing the program that it left him feeling "as politically isolated as the PR industry would have us." He asked, "How do we get organized? Is everybody too tied down by monthly bills to care?" So there are multiple questions and concerns there.*

How do we get organized? There's a simple answer: you go ahead and do it. People have gotten organized under much more onerous conditions than these. Suppose, for example, you're a peasant in El Salvador in a Christian base community which tries to become a peasant cooperative. The conditions under which those things took place are so far beyond anything we can imagine that to talk about the problems we face seems superfluous. Sure, there are problems. People are weighed down with bills, they have personal problems. But most of us live under conditions of extraordinary privilege by comparative standards. The problem of getting organized is a problem of will.

DB *Isn't one of the functions of the media to marginalize people like this listener who wrote and to convince them that affairs must be left to the experts and you stay out of it.*

Of course. But notice that it's done differently in El Salvador. There they send in the death squads. Here what they do is try to hook you on sitcoms. It's

149

true that both are techniques of control, but they are rather different techniques.

DB *You're a scientist. Talk about the notions of objectivity and balance in the media and in scholarship. Who determines those kinds of things?*

There's a big difference between the sciences and humanistic or social science scholarship or the media. In the natural sciences you're faced with the fact of nature as a very hard taskmaster. It doesn't let you get away with a lot of nonsense. At least in the more well developed areas of the sciences, it's difficult for error to perpetuate. Theoretical error, of course, can perpetuate because it's hard to detect. But if a person does an experiment and misstates the results, that's likely to be exposed very quickly, since it will be replicated. There's a fairly stern internal discipline, which by no means guarantees that you're going to find the truth. But it imposes standards that are very hard to break away from. There are external conditions that determine how science proceeds: funding, etc. But it's qualitatively different from other areas, where the constraints imposed by the outside world are much weaker. Much less is understood. The empirical refutation is much harder to come by. It's much easier to simply ignore things that you don't want to hear.

So let's go back to your opening comment about the *Times* taking over the *Globe*. The east-coast press has been flowing with praise for this and saying that because of the *Times*' high journalistic standards there's no concern that this will have any danger. There are thousands of pages of documentation in print which demonstrate that the *Times*' journalistic standards are anything but high. In fact, they're grotesque. But it doesn't matter, because the critical analysis can simply be ignored. It has the wrong message. Therefore you ignore it. That's the kind of thing that's very easy in journalism or any of the other ideological disciplines. You just ignore what you don't like, and if you are on the side of the powerful, it's easy to get away with it.

The other day I read a summary article in the *Washington Post* by a good reporter who knows a lot about Central America, the lost decade in Central America. His article expresses all sorts of puzzlement about why Central America is worse off than it was in 1980 despite the enormous amount of American aid that went into the region. It asks whether this American aid was well-spent, whether it was well-designed, whether it went in the right areas. He asks what went wrong with our enormous effort to bring democracy and social development to Central America.

The author (Douglas Farah) of that article, at least when he's not writing for the *Post*, knows the answer perfectly well. The U.S. led a devastating terrorist war throughout the region to try to prevent democracy and social development. These billions of dollars of aid that he talks about were billions of dollars spent to destroy these countries. That's why they are worse off than before. But the *Post* can't say that. No matter how overwhelming the evidence is, it's perfectly possible simply to disregard it and to go on with fantasies that are much more pleasing to powerful interests and to oneself. In journalism, or in a good deal of what's called "soft scholarship," meaning outside the hard sciences, that's quite easy to do. The controls are very weak, and it's very easy simply to ignore or to deflect critical analysis. In the hard sciences it just won't work. You do that and you're left behind. Somebody else discovers things and you're out of business. Years ago C. P. Snow talked about what he called the two cultures of the humanities and the hard sciences. He was much criticized for that. But there's something to it. They are rather different in character. There are further blurring comments that have to be made, but roughly speaking the difference is real.

So to answer the question, within the more developed natural sciences, although nobody has any illusions about objectivity, there is a kind of peer-pressure control that reflects the constraints imposed by nature. In the other areas, work is commonly considered objective if it reflects the views of those in power.

DB *The concept of objectivity in journalism definitely seems to be something that's situational and mutable.*

If you look at serious monographic work in diplomatic history, the situation is somewhat different. Although there, choices and focus and concentration and framing are themselves often quite ideological and can hardly fail to be. More honest people will recognize that and make it clear. The less honest will make it appear that they're simply being objective.

DB *But of course one of the central myths of the media is that they are objective and balanced.*

Sure. That's part of their propaganda function.

It's obvious on the face of it that those words don't mean anything. What do you mean by balanced? What's the proper measure of balance? There's no answer to that question. If the media were honest, they would say, Look, here are the interests we represent and this is the framework within which we look at things. This is our set of beliefs and commitments. That's what they would say, very much as their critics say. For example, I don't try to hide my commitments, and the *Washington Post* and *New York Times* shouldn't do it either. However, they must do it, because this mask of balance and objectivity is a crucial part of the propaganda function.

In fact, they actually go beyond that. They try to present themselves as adversarial to power, as subversive, digging away at powerful institutions and undermining them. The academic profession plays along with this game. Have a look at academic conferences on the media. One I went through in detail was held at Georgetown University. It was run by a dovish, rather liberal-leaning Quaker. It was about media coverage of Central America and the Middle East. The way the conference is framed is this: First came a series of statements opening the discussion by people who said the media and journalists are overwhelmingly biased against the government. They lie. They try to undermine the U.S. government. They're practically communist agents. After these bitter attacks on the media for their adversarial stance, another set of papers were presented which said, Look, it's pretty bad, we agree. But it's not quite as bad as you say. That's our job, to be subversive, and that's what you have to face up to in a democ-

153

ratic society. Then these two positions were debated.

There is obviously a third position: the media are supportive of power interests. They distort and often lie in order to maintain those interests. But that position can't be expressed. In fact, in the conference I'm talking about, one hundred percent of the coverage on Central America was within the bounds I've described. On the Middle East, where the media are just grotesque, it was only ninety-six percent within those ludicrous bounds. The reason was that they allowed one statement by Eric Hoagland, a Middle East scholar who made an accurate statement, and that's the four percent, which nobody ever referred to again. That's the way the media like to present themselves, naturally, and that's the way the academic profession likes to see them presented. If you can present the media as being critical, antagonistic to power, maybe even subversive, that makes an enormous contribution to the propaganda function. Then they say, Look how critical of power we are. How could anyone go beyond us?

DB *In an article about the acquisition of the* Boston Globe *in the* Times *a few days ago, it was pointed out that the* Globe *was one of the first papers in the United States to lead the crusade against U.S. intervention in Vietnam. You were reading this paper throughout that period. Is that accurate?*

Yes, it's very accurate. They published the first editorial calling for withdrawal from Vietnam. The editor at that time was a personal friend and I followed this quite closely. They did a big study to determine if it would be possible to publish this editorial and still get away with it. They finally agreed to do it. My recollection is that that was in late 1969, that is, about a year-and-a-half after Wall Street had turned against the war. I think it's probably true that that was the first mainstream call for withdrawal of U.S. forces. Of course, it was not framed in terms of a call to withdraw the U.S. forces that had attacked Vietnam, but rather, We should get out, it doesn't make sense, etc. That tells you something about the U.S. media. What it tells you is a year-and-a-half after the business community determined that the government should liquidate the effort because it was harmful to U.S. economic interests, about that time the courageous press timidly began to say, well, maybe we ought to do what the business community announced a year-and-a-half ago, without even conceding the simple truth: that it was a war of U.S. aggression, first against South Vietnam, then all of Indochina. Some elementary truths are too outrageous to be allowed on the printed page.

DB *Do you see knowledge as a commodity? Is it something that's traded and purchased and sold? Obviously it's sold: one sells oneself in the marketplace.*

I'd be a little cautious about the knowledge part. What passes for knowledge is sold. Take, say, Henry Kissinger as an example. He certainly sells himself in the marketplace. But one should be very skeptical about whether that's knowledge or not. The reason is that what's sold in the marketplace tends to be pretty shoddy. It works. It's knowledge or understanding shaped or distorted to serve the interests of power. Or, to go back to the hard sciences, their knowledge is certainly sold. Take American high-tech industry, or the pharmaceutical industry. One of the ways in which the public subsidizes the corporate sector is through university research labs, which do straight research. But the benefits of it, if something commercially viable comes out of it, are handed over to private corporations. I don't know of any university departments which contract out directly to industry, but there are things not too far from that.

DB *Would you say information is a commodity?*

People make such statements. I'm a little leery about them. When you say that information is a commodity, it can certainly be sold, traded, in elementary ways, like a newspaper joins Associated Press and purchases [articles] or you go to a bookstore and buy a book. Information is sold. That's not a deep point, I don't think.

DB *What about ways of acquiring knowledge outside of the conventional structures, the colleges and universities?*

First of all, even within the conventional structures, colleges, universities, the *New York Times*, etc., if you read carefully, you can learn a lot. All of these institutions have an important internal contradiction: On the one hand, they wouldn't survive if they didn't support the fundamental interests of people who have wealth and power. If you don't serve those interests, you don't survive very long. So there is a distorting and propaganda effect and tendency. On the other hand, they also have within them something that drives them towards integrity and honesty and accurate depiction of the world, as far as one can do it. Partly that just comes out of personal integrity of people inside them, whether they're journalists or historians. But partly it's because they won't even do their job for the powerful unless they give a tolerably accurate picture of reality. So the business press, for example, often does quite good and accurate reporting, and the rest of the press too, in many cases. The reason is that people in power need to know the facts if they're going to make decisions in their own interests. These two conflicting tendencies mean that if you weave your way between them you can learn quite a lot.

To get back to your question: Outside these institutions there are all sorts of things people can do. Let's go back to the article I mentioned in the *Washington Post* about Central America. Central American activists in Boulder or plenty of other places, when they look at that article just collapse in laughter. They know the facts. They didn't find out the facts from reading the *Washington Post*, for the most part. They found them out through other sources. The Central American solidarity movements had access to extensive information and still do, through direct contacts, through alternative media, through people travelling back and forth, that is completely outside the framework of the mainstream media. For example, one thing that this article states is that the United States compelled the Marxist Sandinistas to run their first free election in 1990. Everyone in the Central American solidarity movements, and plenty of other people, knows that that's complete baloney and that there was a free election held in 1984, except it came out the wrong way, so therefore it was wiped out of history by the U.S. In fact, the author of this article certainly knows it as well. But for him to say it in the *Washington Post* would be like standing up in the Vatican and saying Jesus Christ didn't exist. You just can't say certain things within a deeply totalitarian intellectual culture like ours. Therefore, he has to say what he says, and maybe even believes it, although it's hard for me to imagine. Everybody has to say that. But people in the popular movements know perfectly well that it's not true and know why it's not true, because they've found other ways to gain understanding of the world.

In case you heard a big bang in the background, that was one of the piles of books in my study collapsing on the floor, as happens regularly.

DB *I can see you surrounded by mountains and stacks of papers and books.*

Occasionally they decide that the laws of physics won't handle it and they fall on the floor, which is what just happened.

DB *You commented to a friend that the amount of material that you lose is "awesome," but it seems to me that the amount of material that you retain is awesome as well.*

It doesn't feel that way to me. I feel mostly the loss. As I see it disappearing it's agonizing. I know if

I don't write about something within a couple of years it will be gone, lost in these piles. The trouble is, all of us feel like this. You're so far out of the mainstream that the few people who follow these issues closely and who write about them know that if they don't deal with something it's out of history. For example, the Nicaraguan election is in history, at least for people who care, primarily because Edward Herman did some very good research on it. It doesn't matter to the *Washington Post*. For them it's out of history, period, because those are the orders from those who are on high. But for people who want to know, you can look at Herman's work.

DB *Something you've been saying over the years strikes me as somewhat contradictory. When you talk about the connection between U.S. aid and human rights abuses, you say that connection is "obvious," and at the same time you say that there's no way to know about these things and you have to be a fanatic, as you describe yourself, to find these things out. Doesn't that leave people intimidated and disempowered?*

If I put it that way I'm being a little misleading. As an individual, you have to be a fanatic to find it out. On the other hand, if you're part of a semi-organized movement, like the Central America solidarity movements, you don't have to be a fanatic, because you have access to alternative sources of information.

Again, take Edward Herman, my friend and colleague, who did an extensive study of the relation between U.S. aid and torture. He found them very

159

highly correlated. We published information about it in jointly written books of ours and elsewhere. He's also published his own books that describe this in detail.

The leading Latin American academic specialist on human rights, Lars Schoultz at North Carolina, published an article in about 1980 on U.S. aid and human-rights violations, primarily torture, in Latin America. He found exactly the same thing. As he put it in his article, U.S. aid tends to flow to the most egregious human rights violators in the hemisphere. They are consistently the highest aid recipients. He also showed that this correlation has nothing to do with need, that it includes military aid, and that it runs through the Carter period. In the Reagan period it shot through the roof. You can find those things out. I've reported them. Herman's reported them.

If an isolated individual like that person you mentioned earlier wanted to figure this stuff out, he'd have to be kind of a fanatic. It would take immense research to even find that anybody ever talked about these topics. You're not going to find them in the *New York Times* index. What you'll find is article after article about our profound commitment to human rights. On the other hand, if you are part of the popular movements you have easy access to such material and you don't have to be a fanatic at all. You just have to have your eyes open.

DB *In the tremendous amount of mail that you receive, are these views of isolation reflected? What is the temper of the mail?*

Overwhelmingly. There is a film (*Manufacturing*

Consent) by Mark Achbar and Peter Wintonick that's been playing around the world, often on national television and around this country, too, though a little less prominently. I get a lot of letters, hundreds, maybe thousands. Very commonly the tone is very much like what the person you mentioned said. This also happens if I occasionally appear on TV in the United States, on Bill Moyers or Pozner/Donahue. I get a lot of letters saying, I was very interested to hear what you had to say. I thought I was the only person in the world who had thoughts like this. Where can I learn more about it? Sometimes I cringe when the letters say, How can I join your movement? Meaning I haven't at all gotten across what I was trying to.

DB *You steadfastly refuse to see the film* Manufacturing Consent. *Why?*

Partly because there's that feeling that however much they might have tried, there's something inherent in the medium which personalizes and gives the false and indeed ridiculous impression that leads to questions like, "How can I join your movement?"

DB *How much time do you spend responding to mail per week?*

I hate to think about it. Probably twenty-five hours or so.

DB *It's actually increased since the last time I*

spoke to you.

It goes up and up. I was away for a couple of weeks in Europe and the Middle East giving lectures. When I came back, I think it took me over two weeks of doing nothing else, just to clear away the mail.

DB *These are individual responses. I know people are absolutely amazed when they do hear from you. They are stunned at the graciousness of your replies.*

These letters are often extremely serious and very thoughtful. I should say that on one topic, finally, I had to write a form letter, saying, Sorry, I can't respond.

DB *What was that?*

Take a guess.

DB *JFK. Conspiracy theories.*

That's it. It just got to the point where I couldn't respond any more. Within the bounds of a twenty-four-hour day I couldn't answer the letters. So much to my regret I had to say, sorry, I can't do it.

DB *Does that interest in conspiracy theories tell you something about the political culture?*

It tells you something about what's undermining

the left. For people who feel a need to believe in conspiracies, here's one sitting there waiting for them. Just imagine the CIA deciding, How can we undermine and destroy all of these popular movements? Let's send them off on some crazy wild goose chase which is going to involve them in extremely detailed microanalysis and discussion of things that don't matter. That'll shut them up. That's happening. In case anybody misunderstands, I don't believe this for one moment, but it's the kind of thing that goes around.

DB *It's curious that there are elements of what is called the "left" in this country that have embraced this so fervidly.*

In my opinion, that's a phenomenon similar to this feeling of impotence and isolation that you mentioned. If you really feel, Look, it's too hard to deal with real problems, there are a lot of ways to avoid doing so. One of them is to go off on wild goose chases that don't matter. Another is to get involved in academic cults that are very divorced from any reality and that provide a defense against dealing with the world as it actually is. There's plenty of that going on, including in the left. I just saw some very depressing examples of it in my trip to Egypt a couple of weeks ago. I was there to talk on international affairs. There's a very lively, civilized intellectual community, very courageous people who spent years in Nasser's jails being practically tortured to death and came out struggling. Now throughout the Third World there's a sense of great despair and hopelessness. The way it showed up there, in very educated circles with European connections, was to become immersed in the latest lunacies of Paris culture and to focus totally on those. For example, when I would give talks about current realities, even in research institutes dealing with strategic issues, participants wanted it to be translated into post-modern gibberish. For example, rather than have me talk about the details of what's going on in U.S policy or the Middle East, where they live, which is too grubby and uninteresting, they would like to know how does modern linguistics provide a new paradigm for discourse about international affairs that will supplant the post-structuralist text. That would really fascinate them. But not what do Israeli cabinet records show about internal planning. That's really depressing.

DB *This was your first visit to Egypt?*

Yes. Incidentally, when that happens in Egypt it's very sad. When it happens all over the West as it does, it's maybe comical or unpleasant but not devastating.

DB *I just got back from Amsterdam, where I did some interviews and gave some talks. Precisely those kinds of convoluted, very pretentious questions were asked.*

I've seen the same in Holland. These are ways in which intellectuals can separate themselves from actual, ongoing struggle and still appear to be lefter than thou. Nobody's radical enough for them. That way you advance your career, you separate yourself from things that are going on. You don't have to get involved in popular activities. You don't have to learn about the world, let alone do anything about it. I'm overstating. I don't want to say this is true of everybody, by any means, but there are elements of it. These are other ways of reacting to the fact that dealing with the problems of the world is hard and unpleasant. Especially if you begin to do it effectively, there are personal costs.

DB *It also creates a tremendous gap between them and so-called "people."*

Sure. Nobody can understand this stuff. That has the effect of intimidating people, especially young people coming into the colleges who look at this and say, My God, to be a radical I'm going to have to understand all these ten syllable words. It's hopeless. I'd better do something else.

DB *What did you learn about the Islamic movement in Egypt?*

I don't want to overstate. I wasn't there long enough to learn a lot. But I should say that I did meet a pretty wide range of people, people I knew and those who were recommended to me, and most of those I came across who were seriously thinking through problems of Egypt and the region were the intellectuals who were associated with the Islamic movement. The ones I met were kind of on the secular wing of those movements. I didn't meet clerics. But these are people who regard themselves, and are regarded as, oppositionists and part of the Islamic movement. They plainly do have grassroots connections. They themselves describe the movement as split between the more progressive sectors and the "rigid" sector, meaning the real deep fundamentalists, who say, We go back to Koranic law, *sharia*, and that's the end of it. But they themselves are thinking about domestic and regional development and local problems in ways which are not at all unrealistic. Furthermore, these movements actually do things. They provide health care, run welfare programs, and try to deal with people's problems. They're almost unique in that respect. Everyone agrees to that, even the people who hate them.

DB *What's the motor that's pushing this movement in Egypt?*

You just walk around Cairo and you can see the motor. There was a period of secular nationalism, of which Nasser was the leading figure. It failed, or was destroyed, partly by itself and partly from outside. Sadat, around 1980, undertook a policy which translates as "opening up," in effect, structural adjustment, neo-liberal policies. There were the usual effects, seen all over the world, completely predictable by now. They increased very sharply the split in the society between great wealth and privilege and enormous misery and suffering, with the proportions being by no means balanced. People are suffering. And they see right next to them enormous wealth and privilege. The government is totally corrupt and doesn't do anything. It's a police state, not a harsh police state, but you can't forget it for long. What happens under those conditions? People turn to something else. It's happening all throughout the region.

DB *Is it not really happening throughout the world as there's global impoverishment?*

These tendencies are going on throughout the world. The rich western countries are imposing these neo-liberal policies, as they're called, on the Third World. They have plenty of power. The debt crisis, for example, is being used as a very effective weapon to try to force most of the Third World into these programs, which are lethal. The rich countries themselves don't accept those policies. They don't accept free market policies for themselves. They're too destructive. However, as the economy becomes more global, more internationalized, there is an automatic effect of bringing back Third World tendencies into the rich countries themselves. It's not very mysterious. American capitalists can be very rich, but American workers are going to have to compete with people in what are, in effect, Third World countries.

DB *There was a photo in the paper here a couple of weeks ago of the University of Colorado graduating class. One senior held up a sign: "Will work for food."*

You see that right outside of rich shopping centers near where I live. The wealthy countries will never, and never have, accepted the neo-liberal principles, the free market principles they impose on the poor. The consequences of imposing them on the poor are slowly to have this Third World model seep back into the rich countries themselves. It's very striking in the U.S. You can see it in Europe, particularly in England, and on the continent you're beginning to see it as well. There's nothing secret about it.

The business press—*Business Week, The Financial Times,* etc.—are very open in saying, American and especially European workers are going to have to give up their "luxurious" social programs. They're going to have to stop being "pampered" and accept labor mobility, meaning lose their security, because corporations can go over to Eastern Europe. In Poland they can get trained workers at ten percent of the wage of the "pampered" west European workers. No benefits, and a highly repressive government that breaks up strikes. Therefore you guys better recognize what's in store for you. There was an article in the *Financial Times* recently with a wonderful headline: "Green Shoots in Communism's Ruins," meaning Communism is a wreck, but there are some green shoots, a few good things. The good thing was that as capitalist reforms are imposed in Eastern Europe, pauperization and unemployment follow, which lowers wages and makes it possible for western corporations to move in and make huge profits. Those are the "green shoots."

DB *There is of course a huge increase in unemployment in western European countries. That has an attendant social component in the many attacks against immigrant communities.*

Unemployment and loss of hope lead to social breakdown. We're much more advanced in that respect. There's a kind of breakdown of social structure in American urban communities which is amazing to most of the world. Take, say, Cairo. Cairo is a very poor city, extremely impoverished. There's nothing like it here. Nevertheless there is a sense of community that exists that doesn't exist here. You feel safer walking through the streets there than here. You don't stumble over homeless people. People are taken care of somehow. It's the same in Nicaragua or many other Third World countries that haven't totally broken down. We are beginning to get Third World characteristics, but under conditions of social breakdown. That's very dangerous. That's why you can have people cheering when someone wins a court trial (in Baton Rouge, Louisiana) after having blasted away somebody (Yoshihiro Hattori) that dared to step on his lawn. That appalled most of the world. They just couldn't understand it.

DB *Your latest book as of this morning—Howard Zinn likes to add that caveat—is* Letters from Lexington. *Do you have any more books planned?*

I promised to write up lectures on international affairs and the Middle East that I gave in Cairo. That will be published by American University Press (Cairo).

DB *Is the summer a good time for you to work, when you're away from the interviews, the phone calls, the classes?*

As you know, I turn off the phone. That's about the only time I can try to get anything done.

DB *Later this year you're going to turn sixty-five.*

You don't believe that propaganda, do you?

KEEPING THE RABBLE IN LINE

DB *Have you thought about slowing down, cutting back on your schedule at all?*

There are an awful lot of things I'd like to do that I'm just not getting to. There isn't all that much time.

DB *You know that anecdote that Mike Albert tells when he went to Poland some years ago, he found people who thought that there were two Noam Chomskys, one who did the linguistics work and the other who did the political work?*

Partly because the name doesn't sound as strange to them there.

DB *There was a serious reactor explosion in a town named Tomsk in central Russia. Is the name of that town at all connected to Chomsky?*

It could be. Nobody really knows the etymology. Roman Jakobson, a great Slavic linguist and scholar, always told me that he was convinced that that was the origin, a corruption of Tomsk, Thomas basically.

DB *Is Avram your actual given name?*

It is, but my parents never used it, so I use my middle name. It's almost become my legal first name by now. Just to show you the good old days of real sexism, I once had to get a copy of my birth certificate and I discovered that a clerk who hadn't believed my name had crossed it out and written in pencil above it "Avrane Naomi." Well, why Avrane? Because girls are allowed to have crazy names, not boys.

DB *Just to back up a little bit. You also went recently to Northern Ireland. What did you find there in terms of economic conditions and the political situation?*

I spent my time either in West Belfast, which is mainly Catholic and a very repressed area, or southern parts of Northern Ireland, within what is called "bandit country," places where the British troops can only go in in fairly substantial force and where there have been plenty of atrocities. I talked to human rights activists. I was at the Center for Human Rights talking to Gerry Adams, the head of Sinn Fein, and others, and to a lot of people. The country is under military occupation. There's no secret about that. There are armored personnel carriers going through the streets, armed blockades right in the middle of Belfast center, etc. There is plenty of killing by paramilitaries on both sides. There is open debate about the extent to which or if the British forces are connected to the loyalists, the mainly Protestant paramilitary, and there is probably some connection, but nobody knows how much. In the Catholic community, listening to the stories was very much like walking around the West Bank a couple of years ago, the same kinds of humiliation and beating and torture. There aren't a lot of ways to have your boot on someone's neck. It always turns out about the same.

DB *It echoes the religious conflicts of the Middle*

Ages in Europe.

The British, back in the mid-seventeenth century, carried out real ethnic cleansing. The indigenous population in what's now Ulster was mostly driven out, often into central Ireland.

DB *Was there settler colonialism?*

Yes. They brought in Scottish and other British settlers to replace them. They took most of the fertile land. Traveling through South Armagh, near the border, I spent some time with a local civil rights group that was set up after several young men were murdered by British troops, who are now coming up for trial, years later. A farmer whose son had been killed took me around and showed me what things were like. They raise cattle, but they can only raise young cattle, because the earth is too infertile to grow grass good enough to raise adult cattle. So they raise calves and send them off somewhere. Every acre is completely reclaimed. You've first got to pull out all the rocks and move them somewhere else and try to level the ground. These are the areas to which the Irish were driven, off into the rocky hills, by the British who cleansed the fertile areas and brought in their own settlers. It was a couple of centuries ago, but the residue is still there.

DB *Do you see any solution to the problem of Northern Ireland?*

There are contrary tendencies going on in

Europe. There's a tendency toward centralization in the European Community executive, which is almost totally insulated from public pressure, and there's a countertendency toward regionalization. So local regions, whether Catalonia, the Basque country, Wales, or whatever, are beginning to become more involved in developing their own cultural authenticity and forms of independence and ways of self-government. In the context of this regionalization and devolution, it's not impossible that the former British Isles could break down into a kind of federal arrangement, maybe as part of a broader European federalism. It would involve a degree of independence in a number of areas: Scotland, Wales, England, Northern Ireland, the Republic, and in that context I think you might imagine a solution. I don't see much else. Within a couple of years the population of Northern Ireland is going to be about fifty-fifty Catholic and Protestant, according to demographic projections.

DB *I have to tell you, going back to the level of mail that you get, some years ago I wrote you a letter, and that was my first contact with you. You responded. That led to a correspondence. Then we starting doing interviews. It really helped to get Alternative Radio going. I can bear witness and give testimony to the enormous efficacy of your efforts. I think I speak for a lot of people who appreciate what you're doing. It does make a difference.*

It's reciprocal. I very much appreciate what thousands of people are doing everywhere, which is making a difference—a big difference. These activities of many, many people around the country and the world have made a tremendous difference over the last thirty years.

DB *It's incremental. People want to see dramatic changes, but the culture and politics change rather slowly.*

They do, but it's very different from what it was. Under conditions like those in the 1960s, you would have had to wait until the fall of 1969 for the first newspaper to timidly suggest that maybe we ought to stop the aggression in Vietnam.

DB *Thank you, and have a restful summer. How's your foot?*

It's OK. It's just a fractured bone.

Crime
and Gun Control

December 6, 1993

DB *I know I didn't get you up because it's well known that you stay up and work through the night, drinking tons and tons of coffee.*

That's why I sound so groggy.

DB *I want to talk to you about a couple of domestic and foreign policy issues and then take calls from our listeners. You can tell a great deal about a society when you look at its system of justice. I was wondering if you would comment on the Clinton crime bill, in which some of the provisions are to hire 100,000 more cops, build boot camps for juveniles, spend more money for prisons, extend the death penalty to about fifty new offenses, and make gang membership a federal crime, which is interesting, considering that there is something about freedom of association in the Bill of Rights.*

One of the consequences of the developments over the past twenty or thirty years has been a considerable increase in inequality. This trend accelerated during the Reagan years. The society has been moving visibly towards a kind of Third World model, which has to do with all sorts of things going on in

175

the international economy as well as very explicit social policy. Huge sectors of the society are simply becoming more or less superfluous for wealth creation, which is considered the only human value. The consequence of this is an increasing crime rate, as well as other signs of social disintegration. People are very worried, and quite properly, because the society is becoming very dangerous. Most of the crime is poor people attacking each other. But it spills over to more privileged sectors. As a result there's a great deal of fear about crime.

A constructive approach to the problem would require dealing with its fundamental causes, and that's off the agenda, because we must continue with social policy aimed at strengthening the welfare state for the rich. So there's no constructive response. The only kind of response that the government can resort to under those conditions is pandering to these fears with increasing harshness and attacks on civil liberties and moves to control the useless population, essentially by force, which is what this is all about.

DB *What are your views on capital punishment?*

It's a crime. I agree with Amnesty International on that one, and indeed with most of the world. The state should have no right to take people's lives.

DB *There's quite a bit of controversy on gun control. Advocates of free access to arms cite the Second Amendment. Do you believe the Second Amendment permits unrestricted, uncontrolled possession of guns?*

176

What laws permit and don't permit is a question that doesn't have a straightforward answer. Laws permit what the tenor of the times interprets them as permitting. But underlying the controversy over guns are some serious questions. Literally, the Second Amendment doesn't permit people to have guns. But laws are never taken literally, including amendments to the Constitution or constitutional rights.

Underlying the controversy is something which shouldn't be discounted. There's a feeling in the country that people are under attack. I think they're misidentifying the source of the attack, but they feel under attack. Decades of intensive business propaganda have been designed to make them see the government as the enemy, the government being the only power structure in the system that is even partially accountable to the population, so naturally you want to make that be the enemy, not the corporate system, which is totally unaccountable. After decades of propaganda people feel that the government is some kind of enemy and they have to defend themselves from it. Many of those who advocate keeping guns have that in the back of their minds. I wouldn't believe it if I hadn't heard it so many times. That's a crazy response to a real problem.

DB *What role do the media play in fostering those attitudes?*

At the deepest level, by contributing to this notion of getting the government off our backs. It's not that that doesn't have its justifications, too. The government is authoritarian and commonly a hostile structure for much of the population, but it is partially accountable and potentially very extensively accountable to the general population.

The media grossly mislead by contributing to the sense that the government is the enemy and displacing real power from view, suppressing the sources of real power in the society, which lie in the totalitarian institutions, by now international in scale, that control the economy and much of social life and in fact certainly set conditions within which government operates and control it to a large extent. This happens sometimes in comical ways and sometimes in deeper ways.

People simply have no awareness of the system of power under which they are indeed suffering. As a result, as intended, they turn against the government. People fear that they're overtaxed. By comparative standards they're undertaxed. When people talk about a tax-based health plan, meaning one that doesn't just soak the poor, like the Clinton plan is intended to do, you get a reflex response: more pointy-headed bureaucrats stealing our money and running our lives. On the other hand, payment of far higher "taxes"—regressive to boot—to a far more bureaucratized and oppressive insurance company that is completely unaccountable, that's OK because you aren't supposed to see it.

To get back to gun control, people have all kinds of motivations, but there is definitely a sector of the population that considers themselves threatened by big forces, ranging from the Federal Reserve to the Council on Foreign Relations to big government to who knows what and are calling for guns to protect themselves.

Crime and Gun Control

DB *I don't know how much you watch local or national network news, but there has been a discernible trend over the last few years. The influence of local news primarily dealing with crimes, rapes, and kidnappings, is now spilling over into the national network news.*

That's true. But it's always the surface phenomenon. Why is there an increase in violent crime? Is that connected to the fact that there has been a considerable decline in income for the large majority of the population and opportunity for constructive work? Is it connected to NAFTA, for example, and the basic phenomena of which NAFTA itself is a symptom? Sure it is. But until you ask why there is an increase in social disintegration and what this has to do with policies that are directing resources towards the wealthy and privileged sectors and away from the general population, until you ask those questions you can't have even a concept of why there's rising crime or how you should deal with it.

DB *There's a juxtaposition I want to pose to you now. Anthony Lewis, in a very strong pro-NAFTA column in the* New York Times, *before the vote, writes that an anti-NAFTA vote would mean "the end of nearly fifty years of rising world prosperity. That's all. Since World War II the world has experienced extraordinary growth. The engine for that growth has been international trade. Vastly increased trade in an age of more and more rapid transportation and communication." Juan de Dias Parra, the head of the Latin American Association for Human Rights, in a meeting in Quito, Ecuador, says, "In Latin America today there are 7 mil-*

179

lion more hungry, 30 million more illiterate, 10 million more families without homes, 40 million more unemployed persons than there were twenty years ago. There are 240 million human beings in Latin America without the necessities of life, and this when the region is richer and more stable than ever, according to the way the world sees it." How do you reconcile those points of view?

It just depends on which people we're worried about. The World Bank came out with a study on Latin America about two months ago in which they warned that Latin America was facing chaos and even the things they're concerned about would be threatened, because of the extraordinarily high inequality, which is the highest inequality in the world, and that's after a period of substantial growth rates. For example, take Brazil, which is a very rich country with enormous resources. It would be one of the richest countries in the world if it weren't for its social and economic system. It is ranked around Albania and Paraguay in quality of life measures, infant mortality, etc.

On the other hand, it's had one of the highest growth rates in the world. It's also been almost completely directed by American technocrats for about fifty years. The inequality that the World Bank describes is not just something that came from the heavens. There was a struggle over the course of Latin American development back in the mid-1940s, when the new world order of that day was being crafted. The State Department documents on this are quite interesting. They said that Latin America was swept by what they called the "philosophy of the

180

new nationalism," which calls for increasing production for domestic needs and reducing inequality. Its basic principle was that the people of the country should be the "first beneficiaries of the development of a country's resources." That's the philosophy of the new nationalism, as the State Department described it.

The U.S. was sharply opposed to that and came out with an economic charter for the Americas that called for eliminating economic nationalism, as it's called, "in all of its forms" and insisting that Latin American development be "complementary" to U.S. development, meaning we'll have the advanced industry and the technology and the peons will produce export crops and do some simple operations that they can manage. But they won't develop the way we did.

The U.S., of course, won, given the distribution of power. In countries like Brazil the U.S. just took over. It was one of the "testing grounds for scientific methods of development on the American capitalist model," as propaganda had it. And so it was, and so you get the consequences you describe. It's true, as Lewis says, that there has been very substantial growth. At the same time there's incredible poverty and misery, which has also increased. Over the past thirty years, there has been a sharp increase in inequality. The growth has slowed down considerably in the last ten years, but there has been growth. Much more dramatic has been the separation of the top sector of the population from the rest. So if you compare the percentage of world income held by the richest twenty percent and the lowest twenty percent, the gap has dramatically increased. That's true whether you consider countries, which is a little mystical, but taking the top twenty percent of countries and the bottom twenty percent of countries, that gap has about doubled. Take the top twenty and the bottom twenty percent of people, the gap has increased far more and is much sharper. That's the consequences of a particular kind of growth.

Incidentally, what Lewis calls "trade"—he's using the conventional term, but it's a bit misleading. In fact, substantially misleading, for reasons we've already discussed. If the Ford Motor Company moves something from an assembly plant in Mexico to an assembly plant in the U.S., that's called trade. But it's not trade in any serious sense, and in fact the centrally managed policies within these totalitarian structures account for about 40% of the interchanges that are called "trade". These policies often involve radical violations of market principles which are not considered by GATT and NAFTA because they are not designed to extend the market system but to extend the power of corporations who want to benefit from this kind of market distortion.

DB *So you see this trend of growth rates and increasing poverty simultaneously continuing?*

Actually, growth rates have been slowing down a lot. In the past twenty years, growth is roughly half of what it was in the preceding twenty years. That tendency of lower growth will probably continue. One factor that has to do with that is the enormous growth of unregulated, speculative capital. That growth has accelerated rapidly basically since Nixon broke down the Bretton Woods system around 1970.

182

By now the unregulated financial capital is estimated by the World Bank at about $14 trillion, and about $1 trillion or so of that moves around every day. That creates pressures for deflationary policies.

That's what that financial capital wants. It wants low growth, low inflation. The huge amounts of capital, which overwhelm national states, make it very difficult to carry out stimulative programs. In the poorer societies it's hopeless. Even in the richer societies it would be very hard. What happened with Clinton's trivial stimulus package was a good indication. It amounted to nothing, $19 billion. It was shot down instantly. Financial capital, which is now an extraordinarily large part of the capital available internationally, has an anti-growth effect. It is driving much of the world into a low-growth, low-wage equilibrium. The figures are really astonishing. John Eatwell, one of the leading specialists in finance at Cambridge University, estimates that in 1970 about ninety percent of international capital was used for trade and long-term investment and ten percent for speculation. In 1990 those figures were reversed: ninety percent for speculation. Also the quantity has grown enormously. The effects of that, as he points out, are what I just said.

DB *The* Boulder Daily Camera *is part of the chain of Knight-Ridder newspapers. In yesterday's edition they ran a box with questions and answers: "What Is GATT?" "What Is the Uruguay Round of GATT?" Here's the part I wanted to ask you about. In the question, "Who would benefit from a GATT agreement?" the answer given is, "Consumers would be the big winners." Does that track with your* *understanding of GATT?*

If you mean by "consumers" rich ones, yes. Rich consumers will gain. People who have lost their jobs, for example—and that will be true both in the rich countries and the poor—obviously are not going to be better consumers. Take a look at NAFTA, where the analyses have already been done, and even appeared in the press after the vote. Before that, there was a huge hype about how important the vote is, of which the Lewis column that you mentioned is a case in point. Do you remember the date of that article?

DB *It was November 5.*

Before the vote. That's the kind of stuff that was appearing before the vote. I noticed a quite striking difference the day after the vote. Immediately after the vote, the *New York Times* and other journals began for the first time discussing the consequences of NAFTA. That was interesting. Not that it was a surprise, but it shows what they knew all along. The day after the vote the *New York Times* had its first article on the expected impact of NAFTA in the New York region. This generalizes for GATT also.

It was a very upbeat article. They talked about how wonderful it was going to be. They said there would be a big improvement in finance and services, particularly. They'll be the big winners. Banks, investment firms, PR firms, corporate law firms will do just great. They said that some manufacturers will benefit, namely the publishing industry and chemical industry, which is highly capital-intensive,

not many workers to worry about Also the pharmaceutical industry, the big beneficiaries of the
increased protectionist elements concerning "intellectual property". They'll all do fine and it will just be
wonderful.

Then they said that, well, there will be some
losers, too. The losers will be women, Hispanics,
other minorities, and semi-skilled workers, who
comprise maybe seventy percent or more of the work
force. They will be losers. But everyone else will do
fine. In other words, exactly as anyone who was paying attention knew, the purpose of NAFTA was to
split the society even further. There will be benefits
for a smaller—it's a rich country, so the small sector's not tiny—but a smaller sector of highly privileged people, investors, professionals, managerial
classes, and so on, the business-related classes. It
will work fine for them, and the general population
will suffer.

The prediction for Mexico is pretty much the
same. The leading financial journal in Mexico, which
is very pro-NAFTA, estimated that Mexico would lose
about twenty-five percent of its manufacturing
capacity in the first few years and about fifteen percent of its manufacturing labor force. In addition,
cheap U.S. agricultural exports are expected to drive
even more people off the land. That's going to mean
a substantial increase in the unemployed workforce
in Mexico, which of course will drive down wages. On
top of that, organizing is essentially impossible.
Notice that although corporations can operate internationally, unions cannot. So though unions can
operate in different states of the U.S., they cannot
cross borders, which means there is no way for the

work force to fight back against the internationalization of production.

The net effect is expected to be a decline in wealth and income for the majority of the population of Mexico and for the majority of the population of the U.S., while there will be exactly that growth and increase in consumption that the Boulder paper talks about, the increase in income that Lewis talks about. Those are completely consistent. A country like Brazil is the extreme example, and a very dramatic example because of its enormous wealth and because of the fact that we've been running it for fifty years. It's a very good model to look at.

Very high growth rates, tremendous prosperity, a lot of consumption in a very narrow sector of the population. And overall, the quality of life at the levels of Albania and Paraguay.

DB *Chile is another country that's recently been heralded in a number of articles as reflecting that model growth rate.*

There was a really funny pair of stories yesterday. The *New York Times* had a story about the election in Chile and about how nobody was paying much attention to it. The headline was something about Chilean satisfaction with the political system. It talked about how everyone is so satisfied and so happy that nobody's paying much attention to the election.

The London *Financial Times*, hardly radical, they had a story on the election which was exactly the opposite. They quoted some data, some polls that showed that seventy-five percent of the population are very unsatisfied, "disgruntled" was their word, with regard to the political system, which allows no options. They said that indeed there is apathy about the election, but that's a reflection of the breakdown of the social structure of Chile, which was a lively, vibrant, democratic society into the early 1970s and then was essentially depoliticized through a reign of fascist terror.

People work alone, the associations were broken down. People are trying to fend for themselves. The economy is not doing badly, but it's based almost entirely on primary exports, fruit, copper, and so on. It's very vulnerable to world markets.

But the crucial thing is the dramatic breakdown of social relations and social structure, which is pretty striking in Chile, because it was a very vibrant and lively society for many, many years. The retreat into individualism and personal gain is the basis for the apathy. Nathaniel Nash wrote the Chile story for the *Times*. There's a section in there, a subheading called "Painful Memories." It said many Chileans have painful memories of Salvador Allende's fiery speeches, which led to the coup in which thousands of people were killed. Notice they don't have painful memories of the torture, the fascist terror, just of Allende's speeches as a popular candidate. These are the ways in which the world is recreated for our edification.

DB *This is a 7 a.m. early edition of Alternative Radio and we're talking to Professor Noam Chomsky. If you'd like to join this conversation, give us a call. One thing you've been talking about is the mystification of the notion of nation and country. You discussed it in a*

187

recent Z Magazine *article. I was struck by a November 15 front-page* New York Times *article. The headline is "Nation Considers Means To Dispose of Its Plutonium. Options are unattractive," we are told, and there are "no easy or quick answers to a problem that will not go away." So the nation is considering how to dispose of essentially what was a creation of private capital, plutonium.*

That's the familiar idea that profit is to be privatized but the cost is to be socialized. So in a sense it's correct to say that the costs are the costs for the nation, the people. But the profits weren't for the people, nor are they making the decisions to produce plutonium in the first place, and they're not making the decisions about how to dispose of it. Nor or they deciding on what ought to be a reasonable energy policy, which is no small issue. There are major questions about energy policy that ought to be right on the top of the social and political agenda today, things connected, say, with global warming.

Let me give you an example. There was a study that came out in *Science* magazine about a month ago reviewing recent studies on global warming. The possibilities they were considering as plausible were that if the year 2000 goals on carbon dioxide emission are met, which is not likely, then within a couple of centuries, by 2300, the world's temperature would have increased by about ten degrees Centigrade, which would mean a rise in sea level that would probably wipe out a good bit of human civilization as it's currently constituted. Of course this doesn't mean that the effects set in in three hundred years. They start setting in much sooner.

Maybe it will be worse. Maybe it will be better. But possibilities like that will not be faced by any sane person with any equanimity. There's nothing being done about them at all. The same study says that in order to avoid this it will be necessary to undertake quite radical changes of a kind not even contemplated. These are what ought to be front-page stories and ought to be the focus of public attention and concern. The matter of disposing of plutonium has largely to do with weapons production. But there are quite serious questions about nuclear power that can't just be dismissed.

CALL-INS

Listener: *You have established a fairly loyal following. I am fearful that there may be this saturation point of despair just from knowing the heaviness of the truth that you impart. I would like to strongly lobby you to begin a process of maybe devoting ten or fifteen percent of your appearances or books or articles towards tangible detailed things that people can do to try to change the world that they're in, even if it does seem like it's potentially useless from time to time. I've heard a few occasions where someone says, What can I do? I live all by myself in Lafayette, Colorado or some other little town, and your response is, Organize. Just do it.*

Your point is quite right. People have been telling me that for a long time. I'll give you an example which goes back about ten years ago. South End Press asked me to write a book called *Turning the Tide*. It came out in 1985. Most of it was just what you were criticizing, and properly, but there was a section at the end called "Turning the Tide: What Can You Do About It?" I try to keep it in the back of my mind and think about it, but I'm afraid that the answer always is the same. It's that person in Lafayette. There is only one way to deal with these things. Being alone, you cannot do anything. All you can do is deplore the situation. If you join with other people, they can be anything from a whole range of possibilities, from Ralph Nader's Public Citizen, to a local activist group to some solidarity group, and there are millions of things that are possible depending on where you want to put your efforts, if you join with other people, you can make changes. I don't know of any other answers.

Listener: *What's happening in Asia, particularly the growing economies in Southeast Asia, China, and so forth. What do you see for the future in terms of the demands of the environment on the political actions in those countries economically? Is it going to be another example of capitalist exploitation, or is the environment going to make such a demand that we could expect to see some kind of change in their awareness?*

Countries like Thailand or China are looming ecological catastrophes. These are countries where growth is being fueled by multinational investment and investor interests and for them the environment is what are called "externalities." You don't pay any attention to it. So if you destroy the forests in Thailand, say, that's OK as long as you make a short-term profit out of it. In China, just because of its scale, the disasters that lie not too far ahead could be extraordinary. The same is true throughout

Southeast Asia.

But the question remains that when the environmental pressures become such that the very survival of the people is jeopardized, do you see any change in the actions?

Not unless people react. If power is left in the hands of transnational investors, the people will just die.

DB *Elaine Bernard and Tony Mazzocchi were in Denver on December 3. They were talking about the possibility of creating a new labor-based party. What are your views on that?*

I think that's an important initiative. It's interesting that right now, we're a little bit like the way Chile is described in the *Financial Times*, not the *New York Times*. The country is becoming very depoliticized and negative. About half the population thinks both political parties should be disbanded. There's a real need for something that would articulate the concerns of that substantial majority of the population which is being left out of social planning and the political process, those, for example, who will be harmed by NAFTA, a substantial majority, as even the *Times* can see. Labor unions have been a significant force for democratization and progress, not always, but often, in fact the main social force. On the other hand, when they are not linked to the political system through a labor-based party, there's a limit on what they can do. Take, say, health care.

191

Powerful unions in the U.S. were able to get fairly reasonable health care provisions for themselves. For example, auto workers were able to get good provisions for themselves. But since they are acting independently of the political system, they did not attempt to or succeed in bringing about decent health conditions for the population.

Compare Canada, where the unions also pressed for health care, but not just for their own industry, but rather for the population. Being linked to labor-based parties they were able to implement health care for the population. That's an illustration of the kind of difference that a politically oriented popular movement like labor can achieve. We're not in the day any longer where the industrial workers are the majority or even the core of the labor force. But the same questions arise. I think Elaine Bernard and Tony Mazzocchi are on the right track in thinking along those lines.

In that same Anthony Lewis column that I referred to earlier, he had this to write: "Unions in this country, sad to say, are looking more and more like the British unions...backward, unenlightened.... The crude, threatening tactics used by unions to make Democratic members of the House vote against NAFTA underline the point."

That brings out Lewis's real commitments very clearly. What he called crude, undemocratic tactics which were assailed by the President and the press, were labor's attempt to get their representatives to represent their interests. By the standard of the elite, that's an attack on democracy, because the political system is supposed to be run by the rich and power-ful. So for example corporate lobbying—which vastly exceeded labor lobbying—was not considered raw muscle or anti-democratic. Did Lewis have a column denouncing corporate lobbying for NAFTA?

I didn't see it.

I didn't see it either. This reached a peak of absolute hysteria before the vote. The day before the vote the *New York Times* lead editorial was exactly along the lines of your quote from Lewis, and it included a little box of the dozen or so representa-tives of the New York region who were voting against NAFTA. It listed their contributions from labor and said, This raises ominous questions about political influence of labor and whether they're being honest, etc.

As a number of these representatives later pointed out, the *Times* didn't have a box listing cor-porate contributions to them or to others nor, we may add, did it have a box listing advertisers of the *New York Times* and their attitudes towards NAFTA. In a way you can't object to Lewis and the *Times*. They are simply taking for granted a principle, which is that the rich and powerful have a right to twist the arms of their legislators and to dictate to them what they should do because that's what democracy is. Democracy is a system where the rich and privileged and powerful make decisions in their own interests, and if the general population tries to press for their interests, that's raw muscle and anti-democratic and are ominous signs.

It was quite striking to watch the hysteria that

built up in privileged sectors, like the *New York Times* commentators and editorials as the NAFTA vote approached. They even allowed themselves the use of the phrase "class lines," which is very rare in elite circles. You're not allowed to admit that the U.S. has class lines. But this was considered a really serious issue, and all bars were let down. So you get columns of the kind by Anthony Lewis that you described, with the real indication of hatred of democracy at the core of it. The tacit assumption is if working people try to press for their interests in the political arena, that's anti-democratic. But if corporate power does so at a vastly greater rate, that's fine.

Listener: *I've often wondered about the people who have power through their extensive financial and economic resources. Are they really as manipulative as you say? Is it possible to reach them with logic and rationale?*

They're acting very logically and very rationally in their own interests. Let's be specific about it. Take the chief executive officer of Aetna Life Insurance. He is one of the guys who is going to be running our health care program and who makes $23 million a year in just plain salary. Could you reach him and convince him that he ought to lobby against having the insurance industry run the health-care program because that's going to be very harmful to the general population, as indeed it will be? Suppose you could. Suppose you could sit down with him and convince him, look, you ought to give up your salary and be a working person. The insurance industry

194

shouldn't run this show and it will be terrible and so on. Suppose he agreed. Then what happens? Then he gets thrown out as CEO and someone else comes in who accepts that position. These are institutional factors.

Listener: *Take it down to the individual, personal level, I got a notice in my Public Service bill that said they're asking for a rate hike. I work, and I really don't have the time to sit down and write a letter of protest. This happens all the time, and not just with me. It happens with most people who have to work. They don't have time to be active politically to change something. So those rate hikes go through without anybody ever really pointing out what's going on. One of the things that I've always thought, and I know this is probably not democratic, is why is there not a limitation on the amount of profit anybody can make, any corporation, any business?*

I think that's highly democratic, in fact. There's nothing in the principle of democracy that says that power and wealth should be highly concentrated so that democracy becomes a sham. But your point is quite correct. If you're a working person you just don't have time, alone, to take on the power company. That's exactly what organization is about. That's exactly what unions are for. That's exactly what political parties of the kind that David was mentioning earlier, based in working people, are for. So if such a party was around, the kind Bernard and Mazzocchi are proposing, they would be the ones speaking for you who would tell the truth about what's going on with the rate hike. Then they would be denounced by the *New York Times* for being anti-democratic, for representing popular interests rather than power interests.

Since the Kennedy assassination there is a bureaucratic philosophy that business and elite power circles control our so-called democracy. Has that element changed at all with the Clinton administration coming in?

First of all, it didn't change with the Kennedy administration. It was very much the case for Kennedy. Kennedy himself was very pro-business. He was essentially a business candidate. Nothing changed with the assassination in this respect. The Kennedy assassination had no significant effect on policy that anybody has been able to detect.

There was a change in the early 1970s, but that was under Nixon. It had to do with changes in the international economy, the kind that I talked about earlier. Clinton is exactly what he says he is, a pro-business candidate. The *Wall Street Journal* had a very enthusiastic big front-page article about him right after the NAFTA vote. They pointed out that the Republicans tend to be just the party of business, period, but the Democrats were a little more nuanced. They tend to be the party of big business with less concern for small business. They said that Clinton is typical of this. They quoted executives of the Ford Motor Company and the steel industry and so on as saying this is the best administration they ever had. They ran through his achievements, and you can see it.

The day after the House vote the *New York Times*

had a very revealing front-page pro-Clinton story by their Washington correspondent, R. W. Apple. People had been criticizing Clinton because he just didn't have any principles. He backed down on Bosnia, on Somalia, on his economic stimulus, on Haiti, on the health program. He was willing to give things up. It seemed like this guy had no bottom line at all. Then he proved that he really was a man of principle and he really has backbone and he silenced his detractors, namely by fighting for the corporate version of NAFTA. So he does have principles, namely, he listens to the call of big money. They thought that was great. The same was true of Kennedy.

Is there any element of the large corporate conglomerates that would have beneficial effect?

That's not the right question to ask. A lot of what's done by corporations will happen to have, by accident, beneficial effects for the population. The same is true of the government or anything else. But what are they trying to achieve? They're not trying to achieve a better life for workers and the firms in which they work, as the Clinton people have it. What they're trying to achieve is profits and market share. That's not a big secret. That's the kind of thing people should learn in third grade. In the business system, people are trying to maximize profit, power, market share, control over the state. By accident, sometimes that will help other people. It's just accidental.

Listener: *I'd like to ask Mr. Chomsky about the U.S. support for Yeltsin versus democracy in Russia,* *and if this country has a vested interest in continuing support for the drug trade in the world?*

On Yeltsin, it's pretty straightforward. Yeltsin was the tough, autocratic Communist party boss of Sverdlosk. He has filled his administration with the old party hacks who ran the place under the earlier Soviet system. The West likes him a lot. For one thing, he's tough and ruthless and autocratic. For another, he's going to ram through what are called "reforms," a nice word, the policies which are designed to return the former Soviet Union to the Third World status that it had for five hundred years prior to the Bolshevik Revolution. The Cold War was largely about the demand that this huge region of the world once again become what it had been, offering resources, markets and cheap labor, serving the West. Yeltsin is leading the pack on that one. Therefore he's democratic. That's standard. That's what we call a democrat anywhere in the world, someone who follows the Western business agenda.

On the drug trade, it's complicated. I don't want to be too brief about it. When you say does the government support the drug trade, of course not. Although even here, there are complexities. You can't talk about marijuana and cocaine in the same breath. Marijuana simply doesn't have the lethal effects of cocaine. You can debate about whether it's good or bad, but out of about sixty million users, I don't think there's a known case of overdose. The criminalization of marijuana has purposes and motives beyond concern over drugs. On the other hand, hard drugs, to which people have been driven to a certain extent by the prohibitions against soft drugs, those are very harmful, although deaths are nowhere near the level of tobacco and alcohol. And here it's kind of complex. There are sectors of American society that profit from the hard drug trade, like the big international banks that do the money laundering or the chemical corporations that provide the chemicals for the industrial production of hard drugs. On the other hand, people who live in the inner cities are being devastated by them. So there are different interests.

Listener: *Two things: One is just a comment. That is that on this issue of gun control, I believe that in fact the U.S. is becoming much more like a Third World country. There's nothing that's going to put a stop to it, necessarily. I look around and I see a lot of Third World countries where if the citizens had weapons they wouldn't have the government they've got. I think that maybe people are being a little short-sighted in arguing for gun control and at the same time realizing that the government they've got is not exactly a benign one. The other thing is that I think that a lot of this stuff correlates with work that the social revolutionary party did as early as 1914 in trying to understand business cycles. Kondratieff pointed out that there's a sixty-year cycle of prosperity in the U.S. and in the world. It's inversely tied in with real interest rates. Real interest rates started to rise in the U.S. in October of 1979. They've been rising ever since. And that in one sense tells the whole story.*

Interest rates are important. There's some evidence for the Kondratieff cycle. But I don't really think those are the big issues. However, on your first point, it illustrates exactly what I think is a major fallacy. You pointed out that the government is far from benign. That's true. On the other hand, the government is at least partially accountable and could become as benign as we make it.

What is not benign and is extremely harmful is what you didn't mention, namely business power, highly concentrated, by now largely transnational power both in the producing and financial sectors. That's very far from benign. Furthermore, it's completely unaccountable. It's a totalitarian system. It has an enormous effect on our lives and also on why the government is not benign.

As for guns being the way to respond to this, that's frankly outlandish. It's true that people think that. They think if we have guns we can make it more benign. If people have guns, the government has tanks. If people have tanks the government has atomic weapons. There's no way to deal with these issues by violent force, even if you think that that's morally legitimate. Guns in the hands of American citizens are not going to make the country more benign. They're going to make it more brutal, ruthless and destructive. So while one can recognize the motivation that lies behind some of the opposition to gun control, I think it's sadly misguided.

DB *In a review of a book we did,* Chronicles of Dissent, *it was suggested by the reviewer that I ask you tougher questions. So I thought I would save my toughest question for you right at the end. Are you ready?*

I'm ready to hang up. (chuckles)

DB *I want to know what MIT professor was born on December 7, 1928 in Philadelphia. You've got five seconds.*

How would I know anything about MIT professors?

DB *Happy Birthday tomorrow, Noam!*

The Emerging Global Economic Order

February 1, 1994

DB *In the fall of 1993 the* Financial Times *trumpeted, "The public sector is in retreat everywhere." This is before the passage of the two major corporate-state initiatives, NAFTA (North American Free Trade Agrrement) and GATT (General Agreement on Trade and Tariffs). How were they able to do it and what are the consequences?*

First of all, it's largely true, but major sectors of the public sector are alive and well, in particular those parts that cater to the interests of the wealthy and the powerful. They're declining somewhat, but they're still very lively. They're not going to disappear. How were they able to do it? These are developments that have been going on for about twenty years now. They had to do with major changes in the international economy that we've talked about in earlier discussions. For one thing, the period of U.S. global economic hegemony had pretty much ended by the early 1970s. Europe and Japan had reemerged as major economic and political entities. There was pressure on profits. The costs of the Vietnam War were very significant for the U.S. economy, and extremely beneficial for its rivals. That tended to shift the world balance. In any event, by the early 1970s the U.S. felt that it could no longer sustain its traditional position as essentially international banker, which was codified in the Bretton Woods agreements at the end of the Second World War. Nixon dismantled that system. That led to a period of tremendous growth in unregulated financial capital. It was accelerated by the short-term rise in commodity prices, which led to a huge flow of petrodollars into the now largely unregulated international system.

There were technological changes that took place at the same time which were significant. The telecommunications revolution made it extremely easy to transfer capital or paper equivalents of capital, in fact, electronic equivalents of it, from one place to another. There has been an enormous expansion of unregulated financial capital in the past twenty years. What's more, its constitution changed radically. Whereas in the early 1970s about ninety percent of financial transactions were devoted to long-term investment and trade, basically more or less productive things, by now that's reduced to ten percent. About ninety percent is being used for speculation. This means that huge amounts of capital, $14 trillion, according to a recent World Bank estimate, are now simply very quickly moveable around the world basically seeking deflationary policies. It is a tremendous attack against government efforts to stimulate the economy. I think it was pointed out in the same *Financial Times* article to which you referred. That's one factor.

Related to that was a very substantial growth in the internationalization of production, so it became a lot easier than it had been in the past to shift production elsewhere to places where you get much cheaper labor, generally high-repression, low-wage areas. So it becomes much easier for, say, a corporation executive who lives in Greenwich, Connecticut to have corporate and bank headquarters in New York but the factory is in some Third World country. That now includes Eastern Europe. These developments placed powerful weapons in the hands of corporate and financial power. With the pressure on corporate profits that began in the early 1970s came a big attack on the whole social contract that had developed through a century of struggle and had been kind of codified around the end of the Second World War with the New Deal and the European social welfare states and so on. There was a big attack on that, led first by the U.S. and England, and by now going to the continent. It's had major effects. One effect has been a serious decline in unionization, which carries with it a decline in wages and other forms of protection of rights. That's led to polarization of the society, primarily in the U.S. and Britain, but it's extending.

Just this morning driving in I was listening to the BBC. They reported a new study of children in Britain which concluded that children living in work houses a century ago had better nutritional standards than millions of children in Britain today living in poverty. That's one of the grand achievements of the Thatcher revolution, in which she succeeded in devastating British society and destroying large parts of British manufacturing capacity and driving England into, as the *Financial Times* puts it, the poorhouse of Europe. England is now one of the poorest countries in Europe, still above Spain and

Portugal, but not much. It's well below Italy. That's the British achievement.

The American achievement was rather similar. We're a much richer, more powerful country, so it isn't possible to achieve quite what Britain achieved. But the Reaganites succeeded in driving U.S. wages down so we're now the second lowest of the industrial countries. Britain is the lowest. Wages in Italy are about twenty percent higher than in the U.S., Germany maybe sixty percent higher. Along with that goes a deterioration of the general social contract. The breakdown in public spending or the kind of public spending that goes to the less privileged. That's rather crucial. That's just a concomitant. We should bear in mind, and it's important to say, that the kind of public spending that goes to the wealthy and the privileged, which is enormous, remains fairly stable. That's a major component of state policy.

DB *What was the extent and quality of domestic opposition and resistance to NAFTA and GATT?*

That was quite interesting. The original expectation was that NAFTA would just sail through. Nobody would ever even know what it is. So it was signed in secret. It was put on a fast track in Congress, meaning essentially no discussion. There was virtually no media coverage. Who was going to know about a complex trade agreement? So the idea was, We just ram it through. That didn't work. And it's interesting that it didn't work. There are a number of reasons. For one thing, the labor movement got organized for once and made an issue of it. Another was the maverick third party candidate Ross Perot, who managed to make it a public issue. And it turned out that as soon as the public heard about it and knew anything about it they were pretty much opposed. The media coverage on this was extremely interesting. Usually the media try to keep their class loyalties more or less in the background. But on this issue the bars were down. They just went berserk, especially toward the end when it looked like there was going to be a problem. There was a very quick transition after it passed, incidentally. I've written about this in *Z Magazine*. But nevertheless, despite this enormous media barrage and the government attack and huge corporate lobbying, which totally dwarfed anything else, of course, despite that the level of opposition remained pretty stable. If you look at polls right through the period, roughly sixty percent or so of those who had an opinion remained opposed. It varied a little bit here and there, but that's quite substantial. In fact, the end result is very intriguing. There was a poll published a couple of days ago in which people had to evaluate labor's actions with regard to NAFTA. The public was overwhelmingly opposed to the actions of the labor movement against NAFTA, about seventy percent opposition to it. On the other hand, the public also took exactly the same position that labor was taking. So why were they opposed to it?

I think it's easy to explain that. The media went berserk. From Bill Clinton down to Anthony Lewis, as you pointed out to me in an earlier interview (December 6, 1993), there was just hysteria about labor's musclebound tactics and these backward labor leaders trying to drive us into the past, jingoist fanatics and so on. In fact, the content of the labor critique has virtually not appeared in the press. But there was plenty of hysteria about it all over the spectrum. Naturally people see what's in the press and figure labor must be doing really bad things. The fact of the matter is that labor, one of the few more or less democratic institutions in the country, was representing the position of the majority of those who had an opinion on NAFTA. Evidently from polls the same people who approved of the positions that labor was actually advocating, though they may not have known it, were opposed, or thought they were opposed to the labor tactics.

I suspect that if someone had a close look at the Gore-Perot television debate, they might well find the same thing. There were some interesting facts about this debate which ought to be looked at more closely. I didn't watch it, but friends who did watch it thought that Perot did quite well. But the press, of course, instantly had a totally different reaction. The news analysis right after was that Gore won a massive victory. Same thing with next morning's headlines: tremendous victory for the White House. If you look at the polls the next day, people were asked what they thought about the debate. The percentage who thought that Perot had been smashed was far higher than the percentage of people who had seen it, which means that most of the people were getting their impression of what happened in the debate from the front pages the next day or the television news. As the story, whatever it may have been, was filtered through the media system, it was turned into what was needed for propaganda purposes, whatever may have happened. That's a topic for research. But on the reaction of the public to labor's tactics, it's quite striking.

DB *One of the mass circulation journals that I get is* Third World Resurgence, *out of Penang, Malaysia. In that I learned that in Bangalore, India, half a million farmers demonstrated against GATT. I wonder if your local paper, the* Boston Globe, *featured that.*

I also read it in *Third World Resurgence* and in Indian journals. I don't recall having seen it here. Maybe there was something. I wouldn't want to say it wasn't reported without checking. But there is plenty of public opposition in India to GATT. The same in Mexico on NAFTA. Incidentally, you asked about GATT. What they had planned for NAFTA worked for GATT. So there was virtually no public opposition to GATT, or even awareness of it. I doubt a tiny fraction of the country even knows what it's about. So that may be rammed through in secret, as intended. Strikingly, they couldn't quite do that in the case of NAFTA. It took a major effort to get it through, one which was very revealing about class loyalty and class lines. In Mexico there was substantial public opposition. That was barely reported here. What happened in Chiapas doesn't come as very much of a surprise. There has been an attempt to portray the Chiapas rebellion as something about the underdeveloped south as distinct from the developed modern north. At first the government thought they'd just destroy it by violence, but they backed off and they'll do it by more subtle violence, when nobody's looking. Part of the reason they backed off is surely they were afraid that there was just too much sympathy all over the country and that if they

209

were too up front about suppression they'd cause themselves a lot of problems all the way up to the Mexican border. The Mayan Indians in Chiapas are in many ways the most oppressed people in Mexico. Nevertheless, the problems they are talking about are the problems of a large majority of the Mexican population. Mexico too has been polarized by this decade of neo-liberal reforms which have led to very little economic progress but have sharply polarized the society. Labor's share in income has declined radically. The number of billionaires is shooting up.

DB *But I found the mainstream media coverage of Mexico during the NAFTA debate somewhat uneven. You mentioned the* New York Times. *They have allowed in a number of articles that official corruption was and is widespread in Mexico. In fact, in one editorial they virtually conceded that Salinas stole the 1988 presidential election. Why did that information come out?*

I think that that's impossible to repress. Furthermore, there were scattered reports in the *Times* of popular protest against NAFTA. Tim Golden, their reporter in Mexico, had a story a couple of weeks before the vote, probably early November, in which he said that lots of Mexican workers are concerned that their wages would decline after NAFTA. Then came the punch line. He said that undercuts the position of people like Ross Perot and others who think that NAFTA is going to harm American workers for the benefit of Mexican workers. In other words, they're all going to get screwed. It was presented in that framework as a critique of the people who were opposing NAFTA here. But there was very little discussion here of the large-scale popular opposition in Mexico, which included, for example, the largest non-governmental trade union. The main trade union is about as independent as the Soviet trade unions were. There were large public protests not reported here. The environmental movements were opposed. Most of the popular movements were opposed. The Mexican Bishops' Conference came out with quite a strong statement criticizing NAFTA and endorsing the position of the Latin American bishops at Santo Domingo in December 1992. There was a conference of Latin American bishops, the first one since Puebla and Medellin back in the 1960s and 1970s, which was quite important. It was not reported here, to my knowledge. The Vatican tried to control it this time to make sure that they wouldn't come out with these perverse ideas about liberation theology and the preferential option for the poor. But despite a very firm Vatican hand the bishops came out quite strongly against neo-liberalism and structural adjustment and these free-market-for-the-poor policies. The Mexican bishops reiterated that in their critique of NAFTA. If there was anything about that here, I didn't see it.

DB *What about the psychological and political position people like us find ourselves in of being "against," of being anti, re-active rather than pro-active?*

NAFTA's a good case, because in fact the NAFTA critiques were pro-active. Very few of the NAFTA critics were saying, No agreement. Not even

Perot. He had constructive proposals. The labor movement, the Congressional Office of Technology Assessment, which issued another major report that was also ignored, and other critics, in fact, virtually every critic I saw, were saying there would be nothing wrong with a North American Free Trade Agreement. But not this one. It should be different. The respects in which it should be different were outlined in some detail. It's just that it was all suppressed. What's left is the picture that, say, Anthony Lewis portrays, jingoist fanatics screaming about NAFTA. Incidentally, what's called the left played the same game. James Galbraith is a left-liberal economist at the University of Texas. He wrote an article in which he also denounced the jingoist left. He picked me out as the main person, quoting an article in which I said the opposite of what he attributed to me, of course, but that's normal. It was in a sort of left-liberal journal, *World Policy Review*. He said there's this jingoist left, nationalist fanatics, who don't want Mexican workers to improve their lives. Then he went on with how the Mexicans are in favor of NAFTA. By the Mexicans he meant Mexican industrialists and executives and corporate lawyers. He didn't mean Mexican workers and peasants. He doesn't have a word about them. All the way over from people like James Galbraith and Anthony Lewis, to way over to the right, you had this very useful fabrication, that critics of NAFTA were just reactive and negative and that they were jingoist and were against progress and wanted to go back to old-time protectionism. When you have essentially total control of the information system, it's rather easy to convey that image. It leads to the conclusion that you describe, that the critics are re-active and not pro-active. It isn't true. You read the reports and studies and analyses and you see that they had very constructive proposals.

DB *In early January you were asked by an editor of the* Washington Post *to submit an article on the New Year's Day uprising in Chiapas. Was this the first time they had asked you to write something for them?*

That was the first time ever. It was for the Sunday *Outlook* section. I was kind of surprised. I'm never asked to write for a major newspaper. I wrote it. It didn't appear.

DB *Was there an explanation?*

No. It went to press, as far as I know. The editor who had asked me called me saying it looked OK and then later told me that it had simply been cancelled at some higher level. I don't know any more about it than that. Although I can guess. That article was about Chiapas, but it was also about NAFTA, and I think the *Washington Post* has been even more extreme than the *Times* in keeping discussion of this topic within narrow bounds.

DB *In that article you write that the protest of Indian peasants in Chiapas gives "only a bare glimpse of time bombs waiting to explode, not only in Mexico." What did you have in mind?*

Take South Central Los Angeles, for example. In many respects, different societies and so on, but

213

there are points of similarity to the Chiapas rebellion. South Central Los Angeles is a place where people once had jobs and lives. Those jobs and lives have been destroyed. They have been destroyed in large part by the socio-economic processes that we have been talking about. For example, say, furniture factories went to Mexico where they can pollute more cheaply. Military industry, the big public input into the high-tech system, has somewhat declined, especially in the L.A. area. People used to have jobs in the steel industry. They don't any more. They rebelled. The Chiapas rebellion was quite different. It was much more organized, much more constructive, and it's the difference between an utterly demoralized society, like South Central Los Angeles, the kind we have, and a society that still retains some sort of integrity and community life and so on, though objectively poorer. When you look at consumption levels, doubtless Mexican peasants are poorer than people in South Central Los Angeles. There are fewer television sets per capita. By other, more significant criteria, mainly social cohesion, integrity of the community, they're considerably more advanced. We have succeeded in the U.S. not only in polarizing but also in destroying community structures. That's why you have such rampant violence. That's one case.

Take another which is even more dramatic. A couple of days after the NAFTA vote, the Senate overwhelmingly passed the most extraordinary crime bill in history. It was hailed with great enthusiasm by the far right as the greatest anti-crime bill ever. I think that it greatly increased, by a factor of five or six, federal spending for "fighting crime". There's nothing constructive in it. There are more prisons, more police, heavier sentences, more death sentences, new crimes...

DB *Three strikes and you're out.*

Three strikes and you're out. Membership in a gang is a crime. Clinton has quickly moved to pick this up as his major social initiative. That makes a lot of sense, and it makes a lot of sense that it should appear right after NAFTA. NAFTA will continue, maybe accelerate the polarization of society. No one has any plans for these people who are being marginalized and suppressed. There will be more South Central Los Angeles-type situations. It's unclear how much pressure and social decline and deterioration people will accept. One tactic is just drive them into urban slums, concentration camps, in effect, and let them prey on one another. But that has a way of breaking out and affecting the interests of wealthy and privileged people. So we'd better build up the jail system, which incidentally is also a shot to the economy. That's public spending, which gives a kind of economic stimulus as well. It's natural that Clinton should pick exactly that as his topic. Not only for a kind of ugly political reason. It's easy to whip up hysteria about that. But also because it reflects the general point of view of the so-called New Democrats, the business-oriented segments of the Democratic Party.

DB *One last point on Mexico: You talked about the wages being depressed. There has also been significant union busting and smashing. Describe what happened at a couple of auto plants in Mexico, one* *involving Ford and one involving Volkswagen.*

Ford and VW are two big examples. Within the last few years, I think for VW it was 1992 and Ford a few years earlier, Ford just fired its entire work force and would rehire at a much lower wage level only those who agreed to be non-unionized. They're backed by the always ruling party when they do this. In VW's case it was pretty much the same. They fired workers who supported an independent union. They were willing to allow the fraudulent government union. But those who sought to get an independent union were kicked out and only those who agreed not to support it were rehired at lower wages.

A few weeks after the NAFTA vote in the U.S., workers at a GE and Honeywell plant in Mexico were fired for union activities. I don't know what the outcome is, but that was again symbolic. That's exactly what things like NAFTA are about. Whether NAFTA in the long term will lower the wages of Mexican workers is kind of hard to predict. There are a lot of complicated factors. I think it may very well. That it will lower the wages of American workers is hardly in doubt. The strongest NAFTA advocates point that out in the small print. My colleague at MIT, Paul Krugman, is a specialist in international trade and interestingly one of the economists who had done some of the theoretical work showing flaws in free trade. He nevertheless was an enthusiastic advocate of NAFTA, which is, I should stress, *not* a free trade agreement. But he did point out, if you look, that the only people who will lose will be unskilled workers. A footnote: Seventy percent of the work force is classified as "unskilled." They're the only ones who will lose.

The Emerging Global Economic Order

The Clinton Administration has various, I don't know if they believe it or not, fantasies about retraining. They aren't doing anything about that, but even if they did, it would probably have very little impact. What's true of industrial workers is also true of skilled white-collar workers. You can get software programmers in India who are very well trained at a fraction of the cost of American programmers. Somebody involved in this business recently told me that Indian programmers are actually being brought to the U.S. and kept at Indian salaries, a fraction of American salaries, in software development. So that can be farmed out just as easily.

The chances of retraining having much of an effect are slim. The problems are quite different. The problems are that in the search for profit, you will try to repress people's lives as much as possible. You wouldn't be doing your job otherwise.

DB *An interesting thing happened in Alabama involving Daimler-Benz, the big German auto manufacturer.*

This deterioration of the policies that destroy unions and undermine wages have a whipsaw effect. It's not only Mexico and the U.S. It's also across the industrial world. So now that the U.S. has managed, under Reagan, to drive wages down way below the level of its competitors, except for Britain, that's had its international effects. So one of the effects of the so-called free trade agreement with Canada was to stimulate a big flow of jobs from Canada to the southeast U.S. because these are essentially non-union areas. Wages are lower. You don't have to worry about benefits. Workers can barely organize. So that's an attack against Canadian workers. What you're describing now simply shows the internationalization of these effects. Daimler-Benz, which is Germany's biggest conglomerate, was seeking essentially Third World conditions. They managed to get the southeastern states to compete against one another to see who could force the public to pay the most to bring them there. Alabama gave the biggest package. They offered them hundreds of millions of dollars in tax benefits. They practically gave them the land for free. They agreed to build all sorts of infrastructure for them. The cost to the citizens of Alabama is substantial. But there will be people who benefit. The small number of people who are employed there, some spillover to hamburger stands and so on, but primarily bankers, corporate lawyers, people involved in investment and finance and financial services and so on, they'll do very well.

It was interesting that even the *Wall Street Journal*, which is rarely critical of business, pointed out that this is very much like what happens when rich corporations go to Third World countries and questioned whether there were going to be overall benefits for the state of Alabama. Probably not, although for sectors of Alabama, especially the corporate, financial and skilled professional sectors, there will be benefits. The general public will pay the costs.

Meanwhile Daimler-Benz can use that to drive down the living standards of German workers. That's in fact the way the game is played. Southeastern U.S. is one case. But of course Mexico, Indonesia, and now east Europe are much better cases. For

218

example, VW will throw out their work force in Mexico and rehire it. But they'll also set up factories in the Czech Republic, as they are now doing, where they can get workers for about ten percent of the cost of German workers. It's right across the border. It's a westernized society. High educational levels. Nice white people with blue eyes. You don't have to worry about that. Of course, they insist on plenty of benefits. They don't believe in the free market any more than any other rich people do, so they leave the Czech Republic to pay the social costs of pollution, debts, etc. They'll just pick up the profits. It's exactly the same when GM moves to Poland. GM is building plants in Poland, but of course insisting on thirty percent tariff protection. The free market is for the poor. We have a dual system. Free markets for the poor and state socialism for the rich.

DB *After your return from a recent trip to Nicaragua you told me it's becoming more difficult to tell the difference between economists and Nazi doctors. What did you mean by that?*

A report from UNESCO just appeared, which I haven't seen reported here. It was reported in the *Financial Times* of London, which estimated the human cost of what are called reforms, a nice-sounding word, in Eastern Europe since 1989. "Reforms" is a propaganda term. It implies that the changes are good things. If a populist government took over private industries, that wouldn't be called "reform." By referring to the policies as "reforms," the press is able to avoid any discussion of whether they are good or bad policies. They are good, by stipulation. But the so-called reforms, meaning returning Eastern Europe to its Third World status, have had social costs. The UNESCO study tries to estimate them. For example, in Russia they estimate about a half-a-million deaths a year as a direct result of the reforms, meaning the effect of the collapse of health services, the increase in disease, the increase in malnutrition, and so on. Killing half-a-million people a year, that's a fairly substantial achievement for reformist economists. You can find similar numbers, though not quite that bad, in the rest of Eastern Europe, if you look at death rates from malnutrition, polarization, suffering. It's a great achievement.

If you go to the Third World, the numbers are fantastic. So for example, another UNESCO report estimated that in Africa about half-a-million children die every year simply from debt service. Not from the whole array of "reforms," just debt service. About eleven million children are estimated to die every year from easily treatable diseases. Most of them could be overcome by a couple of cents' worth of materials. But the economists tell us that to do this would be interference with the market system. It's not new. It's very reminiscent of British economists during the Irish famine in the mid-nineteenth century, when economic theory dictated that famine-struck Ireland must export food to Britain, which it did, right through the Irish famine, and should not be given food aid because that would violate the sacred principles of political economy. These principles typically have this curious property of benefiting the wealthy and harming the poor.

DB *You'll recall the uproar in the 1980s about*

Sandinista abuses of the Miskito Indian population on the Atlantic coast. President Reagan, in his inimitable style of understatement, said it was "a campaign of virtual genocide." UN Ambassador Jeane Kirkpatrick was a bit more restrained. She called it the "most massive human rights violation in Central America." What's happening now with the Miskito Indians in Nicaragua?

They were talking about an incident in which, according to Americas Watch, several dozen Miskitos were killed and lots of people were forcefully moved in a very ugly way in the course of the *contra* war. The U.S. terrorist forces were moving into the area and this was the reaction. It was certainly an atrocity, but you couldn't even see it in comparison to the atrocities that Jeane Kirkpatrick was celebrating in the neighboring countries at the time, or for that matter in Nicaragua, where the overwhelming mass of the atrocities were committed by the so-called freedom fighters.

What's happening to the Miskitos now? I was in Nicaragua in October. Church sources, the Christian Evangelical Church, primarily, who work in the Atlantic coast, were reporting that 100,000 Miskitos were starving to death, largely as a result of the policies that we are imposing on Nicaragua. Not a word here.

Another problem among the Miskitos is narcotics. One typical consequence of U.S. victories in the Third World, which again includes much of Eastern Europe, is that the countries where we win immediately become big centers for drug flow.

There are good reasons for that. That's part of the market system that we impose on them.

Nicaragua has now become a major drug transshipment center. There's a little concern about that here, so that gets into the press. If you look at the small print, you'll discover that a lot of it goes through the Atlantic coast now that the whole governmental system has collapsed. There's also a drug epidemic. This goes along with being a drug transshipment area.

It's a major epidemic among the Miskitos, in particular, among the divers. Miskito Indian divers, both in Nicaragua and Honduras, are compelled by economic circumstances to carry out diving under horrendous conditions. They are forced to do very deep diving without equipment for lobsters and other shellfish. It's a market system. You've got plenty of superfluous people. So you make them work under these conditions. If they die off fast you just bring in others. That's a standard free-market technique. In order to try to maintain their work rate they stuff themselves with cocaine. Somehow it enables them to bear the pain. So that actually sort of got reported. There was a little report about cocaine use among Miskito Indians. Of course, nobody cared much about the work conditions, or why they are there. That's the situation of the Miskito Indians in Nicaragua today. In Honduras it may even be worse.

DB *This speaks volumes about the whole notion of worthy victims whose plight can be attributed to official enemies, and then when the enemies are eliminated, they become unworthy victims.*

It's a clear example of that. If you want another example, in many ways an uglier one, have a look at today's *Boston Globe*. There's an op-ed by Sidney

Schanberg blasting Senator Kerry of Massachusetts for being dishonest and two-faced because he is refusing to concede that the Vietnamese have not been entirely forthcoming about American POWs.

Nobody, according to Schanberg, is honest enough to tell the truth about this. He says the government ought to finally have the honesty to say that it left Indochina without accounting for all the Americans. Of course, it wouldn't occur to him to suggest that the government should be honest enough to say that we killed a couple of million people and destroyed three countries and left them in total wreckage and have been strangling them ever since. It is particularly striking that this is Sidney Schanberg. He is regarded as the great conscience of the press because of his intrepid courage in exposing the crimes of official enemies, namely Pol Pot. He also happened to be the main U.S. reporter in Phnom Penh in 1973, which was the peak of the U.S. bombardment of inner Cambodia, when tens of thousands of people were being killed and the society was being wiped out.

Nobody knows very much about the bombing campaign and its effects because people like Sidney Schanberg refused to cover it. It wasn't a big effort for him to report it. He didn't have to go trekking off into the jungle to find the appropriate refugees. He could walk across the street from his fancy hotel in Phnom Penh, where there were hundreds of thousands of refugees driven from the countryside into the city. I went through all of his reporting. It's reviewed in detail in *Manufacturing Consent*, my book with Edward Herman. He simply refused to interview refugees to find out what was going on in

inner Cambodia. Only a few sentences of refugee testimony appear in his dispatches.

To heighten the depravity, to make it very clear
just what he is, there happens to be one rather
detailed report of an American atrocity. If you look at
the movie *The Killing Fields*, which is based on his
story, it opens by describing this atrocity, which he
did report for about three days. What's the one
report? American planes hit the wrong village, a government village. That's an atrocity. That was reported. How about when they hit the right village? We
don't care about that. One of the reasons why we
know very little about this monstrous atrocity in
inner Cambodia is that people like Sidney Schanberg
wouldn't report it.

Now he's orating about the lack of honesty and
the two-facedness of people who won't say that we
left POWs behind. Incidentally, take a look at the
U.S. record with POWs. It was atrocious. Not only in
Vietnam, where it was monstrous, but in Korea,
where it was even worse. U.S. treatment of POWs in
Korea was an absolute scandal. It's been well discussed in the scholarly literature. If you go back to
the Pacific war, it's also horrible, including after the
war, when we kept prisoners illegally under confine-
ment, as did the British.

DB Other Losses, *a Canadian book, alleges it
was official U.S. policy to withhold food from German
prisoners. Many of them supposedly starved to death.*

That's James Bacque's book. There's been a lot
of controversy about the details, and I'm not sure
what the facts of the matter are. He did say that. On

the other hand, there are things on which there's no controversy. Ed Herman and I wrote about it back in the late 1970s, in our book *Political Economy of Human Rights*. It was kind of striking. Just at the time that the first uproar was being whipped up about the American POWs, scholarly work was coming out about American and British treatment of German POWs during and after the Second World War. There were some reviews of this material. They were lauding the humanitarian efforts of the Americans and the British.

If you looked at the material, what happened was that the Americans were running "re-education camps" for German prisoners. Since it was in gross violation of international conventions, it was concealed. They finally changed the name. They picked some Orwellian name for it instead of re-education camps. This was hailed as a tremendous example of our humanitarianism, because we were teaching them democratic ways. In other words, we were indoctrinating them into accepting our beliefs. Therefore it's humanitarian in these re-education camps. They kept it secret because they were afraid that the Germans might retaliate and treat American prisoners the same way. Prisoners were being treated very brutally, killed and starved and so on.

Furthermore, it went on after the war. The U.S. kept German POWs until mid-1946, I think. They were used for forced labor, beaten, and killed. It was much worse in England. There they kept them until, I think, mid-1948. All totally illegal—forced labor, violence, and so on.

Finally there was public reaction in Britain. The person who started it off was Peggy Duff, a marvelous woman who died a couple of years ago. She was later one of the leading figures in the CND and the international peace movement during the 1960s and 1970s. She started off her career with a protest against the treatment of German POWs.

Incidentally, why only German POWs? What was happening to the Italian POWs? We don't know anything about that. The reason is that Germany is a very efficient country. So they have published volumes of documents on what happened to German POWs. But Italy's sort of laid back, and at least at that time there was no research on the surely much worse treatment of Italian POWs.

I can remember this as a kid. There was a POW camp right next to my high school. There was controversy among the students over the issue of the students taunting the prisoners. There were a group of us who thought this was horrifying and objected to it, but very few. That's not the worst of it, of course.

DB *At the same time this was going on with the prisoners of war after World War II, there was Operation Paper Clip. Chris Simpson describes this in his book* Blowback, *and you've discussed it as well. It involved the importation, on a large scale, of known Nazi war criminals, rocket scientists, camp guards, etc.*

That was part of it. But it was actually much worse than that. There was also an operation involving the Vatican and the U.S. State Department, and American-British intelligence, which took some of the worst Nazi criminals, like Klaus Barbie, and used them. Klaus Barbie was taken over by U.S. intelli-

226

gence and returned to exactly the operations that the Nazis had him doing. Later, when it became an issue, some of his supervisors pointed out that they didn't see what the fuss was all about.

They said: We needed a guy who would attack the resistance. We had moved in. We had replaced the Germans. We had the same task they did, namely destroy the resistance, and here was a specialist. He had been working for the Nazis to destroy the resistance, the butcher of Lyon, so who would be better placed to continue exactly the same work for us, when we moved in to destroy the resistance?

So Barbie worked for the Americans as he had worked for the Nazis. When they could no longer protect him, they moved over to the Vatican-run ratline operation, with Croatian Nazi priests and others, and managed to spirit him off to Latin America, where his career continued. In fact, he became a big drug lord and narcotrafficker, and was involved in Bolivia in a military coup, all with U.S. support.

Klaus Barbie was basically a small operator. There were much bigger people. We managed to get Walter Rauff, the guy who invented gas chambers, off to Chile. Others went to fascist Spain. This was a big operation involving many top Nazis. That's only the beginning. Reinhard Gehlen was the leading figure. He was the head of German military intelligence on the eastern front. I don't have to tell you what that means. That's where the real war crimes were. Now we're talking about Auschwitz and other death camps.

Gehlen was taken over quickly by American intelligence and returned essentially to the same role. The U.S. was supporting German-established armies in Eastern Europe. The U.S. continued to support them at least into the early 1950s.

It turns out the Russians had penetrated American intelligence, so the air drops didn't work very well. But they were trying to support Hitler's armies in Eastern Europe. Gehlen was returned to the operations that he had carried out under the Nazis. Furthermore, German, as they called them, counterterrorist specialists, meaning people who were fighting the partisans and the resistance, were taken over by the American army. Their records and expertise were used to create counterinsurgency doctrine.

In fact, if you look at the American army counterinsurgency literature, a lot of which is now declassified, it begins by an analysis of textbooks written with the cooperation of Nazi officers recording the German experience in Europe. It describes everything from the point of view of the Nazis, e.g., which techniques for controlling resistance worked, which ones didn't work. That becomes simply transmuted with barely a change into American counterinsurgency literature. This is discussed at some length by Michael McClintock in a book called *Instruments of Statecraft*, a very good book which I've never seen reviewed. It's quite illuminating on this topic.

DB *This makes an interesting counterpoint to the opening of the Holocaust Museum in Washington, D.C. and the current widespread popularity of Stephen Spielberg's film* Schindler's List, *that the U.S. was not passively engaged in recruiting German war criminals but was in fact actively engaged. Is it about this that you say that if a real history of the aftermath of the*

The Emerging Global Economic Order

Second World War were ever written this would be the first chapter?

This would be a part of the first chapter. Recruiting Nazi war criminals and saving them is bad enough, but continuing the activities that they carried out is worse. The first chapter of postwar history, in my view, would be the description of the British and U.S. operations, mostly U.S., given power relations, throughout the world to destroy the anti-fascist resistance and restore the traditional essentially fascist order to power.

That took different forms in different parts of the world. In Korea, where we ran it alone, it meant killing about 100,000 people, just in the late 1940s before what we called the Korean War. In Greece it meant supporting the first major counterinsurgency war, which destroyed the peasant- and worker-based anti-Nazi resistance and restored collaborators to power.

Italy is a very interesting case. A lot of information is just coming out now. The British first, and then the Americans, as they moved in, wanted to destroy the very significant resistance movement. It had liberated most of northern Italy. The Americans essentially wanted to restore the fascist order, as did the British. This is the British Labor Party, incidentally. In the south, they simply restored the fascist order, the industrialists. The Americans tried to get leading fascists in, like Dino Grandi, but the Italians wouldn't accept it, so they took an Italian war hero, Badoglio, and essentially restored the old system.

But the big problem was when they got to the north. There the Italians had already been liberated.

The Germans had been driven out by the Italian resistance. The place was functioning. Industry was functioning. First Britain and then the U.S. had to dismantle all of that and restore the old order. Their attitude is extremely interesting. It's just coming out now in books. There is one by an Italian scholar, Federico Romero, who describes this very positively. The big critique of the resistance was that they were displacing the old owners in favor of popular workers' and community control. This was called "arbitrary dismissal" of the legitimate owners. They were also hiring what was called "excess workers," meaning they were giving jobs to people beyond what's called economic efficiency, meaning maximal profit-making. In other words, they were trying to take care of the population and they were more democratic. That had to be stopped. The prime commitment, as the documents say, was to eliminate this arbitrary dismissal of legitimate owners and the hiring of excess workers.

There was also another problem which they recognized. Of course the most severe problem for Italy at the time was hunger and unemployment. But that's the Italians' problem, the British labor attaché explained. Our problem, the problem of the occupying forces, is to eliminate this hiring of excess workers and arbitrary dismissal of owners. Then they can worry about the other problem, everybody starving. This is, I should say, described very positively, showing how law-abiding we are. It goes right to contemporary neo-liberalism without much change.

The next thing was to try to undermine and destroy the democratic process, which the U.S. was very concerned about in Italy. The left was obviously going to win the elections. It had a lot of prestige from its involvement in the resistance and the traditional conservative order had been discredited. The U.S wouldn't tolerate that. The first memorandum of the first meeting of the newly-formed National Security Council in 1947 is devoted to this. This was a major issue. They decided that they would undermine the election. There were big efforts made to undermine the election, to withhold food and put all sorts of pressure to ensure that the democratic system couldn't function and that our guys would get in.

That's a pattern that's been relived over and over. Nicaragua recently is another case. You strangle them. You starve them. And then you have a free vote and everybody talks about how wonderful democracy is. They were afraid that violence and coercion might not work. The fascist police and strikebreakers were put back. They said: In the event that the communists win a democratic election legitimately, the U.S. will declare a national emergency, put the Sixth Fleet on alert in the Mediterranean and support paramiltiary activities to overthrow the Italian government. That's NSC 1, the first National Security Council Report.

There were other people who were more extreme, like George Kennan, who thought that we just ought to invade the place, not even let them have the election. They managed to hold him back, figuring that subversion and terror and starvation would do it. And it did. Then comes a long follow-up, right into at least the 1970s, when records dry up.

Maybe it's still going on. Probably the major CIA effort in the world was the subversion of Italian democracy, from the 1940s right to the very modern period, including support for ultra-right Masonic Lodges and paramilitary elements and terrorists and so on. A very ugly story.

If you look at France and Germany and Japan, you get pretty much the same thing. That ought to be chapter 1 of postwar history. The person who opened up this topic and many others was Gabriel Kolko, in his classic book *Politics of War* (1968) which has really been shamefully ignored. It's a terrific piece of work. A lot of the documents weren't around then, but his picture turns out to be quite accurate, and it's been by now supplemented by a lot of specialized monographic materials.

DB *Let's talk about human rights in a contemporary framework with one of our major trading partners, China.*

Today's a good day to talk about it. The State Department just came out with its report on human rights in China. I haven't read the whole report, just the newspaper account, but I'm willing to predict. In the Asia Pacific summit in Seattle, the one substantive achievement was sending more high-tech equipment to China, in violation of legislation, which the governemnt would reinterpret to allow it; the legislation was because of China's involvement in nuclear and missile proliferation, so we therefore sent them nuclear generators and sophisticated satellites and Cray supercomputers. Right in the midst of that summit is a little tiny report which you can find tacked on to the articles about the grand vision in Asia, saying that 81 women had been burned to death. They were locked in a factory in what's called booming Guandong province, the economic miracle of China.

A couple of days later sixty workers were killed in a Hong Kong-owned factory. The China Labor Ministry reported that eleven thousand workers had been killed in industrial accidents just in the first eight months of 1993, double the figure of the preceding year.

These atrocities and the women locked into factories never enter the human rights report. On the other hand, it would be unfair to say that labor practices never enter it. They do. There's been a big hullabaloo about the use of prison labor. Front-page stories in the *Times*. It's terrible. Prison labor we're opposed to. But locking women in factories in foreign-owned enterprises where they burn to death, that's just one of those things that happens.

What's the difference? Very simple. Prison labor does not contribute to private profit. That's state enterprise. Prison labor in fact undermines private profit because it competes with private industry. On the other hand, locking women in factories where they burn to death contributes to private profit. So prison labor is a human rights violation. But there is no right not to be burned to death. In fact, that's just part of the capitalist system. We're in favor of that. People might be burned to death, but we have to maximize profit. From that principle everything follows. Opposition to prison labor to silence about eleven thousand workers being killed in industrial accidents.

DB *Notions of democracy fill the air. Clinton's National Security Advisor, Anthony Lake, is encourag-*

*ing democracy enlargement overseas. Might Anthony
Lake extend that to the U.S.?*

I can't tell you what Anthony Lake has in mind,
but the concept of democracy that's been advanced
is a very special one. It's one that the more honest
people on the right describe accurately. For example,
there are some interesting writings recently by
Thomas Carothers, who was involved in the Reagan
administration in what they called the "democracy
assistance project" in the 1980s. He has a book and
several articles about the achievements of the project. He takes the commitment seriously, which is
odd, to say the least, even given his own report and
evaluation.

Carothers gives an assessment which is rather
accurate. He said that the U.S. sought to create a
form of top-down democracy which would leave traditional structures of power with which the U.S. had
always been allied still in effective control. That kind
of democracy is OK. That's the kind of democracy
that's being enhanced, at home as well, a form of
democracy which leaves traditional structures of
power in control and in fact, in greater control.
Traditional structures of power are basically the corporate sector and its affiliates. Any form of democracy that leaves them unchallenged, that's admissible.
Any form that undermines their power is as intoler-
able as ever.

DB *We should have a lexical definition of democracy and then the practical definition.*

The practical definition is something like the one

234

that Thomas Carothers describes and criticizes. The lexical definition is that democracy has lots of different dimensions. But roughly speaking, a society is democratic to the extent that people have meaningful opportunity to take part in formation of public policy. Insofar as that's true, the society's democratic, and there are a lot of different ways in which that can be true. Society can have the formal trappings of democracy and not be democratic at all. The Soviet Union, for example, had elections.

DB *You've commented that the U.S. has a formal democracy with primaries, elections, referenda, recalls, and so on. But what is the content of this democracy in terms of popular participation?*

The content has generally been rather slight. There are changes, but over long periods the involvement of the public in planning or implementation of public policy has been quite marginal. It's a business-run society. For a long time the parties have reflected business interests.

One version of this view which I think has much power behind it is what political scientist Thomas Ferguson calls the investment theory of politics. He argues that since the early nineteenth century the political arena has been a domain in which there's a conflict for power among groups of investors who coalesce together on some common interest and invest to control the state. The ones who participate are the ones who have the resources and the private power to become part of a meaningful coalition of investors. He argues, plausibly, I think, that long periods of apparent political compromise, when not much is going on of a major character in the political system, are simply periods in which the major groups of investors have seen more or less eye to eye on what public policy should look like. The moments of conflict which come along, like the New Deal, are cases where you do have some differences in perspective and point of view among groups of investors.

So in the New Deal period there were various groupings of private capital which were in conflict over a number of issues. He identifies, among others, a high-tech capital-intensive, internationally oriented, export-oriented sector who tended to be quite pro-New Deal and in favor of the reforms. They wanted an orderly work force. They didn't want to be bothered. They wanted an opening to foreign trade. A more labor-intensive, more domestically oriented group, essentially around the National Association of Manufacturers, were strongly anti-New Deal. They didn't want any of these reform measures.

Of course, those groups were not the only thing involved. There was the labor movement, a lot of public ferment and so on, that led to something happening in the political arena.

DB *You view corporations as being incompatible with democracy. You say if we apply the concepts we use in political analysis they are fascist. "Fascist" is a highly charged term. What do you mean?*

I mean fascism pretty much in the traditional sense. So when a rather mainstream person like Robert Skidelsky, the biographer of Keynes, describes the early postwar systems as modeled on fascism, he simply means the system of state coordination of corporate sectors. It integrates labor, capital, and so on, under the control of those who have power, which is the corporate system and with general state coordination. That's what a fascist system traditionally was. It's absolutist. Power goes from top down. Even a fascist system can vary in the way it works, but the ideal state is top down control with the public essentially following orders.

Let's take a look at a corporation. Fascism is a term that applies to the political domain, so it doesn't apply strictly to corporations. But if you look at what they are, power goes strictly top down, from the board of directors to managers to lower managers to ultimately the people on the shop floor, typing messages, and so on. There's no flow of power or planning from the bottom up. People can disrupt and make suggestions, but the same is true of a slave society. The structure of power is linear, from top to bottom, ultimately back to owners and investors. As for those who are not part of that structure, they have nothing to say about it. They can choose to rent themselves to it, and enter into the system at some level, following the orders from above and giving them to those down below. They can choose to purchase the commodities or services that it produces. That's it. That's the totality of their involvement in the workings of the corporation.

That's something of an exaggeration, because corporations are subject to some legal requirements and there is some limited degree of public control. There are taxes and other things. That reflects the parliamentary system to the extent that that's democratic. Corporations are more totalitarian than the things we call totalitarian in the political system.

These are vast. We're not talking about small isolated islands in some huge sea. We're talking about islands which are the size of the sea. Their operations, including much of what is called "trade," are centrally managed by highly visible hands which may introduce severe market distortions. So, for example, a corporation that has an outlet in Puerto Rico may decide to take its profits in Puerto Rico because of tax rebates and change the pricing system, what's called transfer pricing, so they don't seem to be making a profit here. There are severe market distortions, as in fact in any form of central internal planning. It's a very substantial and growing part of interactions across borders, which really shouldn't be called trade.

About half of what are called U.S. exports to Mexico are just intrafirm transfers. They don't enter the Mexican market. There's no meaningful sense in which they're exports to Mexico. It means Ford Motor Company has components constructed here and ships them to a plant which happens to be on the other side of the border where they get much lower wages and don't have to worry about pollution, unions, and that sort of nonsense. Then they ship them back here. Mexico has nothing to do with it.

According to the last figures I saw, about seventy percent of Japanese exports to the U.S. were in that category. These are major market distortions, and growing. When people say that GATT and NAFTA are free trade agreements, there are many respects in which that's not true. Some of the respects in which it's not true is that these investor rights agreements, as they ought to be called, extend the power of international corporations and finance. That means extending their ability to carry out market distorting operations internally.

If you tried to get a measure of the effect of the distortion of market principles, which I don't think anybody has ever done, you'd probably find that it's quite significant. Things like shifting pricing around to maximize profit are more or less functionally equivalent to non-tariff barriers to trade and voluntary export restrictions. There are estimates of the scale of non-tariff barriers. But I know of no estimates of internal corporate interference with market processes that way. They may be large in scale and are sure to be extended by the trade agreements. These are huge totalitarian institutions which are in a kind of oligopolistic market with plenty of government interference. There are market factors that affect them, but internally, they have little to do with market principles, and they are totalitarian. So when people like Anthony Lake, to get back to the original point, talk about enlarging market democracy, they are enlarging something, but it's not simply markets and it's not democracy.

DB *You describe free trade as protection for the rich and market discipline for everyone else.*

That's what it comes down to. So the poor are indeed subjected to market discipline. The rich are not. The ideology calls for what are called flexible labor markets. Flexible labor markets is a fancy way of saying, when you go to sleep at night you don't know if you'll have a job tomorrow morning. That's a flexible labor market. That increases efficiency. Any economist can prove that it increases efficient use of resources if people have no job security, if you can get thrown out and somebody cheaper can come in the next morning. That's the kind of market discipline that the poor are to be subjected to. But the rich have all sorts of forms of protection. This was dramatically illustrated at Clinton's great triumph at the Asia Pacific summit, when he presented what the press called his grand vision for the free market future. He picked as his model for the free market future the Boeing Corporation, whose wealth and power derive substantially from state intervention. That's protection for the rich.

Reflections on Democracy

April 11, 1994

DB *You just returned from the San Francisco Bay area where you had the usual rounds of speeches, interviews, and receptions. Anything different about this particular trip?*

There was a noticeable effect of people having seen the Achbar-Wintonick film *Manufacturing Consent*. Lots of people recognized me on campus and the streets. Otherwise, it's similar to what I find around the country. It takes a little different form in different places. It's a combination of dismay ranging to hopelessness on the one hand and hunger for something to do and some suggestion as to a way to proceed on the other.

DB *Are you concerned that this increased visibility and recognition might inhibit you in some way?*

It has a feature that I think is extremely unfortunate and that may actually be inherent in the film medium and also in the general collapse of a left intelligentsia, namely a tendency to personalize issues and to impose a serious misunderstanding of the way things happen, as if they happen because individuals show up and lead people, whereas in fact

241

what happens is that people organize and occasionally will toss up a spokesperson.

DB *Let's talk about democracy. When democratic theorists talk about the "rabble," who do they mean?*

They mean the general population, who they in past years called the rabble and in more recent years have called "ignorant and meddlesome outsiders." If they're more polite, they call them the "general public."

DB *Why is it important to keep the rabble in line?*

Any form of concentrated power, whatever it is, is not going to want to be subjected to popular democratic control or, for that matter, to market discipline. Powerful sectors, including corporate wealth, are naturally opposed to functioning democracy, just as they're opposed to functioning markets, for themselves, at least. It's just natural. They do not want external constraints on their capacity to make decisions and act freely. It entails that the elites will be extremely undemocratic.

DB *And has that always been the case?*

Always. Of course, it's a little more nuanced because certain forms of democracy are favored, what is sometimes called "formal democracy." Modern democratic theory is simply more articulate and sophisticated than in the past. It takes the view that the role of the public, the "ignorant and meddlesome outsiders," as Walter Lippmann called them, is to be "spectators," not "participants," who show up every couple of years to ratify decisions made elsewhere or to select among representatives of dominant sectors in what's called an election. That form of democracy is approved and is indeed helpful to certain kinds of ruling groups, namely those in more or less state capitalist societies, and indeed the rising bourgeoisie a century or two ago. For one thing it has a legitimizing effect, and for another, it does offer significant options for the more privileged sectors, sometimes called the political class or the decision-making sectors, maybe something like a quarter of the population in a wealthy society.

DB *In discussions on democracy you refer to a couple of comments from Thomas Jefferson.*

Near the end of his life, (he died in 1826), and a little before that, Thomas Jefferson had spoken with a mixture of concern and hope about what had been achieved. This is roughly fifty years after the Declaration of Independence. He said many interesting things. He made a distinction between two groups, what he called "aristocrats" and "democrats." The aristocrats are, in his words, "those who fear and distrust the people and wish to draw all powers from them into the hands of the higher classes." The democrats are those who "identify with the people, have confidence in them, cherish and consider them as the most honest and safe, although not the most wise depository of the public interest." So the democrats say, Look, people must be in control, whether or not I think that they're going to make the right decisions. The aristocrats fear and distrust the people and say that the higher classes shall take all powers into their hands.

What he called the aristocrats include the modern intelligentsia, whether in their Leninist variety or in the variety that appears in state capitalist democracies. So those who warn us of the "democratic dogmatisms about men being the best judges of their own interests" say that *they* are not the best judges; *we* are. I'm quoting one of the founders of contemporary political science, Harold Lasswell, representing a standard view. They are what Jefferson called the aristocrats. Their view has a close similarity to the Leninist doctrine that the vanguard party of radical intellectuals should take power and lead the stupid masses to a bright future. Those views run across the board in the groups that are considered respectable intellectuals in their own societies. In fact this is the victory of Thomas Jefferson's aristocrats, something which he feared and hoped might not happen, but indeed did happen, not entirely in the forms he predicted, but in the general character. These insights, of which Jefferson was one of the earliest articulate spokespersons, continued through the nineteenth century.

Later on Bakunin made a similar distinction, predicting that the intellectual classes more or less becoming visible as an independent element in the world would separate into two groups, those that he called the "red bureaucracy," who would take power into their own hands and create one of the most malevolent and vicious tyrannies in human history, and those who would conclude that power lies in the private sector and would become the intellectual servants of state and private power in what we now call state capitalist societies and, in his term, would "beat the people with the people's stick," meaning they would profess democracy while serving as what were later called the "responsible men" (Lippmann) who would make the decisions and the analysis and keep the "bewildered herd" (Lippmann) in hand. Those are two categories of what Jefferson called aristocrats. Democrats do exist, but they're increasingly marginal.

DB *You also cite the twentieth-century philosopher and educator John Dewey in a kind of link with Jefferson. What did Dewey have to say about this subject?*

Dewey was one of the last spokespersons of what you might call the Jeffersonian view of democracy. Of course, he was writing a century later. Jefferson himself, some years before the remarks I quoted, warned of the danger that the government would fall into the hands of what he again called an aristocracy of "banking institutions and monied incorporations," what we would nowadays called corporations. He warned that that would be the end of democracy and the defeat of the American revolution. That's pretty much what happened in the century that followed, far beyond his worst nightmares.

Dewey was writing in the early part of the twentieth century. His view was that democracy is not an end in itself, it's a means by which people discover and extend and manifest their fundamental human nature and human rights, which is rooted in freedom and solidarity and a choice of both work and other forms of participation in a social order and free individual existence. Democracy produces free people, he said. That's the "ultimate aim" of a democratic society; not the production of goods, but "the production of free human beings associated with one another on terms of equality." He recognized that democracy in that sense was a very withered plant.

He described politics as "the shadow cast on society by big business," namely by Jefferson's "banking institutions and monied incorporations," of course vastly more powerful by this time. He felt that that fact made reform very limited if not impossible. Here are his words: As long as "politics is the shadow cast on society by big business, the attenuation of the shadow will not change the substance." So reform may be of some use, but it's not going to bring democracy and freedom. These are undermined by the very institutions of private power, which of course he recognized, as did Jefferson and other classical liberals, as absolutist institutions. They're unaccountable. They're basically totalitarian in their internal structure. They're powerful far beyond anything that Dewey dreamed, for that matter. He also spelled out exactly what they were. He made it quite clear that as long as there is no democratic control of the workplace, of the banking institutions and monied incorporations, there will be only the most limited democracy.

DB *A question about your methodology and research. You retrieve and resurrect very valuable material, for example on Jefferson and Bakunin and Dewey and Adam Smith. There is that great St. Augustine story on pirates and emperors that you use. When did you read St. Augustine on the difference*

246

between pirates and emperors?

The St. Augustine story was actually brought to my attention by a friend, Israel Shahak, the Israeli dissident. He mentioned that to me. It was a nice story.

DB *Do you file these away? You dug out a quote from John Jay, "Those that own the country ought to govern it." Where did you find that?*

I read it somewhere.

DB *It's a very impressive service.*

This literature is all accessible. Thomas Jefferson and John Dewey, for example, it's hard to think of more leading figures in American history. All of these things are as American as apple pie. When you read John Dewey today, or Thomas Jefferson, their work sounds like that of some crazed Marxist lunatic. But that just shows how much intellectual life has deteriorated. These are straight developments from the classical liberal period. In many ways they received their earliest, and often most powerful formulation, in people like Wilhelm von Humboldt, somebody who I've been greatly interested in, and who inspired John Stuart Mill.

Von Humboldt was one of the eighteenth-century founders of the classical liberal tradition. He, like Adam Smith and other basically pre-capitalist classical liberals, felt that at the root of human nature is the need for free creative work under one's own control. That must be at the basis of any decent society. Those ideas run straight through to Dewey. They are of course deeply anti-capitalist in character. In the eighteenth century, Adam Smith didn't speak of himself as anti-capitalist because this was pre-capitalist, but you can see exactly where it's leading. It's leading to the left-libertarian critique of capitalism, which in my view grows straight out of classical liberalism and takes various forms. It takes the Deweyian form of a sort of workers' control version of democratic socialism. It takes the left Marxist form of people like Anton Pannekoek and Rosa Luxemburg, and it feeds directly into the libertarian socialist-anarchist tradition. All of this has been grossly perverted or forgotten in modern intellectual life. I think that those traditions are rich and internally fairly consistent, and I even think they can be traced back to earlier origins in seventeenth-century rationalism.

DB *Let's take Adam Smith, for example. He of course is the icon celebrated by the corporate community as the godfather of capitalism. But your research reveals some very startling information about Adam Smith.*

It's not really startling. It's well known in Smith scholarship. Recall that Smith, for example, had even given an argument to show that a properly functioning market will tend towards equality and that the perfect system will be one of very extensive and pervasive equality. The closer you reach equality the closer you reach a perfect society. He also argued that only under those conditions would a market function efficiently. He was very critical of what he called "joint stock companies," what we would call corporations, which existed in quite a different form in his day. He had a good deal of skepticism about them because of the separation of managerial control from direct participation and also because they might, he feared then, turn into, in effect, immortal persons, which indeed happened in the nineteenth century, not long after his death.

It happened not through parliamentary decisions. Nobody voted on it in Congress. This was a significant change in American society, and elsewhere in the world as well, through judicial decisions. Judges, corporate lawyers, and others, simply crafted a new society in which immortal persons, namely corporations, have immense power. By now the top two hundred corporations in the world control over a quarter of total assets, and this is increasing. Just this morning *Forbes* magazine came out with its annual listing of the top American corporations and their assets, their behavior, and their welfare, and found increasing profits, increasing concentration, and reduction of jobs, a tendency that's been going on for some years.

DB *You suggest that to further democracy people should be "seeking out authoritarian structures and challenging them, eliminating any form of absolute power and hierarchic power." How would that, for example, work in a family structure?*

In any structure, including a family structure, there are various forms of authority. A patriarchal family, that kind of family structure, may have very rigid authority, from the father usually, setting rules that others adhere to, in some cases administering severe punishment if there's a violation of them. There are other hierarchical relations among siblings, between the mother and father, gender relations, and so on. These all have to be questioned. Sometimes I think you can find that there's a legitimate claim to authority, that is, the challenge to authority can sometimes be met. But the burden of proof is on the authority. So for example, some form of control over children is justified. It's fair to prevent the child from putting his or her hand in the oven, let's say, or from running across the street in traffic. It's even proper to place clear bounds on children. They want them. They want to understand where they are in the world. However, all of these things have to be done with sensitivity and with self-awareness and recognition that any authoritarian role that one plays, or that someone else plays, does require justification. It's not self-justifying.

DB *This is a difficult question. When does that child move to an autonomous state where the parent doesn't need to provide authority?*

I don't think there are formulas for this. For one thing, it's not that we have solid scientific knowledge and understanding of these things. We don't. There's a mixture of experience and intuition plus a certain amount of study which yields a limited framework of understanding, about which people may certainly differ. Beyond that there are plenty of individual differences. So I don't think there's a simple answer to that question. The growth of autonomy and self-control and expansion of the range of legitimate choices and the ability to exercise them, that's growing up.

DB *Let's talk about media and democracy. In your view, what are the communications requirements of a democratic society?*

I would agree with Adam Smith on this. We would like to see a tendency toward equality. Equality doesn't just mean the extremely spare form of equality of opportunity that's considered part of the dominant value system here. It means actual equality and the ability at every stage of one's existence for access to information and choices and decisions and participation on the basis of that information. So a democratic communications system would be one that involves large-scale public participation, that reflects on the one hand public interests and on the other hand real values, like truth and integrity and discovery and so on. Pursuit and dissemination of scientific understanding, for example, isn't something that results from parliamentary choices. It does in part because of funding and so on, but it also pursues its own path. And it's pursuing values that are significant in themselves.

DB *Bob McChesney, in his recent book* Telecommunications, Mass Media and Democracy, *details the rather contentious debate between 1928 and 1935 for control of radio in the U.S. How did that battle for radio play out?*

That's a very interesting topic, and he's done an important service by bringing it out. It's very pertinent today, because we're involved in a very similar battle over this so-called "information highway." In the 1920s, the first major means of mass communication came along after the printing press, which was radio. It's obvious that radio is a bounded resource. There was no question in anyone's mind that the government was going to have to regulate it. There's only a fixed bandwidth. The question was, What form would this government regulation take?

There were essentially two choices: It could offer this new technology, this new form of mass communication, as, in effect, a public service, meaning that it would be public radio, with popular participation, and as democratic as the society is. Public radio in the Soviet Union would have been totalitarian, and public radio in, say, Canada or England would be partially democratic insofar as the societies are democratic, which they are to an extent. That debate was pursued all over the world, at least in the wealthier societies that had choices, and it split.

The U.S. went one way, and the rest of the world, maybe all of it, I can't think of an exception, went the other way. Almost the entire world went in the direction of public radio. The U.S. chose private radio. "Chose" is a funny word. The distribution of power in the U.S. led to commercialization of radio. Not a hundred percent, so you were allowed to have small radio stations, say, a college radio station, which can reach a few blocks. But in effect it was handed over to private power. There was, as McChesney points out, a considerable struggle about that. There were church groups and some labor groups and other public interest groups that felt that the U.S. should go the way the rest of the world was going. They lost out. This is very much a business-run society. That shows itself in many differences between the U.S. and the rest of the industrial world. Lack of comprehensive health care is another well-known example.

In any event, business power won. Rather strikingly, it also won an ideological victory, claiming that handing radio over to private power was democracy because you have choices in the market. That's a very weird concept of democracy, which means that your power in this democracy depends on the number of dollars you have, and the choices are limited to selection among options that are highly structured by the real concentration of power. So it's a very odd notion of democracy, sort of the kind of democracy you get in a totalitarian system. But nevertheless that was considered democracy. It was widely accepted, including by liberals, as the democratic solution. By the mid- and late 1930s that game was essentially over.

It replayed, in the world, at least, about a decade later, when television came along. In the U.S. this wasn't a battle at all. It was completely commercialized without any conflict. But again in the rest of the world, maybe in the entire rest of the world, it moved into the public sector, again a big split between the U.S. and other countries. There was a slight modification of this in the 1960s. For one thing, television and radio were becoming by then partly commercialized in other societies, too, as an effect of the same concentration of private power that we find in the U.S. So it was chipping away at the public service function of radio and television. In the U.S. in the 1960s there was a slight opening to public radio and television. The reasons for this have never been explored in any depth, as far as I know, but what seems to have happened is that corporations recognized that it was a nuisance for them to have to satisfy the formal requirements of the Federal Communications Commission that they devote part of their functioning to public interest purposes. So CBS and so on would have to have a big office with a lot of employees and bureaucrats who every year would put together a collection of fraudulent claims about how they had met this legislative condition. That's just a pain in the neck. Presumably they decided at some point that it would be easier to get the entire burden off their backs and permit a small and underfunded public broadcasting system. They could then claim that they don't have to fulfill this service any longer. That's what happened. So you get public radio and public television, small, underfunded, and by now largely corporate-funded in any event.

DB *That's happened more and more. PBS is sometimes called Petroleum Broadcasting Service.*

That's again a reflection of the interests and power of a highly class-conscious business system which is always fighting an intense and self-conscious class war. These issues are coming up again in the decisions that are going to be made about the new communications technology, the Internet, the interactive technologies that are being developed and so on. And again we're going to find exactly the same conflict. It's going on right now.

DB *Lorenzo Milam is one of the pioneers of com-*

munity radio in the U.S. He had this to say about public broadcasting: "Our freedom to be heard has been replaced on radio by mindless call-in programs, endless repeats of the car culture by illiterate Bostonians," sorry, Noam, "and national news programs ground out like commercial sausage. On television, any access by the poor and dispossessed is replaced by lions eating wildebeests, Lawrence Welk, and hour-long programs dedicated to the wonders of theme parks. Those of us who once hoped that commercial radio and television would live up to their initial hopes now have to be satisfied with the exposure of our most lurid preoccupations on the likes of Oprah, Geraldo, Arsenio, sandwiched between the prime-time ritual murder of our children."

I don't see any reason why one should have had any long-term hopes for anything different. Commercially run radio is going to have certain purposes, namely the purposes designed and determined by those who own and control it. Their purposes are to have a passive, obedient population of spectators in the political arena, not participants, consumers in the commercial arena, certainly not decision makers and participants, a community of people who are atomized and isolated so they cannot organize to put together their limited resources so as to become an independent and powerful force that will chip away at concentrated power. That's exactly what private business power will naturally want. From that you can pretty well predict the kind of system that will emerge.

DB *Does ownership always determine and drive*

content?

In some far-reaching sense it does. That is, if content ever goes beyond the bounds that ownership will tolerate, it will surely move in to limit it. On the other hand, that permits a fair amount of flexibility. So investors don't go down to the television studio and make sure that the local talk show host or news director is doing what they want. On the other hand, there are other complex mechanisms which make it fairly certain that they *will* do what the owners and investors want. There's a whole filtering process that enables people to rise through the system into managerial roles only if they've demonstrated that they've successfully internalized the values demanded by private power.

At that point they can describe themselves as quite free. So you'll occasionally find the sort of flaming independent liberal type. I remember columns by Tom Wicker saying, Look, nobody tells me what to say. I do anything I feel. It's an absolutely free system. And for him that's just right. After he had demonstrated to the satisfaction of the bosses that he had internalized their values, he was entirely free to write anything he wanted.

DB *Within the ideological framework, both PBS and NPR frequently come under attack as being left-wing.*

This is an interesting sort of critique. The fact is that they are elite institutions, reflecting by and large the points of view and interests of wealthy professionals who are very close to business circles, including corporation executives. Their circles happen to be liberal by certain criteria. That is, if you took a poll among corporation executives on matters like, say, abortion rights, I've never seen this done, but I presume that they would be together with what's called the liberal community. The same on lots of social issues. They would tend not to be fundamentalist, born-again Christians, for example. They might tend to be more opposed to the death penalty than the general population. You'll find the wealthy and the privileged, including CEOs of corporations and big investors and so on, at the liberal fringe on a whole series of issues. The same will be true on things like civil rights and freedom of speech, I suspect. Since those are aspects of the social order from which they gain, they will tend to support them. If you look at support for the American Civil Liberties Union, I'm sure you'll find plenty of private wealth backing it. So by these criteria, by these standards, the powerful elites who basically dominate the country and own it tend to be liberal. That reflects itself in an institution like PBS.

DB *You've been on National Public Radio twice in twenty-three years, on MacNeil-Lehrer once in its almost twenty years. What if you were on MacNeil-Lehrer ten times? Would it make a difference?*

Not a lot. I'm not quite sure of those numbers. I don't know where they come from, and my own memory is not that precise. For example, I've been on local PBS stations in particular towns.

DB *I'm talking about the national network.*

257

Probably something roughly like that is correct. I don't know the exact numbers. It wouldn't make a lot of difference. In fact, in my view, if the managers of the propaganda system were more intelligent, they would allow more leeway to real dissidents and critics. Because it still wouldn't make much of a difference, given the overwhelming weight of propaganda on the other side and the constant framing of issues, even in the news stories and in that huge mass of the media system that is simply devoted to diverting people and making them more stupid and passive. It would also give the impression of broader debate and discussion and hence would have a legitimizing function. That's not to say I'm against opening up these media a bit, but I would think it would have a limited effect.

What you need is something that presents every day, in a clear and comprehensive fashion, a different picture of the world, one that reflects the concerns and interests or ordinary people, that takes something like the point of view on democracy and participation that you find from people like Jefferson or Dewey. Where that happens, and it has happened, even in modern societies, it has effects. Let's say, in England, where up until the 1960s you did have major mass media of this kind. It helped sustain and enliven a working-class culture, which had a big effect on British society.

DB *In 1990 we did one of our many interviews. We had a brief discussion about the role and function of sports in American society. I've probably gotten more comments about your comments than practically anything else. Part of it was excerpted in* Harper's. *You* *really pushed some buttons on this issue of sports. What's that about?*

I got some funny reactions, a lot of irate reactions, as if I were somehow taking people's fun away from them. I have nothing against sports. I like to watch a good basketball game and that sort of thing. On the other hand, we have to recognize that there is a role that this mass hysteria about spectator sports plays. It's a significant role. It plays a role first of all in making people more passive, because you're not doing it. You're watching somebody doing it.

Secondly, it plays a role in engendering jingoist and chauvinist attitudes, sometimes to quite an extreme level. I saw something in the newspapers just a day or two ago about how high school teams are now so antagonistic and passionately committed to winning at all costs that they can't even do civil things like greeting one another because they're ready to kill one another. So they had to abandon the standard handshake before or after the game.

Those are the things that spectator sports engender, particularly when they're designed to organize a community to be hysterically committed to their gladiators. That's very dangerous, and it has lots of deleterious effects. Furthermore, I think things like that are understood and are part of the planning system, part of the public relations control system.

I was reading something about the glories of the information highway not too long ago. I can't quote it exactly, but I'll paraphrase the general tone. It was talking about how wonderful and empowering it's going to be with these new interactive technologies. Two basic examples were given. For women, what it's going to offer is highly improved methods of home shopping. So you'll be able to watch the tube and some model will appear with a commodity and you're supposed to think, God, I've got to have this or my children won't go to college, or whatever the reasoning is supposed to be. So you press a button and they deliver it to your door within a couple of hours. That's interactive technology liberating women. On the other hand, for men the example that was given was the Superbowl. Every red-blooded American male in the country is glued to it. Now all they can do is watch and cheer and drink beer. But once we have interactive technology, they can be asked, while the quarterback is getting his instructions from the coach about the next play, what the play ought to be. He should throw a pass, or something. They will be able to punch that into their computer and it will go to some central location. It won't have any effect on what the quarterback does, but after the play the television channel will be able to put up the numbers, sixty-three percent say he should have passed. That's interactive technology for men. Now you're really participating in the world. Forget about all this business of deciding what ought to happen for health care. Now you're doing something really important: deciding what play the quarterback should have called. That reflects the understanding of the stupefying effect of these systems in making people passive, atomized, obedient, non-participants, non-questioning, and easily controlled and disciplined.

DB *You also have, at the same time, the lionization of these athletes, or, in the case of Tonya Harding, for example, the demonization.*

If you can personalize events, whether it's Hillary Clinton or Tonya Harding, you are directing people away from what matters and what is important. The John F. Kennedy cult is a good example, with the effects that that's had on the left.

DB *You were at American University in Washington, D.C. in December 1993. A student got up and said, Isn't it just great? We now have all these computer bulletin boards and the opportunity to be on e-mail and expand our information and awareness, etc. I was very struck by your response. You were talking about our need to have more human contact and that there was a danger in the new technologies.*

I think that there are good things about these Internet communications. There are also aspects of them that concern and worry me. These are intuitive responses. I can't prove it. But my feeling is that people are not Martians, they are not robots, and that direct human contact, and I mean by that face-to-face contact, is an extremely important part of human life and existence and developing self-understanding and the growth of a healthy personality and so on. You just have a different relationship to somebody when you are looking at them than when you're punching away at a keyboard and some symbols come back. Extending that form of abstract and remote relationship, instead of direct personal contact, I suspect that that's going to have unpleasant effects on what people are like. It will diminish people, I think.

DB *Let's move on to another area. Historian Paul*

261

Boyer, in his book When Time Shall Be No More, *writes, "Surveys show that," and I find this absolutely stunning, "from one third to one half of the population," he's talking about Americans, "believes that the future can be interpreted in biblical prophecies." Have you heard of these things?*

I haven't seen that particularly number, but I've seen plenty of things like it. I saw a cross-cultural study a couple of years ago, I think it was published in England, which compared a whole range of societies in terms of beliefs of that kind. The U.S. stood out. It was unique in the industrial world. In fact, the measures for the U.S. were similar to pre-industrial societies.

DB *Why is that?*

That's an interesting question, but it's certainly true. It's a very fundamentalist society. It's like Iran in the degree of fanatic religious commitment. You get extremely strange results. For example, I think about seventy-five percent of the population has a literal belief in the devil. There was a poll several years ago on evolution. People were asked their opinion on various theories of evolution, of how the world came to be what it is. The number of people who believed in Darwinian evolution was less than ten percent. About half the population believed in a church doctrine of divine-guided evolution. Most of the rest presumably believed that the world was created a couple of thousand years ago. This runs across the board. These are very unusual results. Why the U.S. should be off the spectrum on these issues has been discussed and debated for some time.

I remember reading something by a political scientist who writes about these things, William Dean Burnham, maybe ten or fifteen years ago. He had also done similar studies. He suggested that this may be a reflection of depoliticization, that is, inability to participate in a meaningful fashion in the political arena, which may have a rather important psychic effect, heightened by the striking disparity between the facts and the ideological depiction of them. What's sometimes called the ideal culture is so radically different from the real culture in terms of the theory of popular participation versus the reality of remoteness and impotence. That's not impossible. People will find some ways of identifying themselves, becoming associated with others, taking part in something. They're going to do it some way or other. If they don't have the options of participation in labor unions, political organizations that actually function, they'll find other ways. Religious fundamentalism is a classic example.

We see that happening in other parts of the world right now. The rise of what's called Islamic fundamentalism is to a significant extent a result of the collapse of secular nationalist alternatives which were either discredited internally or destroyed, leaving few other options. Something like that may be true of American society. This goes back to the nineteenth century. In fact, in the nineteenth century you even had some conscious efforts on the part of business leaders to promote and encourage fire and brimstone-type preachers who would lead people into looking in another way. The same thing happened in the early part of the Industrial Revolution in England. E.P. Thompson writes about this in his classic *The Making of the English Working Class*.

DB *What is one to make of Clinton's comment in his recent State of the Union speech. He said, "We can't renew our country unless more of us, I mean all of us, are willing to join churches."*

I don't know exactly what's in his mind, but the ideology is very straightforward. If you devote yourself to activities out of the public arena, we folks will be able to run it straight. It's very interesting to see the way this is done in the slick PR productions of the right-wing corporations. One of the biggest ones is the Bradley Foundation, which is devoted to trying to narrow still further the ideological spectrum that shifted to the right in the schools and colleges and the ideological institutions generally in the 1980s, in part as a result of dedicated ideological warfare by the business sector. That's their mission. Their director, Michael Joyce, recently published an article on this which I found fascinating. I don't know whether he wrote it or one of his PR guys. It was very revealing in this respect, done in a very slick fashion.

It starts off with rhetoric drawn, probably consciously, from the left. When left liberals or radical activists start reading it they get a feeling of recognition and sympathy. I suspect it's directed to them and to young people. It starts off talking about how remote the political system is from us, how we are asked just to show up every once in a while and cast our votes and then go home. This is meaningless. This isn't real participation in the world. What we

Reflections on Democracy

need is a functioning and active civil society in which people come together and do important things and not just this business of pushing a button now and then. That's the way it's starts. Then you get to page 2. It says, "How do we overcome these inadequacies."

Strikingly, the inadequacies are *not* to be overcome by more active participation in the political arena. They're to be overcome by *abandoning* the political arena and joining the PTA and going to church and getting a job and going to the store and buying something. That's how you fulfill your function as a citizen. That's the way to become a real citizen of a democratic society, by becoming engaged in activities like finding a job and going to the PTA.

Nothing wrong with going to the PTA. But there are a few gaps here. What happened to the political arena? That disappears from the discussion after the first few comments about how meaningless it is. Of course, if you abandon the political arena, *somebody* is going to be there. The somebody who is going to be there is the missing element in the entire discussion—namely, private power, corporations. They're going to be there. They're not going to go home and join the PTA. So they're going to be there and they're going to run it. Nothing is said about this. This is abandoned.

As the discussion continues, there is some reference to the political arena and the way the people in it are oppressing us. But who are the people who are oppressing us? The liberal bureaucrats, the social scientists, the people who are trying to design social programs. They're the ones who run the country. They're ordering us around and kicking us in the pants and we've got to defend ourselves from them

265

and so on. So there is a form of external power, namely, English departments somewhere or bureaucrats administering the IRS or social planners who are trying to talk about doing something for the poor. They're the ones who are really running the society. They're that impersonal, remote, unaccountable power that we've got to get off our backs as we go to the PTA and look for a job and in such ways fulfill our obligations as citizens.

Meanwhile the *real* public arena and the *real* centers of power in the country are totally missing from the discussion. This is done not quite step-by-step. I'm collapsing it. When you go through you see very clever propaganda, well-designed, well-crafted, plenty of thought behind it. Its goal, surely, is to make people as stupid and ignorant as possible and also as passive and obedient as possible, while at the same time making them feel that they are somehow moving towards higher forms of participation by abandoning the public arena. It also serves the crucial role of displacing attention from actual power. This is the kind of thing that really can't be achieved in a totalitarian state, where central power is just too visible. But it's achieved very commonly in the U.S. This is the right wing.

You see it at the liberal extreme, too. The campaign literature of the Clinton administration was interesting, since you mentioned Clinton. They put out a book called *Mandate for Change*, the kind of thing you pick up at airport newsstands for twenty-five cents, right before the election. We've talked about it before, but it's worth recalling in this context, to illustrate the actual breadth of the spectrum in a business-run society. It was about what great things they were going to do. The first chapter was on entrepreneurial economics and all their great plans for this. They explained that they're not going to be old-fashioned tax-and-spend liberals. They realize what's wrong with that. On the other hand, they're not going to be hard-hearted Republicans. They're forging a new path, entrepreneurial economics, which is concerned just for working people and their firms. The Clinton Administration is going to do something for them. The word "profits" appears once, I think, namely in a reference to the bad days when the Republicans were trying to make too much profit. The word "bosses" doesn't appear. "Managers" doesn't appear. "Owners" and "investors" don't appear. They're not there. It's just the workers and the firms in which they work, their own firms. What about the entrepreneurs? They're there. The entrepreneurs are people who come in every once in a while and help out the workers and improve the firms in which they work and then apparently disappear. That's the picture. Here's the workers and their firms and the entrepreneurs helping them now and then and the Clinton administration coming in to benefit them. The actual structure of power and authority is totally missing, just as much as it is in the publication of the Bradley Foundation. This makes sense if you're trying to turn people into passive and obedient automata.

DB *To tie up this discussion about religion and irrational belief and state capitalism, I recently read an article on MITI, the Ministry of International Trade and Industry in Japan. There was a fascinating discussion by a MITI bureaucrat who was trained in the U.S. at* *the Harvard Business School. He says his class at Harvard was studying a failed airline, maybe Eastern or Pan Am, that went out of business. The class was shown a taped interview with the company's president, who noted with pride that through the whole financial crisis and eventual bankruptcy of the airline he had never asked for government help. The class, the Japanese man recalls with astonishment, erupted into applause. Then he says, "There's a strong resistance to government intervention in America. I understand that. But I was shocked. There are many shareholders in companies. What happened to his employees, for example?" Then he reflects on what he views as America's blind devotion to a free-market ideology. He says, "It is something quite close to a religion. You cannot argue about it with most people. You believe it or you don't." It's interesting.*

It's interesting in part because of the failure to understand what happens in the U.S., which may well be shared by the students in his business class. If that was Eastern Airlines that they were talking about, Frank Lorenzo, the director, was in fact trying to put it out of business. He made a personal profit out of that, but he wanted to break the unions and to support his other enterprises, which he ripped off profits from Eastern Airlines for to leave the airline industry less unionized and more under corporate control and to leave himself wealthier, all of which happened. So naturally he didn't ask for government intervention because it was working the way he wanted. On the other hand, the belief that corporations don't call for government intervention is a joke. They *demand* government intervention and government power at an extraordinary level. The Chrysler bailout is a famous example, but a minor one. That's largely what the whole Pentagon system is about.

Take the airline industry. It was created by government intervention. A large part of the reason for the huge growth in the Pentagon in the late 1940s was to salvage the collapsing aeronautical industry, which obviously couldn't survive in a civilian market. There's an interesting and important book by Frank Kofsky which just came out on this, running through the details of the war scares that were manipulated in 1947 and 1948 to try to ram spending bills through Congress that would save the aeronautical industry. It's not the only thing they were for, but it was a big factor. That's continued. The aeronautical industry is the leading American export industry. Boeing is the leading American exporter without government intervention it might be producing one-seaters for sport.

Furthermore, the real U.S. comparative advantages in what's called "services." About a third of the trade benefits and services are aeronautical related, things like tourism, travel, and so on. These are huge industries spawned by massive government intervention and maintained that way. The corporations demand it. They couldn't survive without it, even if for some of them it's not a huge part of their profits right now. But it's a cushion. And the public also provides the basic technology, metallurgy, avionics, and so on, via the public subsidy system. The same is true just across the board. You can't find a functioning sector of the American economy which hasn't gotten that way and isn't sustained that way by state intervention. Just a day or two ago the lead story in the *Wall Street Journal* was about how the Clinton administration is reviving the National Bureau of Standards and Technology and pouring new funds into it to try to replace the somewhat declining Pentagon system. It's harder to maintain the Pentagon, but you've got to keep the subsidy going to big corporations. You have to have the public pay the research and development costs. So they're shifting over to the National Bureau of Standards, which used to try to work out how long a foot is and will now be more actively involved in serving the needs of private capital. It describes how hundreds of corporations are beating on their doors asking for grants. The idea that a Japanese investigator could fail to see this is pretty remarkable. It's pretty well known in Japan. And it's hard to imagine that they don't teach it in business school.

DB *I remember you telling me about when you were a kid in Philadelphia, the first baseball game you ever attended. The Philadelphia Athletics were playing the New York Yankees. Tell me about that, if you don't mind.*

I can still remember it. It must have been around 1937, I guess. My closest friend and I were taken to this game by the fourth-grade teacher, whose name was Miss Clark and who we were madly in love with. It was a great occasion. Not only were we being taken to our first baseball game, but Miss Clark was taking us. We sat in the bleachers, the cheap seats, in center field, right behind Joe DiMaggio and the A's equivalent star, whose name I think was Bob Johnson. We were naturally rooting for the home team, the Philadelphia A's, who were winning 7-3 going into the seventh inning when the Yankees had a seven-run explosion and won the game 10-7. Big disaster, except that we saw all of our heroes, Joe DiMaggio, Lou Gehrig, Red Ruffing and the rest of them. I can remember it pretty clearly.

DB *The A's were always losing in those years, right?*

For a boy growing up in Philadelphia in those years, given the way the culture works, they were hard times. Not only the A's, but every team in Philadelphia was always losing. So we were an object of considerable mockery when we met our friends and cousins from New York, where they were always winning. I have a certain suspicion that young boys who grew up in Philadelphia in those days must have a kind of deep inferiority complex.

DB *Things got so bad for the Athletics that they eventually left town.*

So I heard. After my day.

Health Care

DB *So I guess you're finished with the sports pages and ready to get into a day's work.*

Only some of the sports pages. There's still the weeklies. (chuckles)

DB *It's becoming increasingly difficult to do interviews with you. That's because I don't know where we left off in conversations that we have and what we've talked about during interviews. So sometimes there's this blurring. Do you do all these interviews in your office upstairs in your home?*

They're mostly here. Sometimes people come to my office at work, the ones with television cameras and stuff.

DB *I don't suppose you can see the Boston skyline from your home in Lexington. But if you could, do you know the two tallest buildings in Boston?*

Yes.

DB *What are they?*

The John Hancock and the Prudential.

DB *And what does that tell you? They happen to be two types of what?*

They're going to be running our health program if Clinton has his way.

DB *There is a general consensus that the U.S. health care system needs to be reformed. How and why did that evolve?*

It evolved very simply. Healthcare is never fully privatized. It can't be. It's not a commodity. But on the spectrum we have a relatively privatized health system. As a result it's hopelessly inefficient and extremely bureaucratic, with huge administrative expenses, and it's geared towards high-tech intervention rather than public health, prevention, and so on. It's just gotten too costly for American business. In fact, a little bit to my surprise, *Business Week*, the main business journal, has come out recently with several articles advocating a Canadian-style national government insurance program, what we call a single-payer program.

DB *What is that Canadian-style single-payer program?*

The Canadian style is one of various plans that exist around the industrial world. It's basically a government insurance program. Health care is still individual, but the government is the insurer.

DB *The Clinton plan is called "managed competi-*

tion." The big insurance companies are backing it in one form or another. What is managed competition and why are the big insurance companies supporting it?

Managed competition essentially will drive the little insurance companies out of the market, which is why they're opposed to it. It will mean that the big insurance companies will put together big conglomerates of health care institutions, hospitals, and clinics, labs, and so on. They will be in charge of organizing your health care. Various bargaining units will be set up to determine which of these conglomerates to work with. That's supposed to introduce some kind of market forces. But in effect, the big insurance companies will be pretty much running the show. It means an oligopolistic system, a very small number of big conglomerates in limited competition with one another and doubtlessly micromanaging health care, because they're business operations, they're in business for profit, not for your comfort.

DB *According to a Harris poll, Americans prefer, by a huge majority, the Canadian single-payer health-care system. Those results are kind of remarkable, given the minimal amount of media attention.*

Polls, of course, depend on exactly how the question is asked. But there have been some surveys of polls over the years. The best work on this that I know is by Vicente Navarro. Have you ever interviewed him on this? You should if you haven't. He's extremely good.

DB *Yes. He's at Johns Hopkins.*

He's done a lot of work on this. He has among other things surveyed many poll results. He has pointed out that even putting aside the variations depending on phrasing, there has been quite consistent support for something like a Canadian-style system ever since polls began on this business, which is now over forty years ago. In fact, Truman tried to put through such a program in the 1940s that would have brought the U.S. into line with the rest of the industrial world. It was beaten back by a huge corporate offensive with tantrums about how we were going to turn into a Bolshevik society and so on. Every time the issue has come up there has been a major corporate offensive. Occasionally it fails. One of Ronald Reagan's great achievements back in the late 1960s was to read the messages written for him by the insurance companies over radio and television about how if Medicare was passed we would all be telling our children and grandchildren decades hence what freedom used to be like.

DB *David Himmelstein and Steffie Woolhandler also cite another poll result: When Canadians are asked if they would want a U.S.-style system, only five percent say yes.*

By now, even the business community doesn't want it. It's just too inefficient, too bureaucratic and too costly for them. The auto companies estimated a couple of years ago that it was costing them about $500 extra per car just because of the inefficiencies of the U.S. health system, as compared with, say,

276

their Canadian operations. When business starts to get hurt, then the thing moves into the public agenda. The public has been in favor of a big change for a long time.

The public is sufficiently out of the political system so it doesn't matter much. There's a nice phrase about this sort of thing in a recent issue of the London *Economist*, the British business journal. It was about Poland. Their constituency is apparently worried about the fact that Poland has degenerated into this system where they have democratic elections, which is sort of a nuisance. The populations of all the East European countries are being smashed by the economic changes called "reforms"—that's supposed to make them sound good—that are being rammed down their throats. The Poles are opposed to the reforms. They voted in an anti-reform government. The *Economist* pointed out that this really wasn't too troublesome because "policy is insulated from politics." And that's a good thing. That's the way it is here, too. Policy is insulated from politics. People can have their opinions. They can even vote if they like. But policy goes on its merry way, determined by other forces.

DB *You have commented on another term, called "politically unrealistic."*

What the public wants is called "politically unrealistic," meaning, when you translate that into English, that the major centers of power and privilege are opposed to it. A change in the health care system is now politically realistic because major systems of power, including the U.S. corporate community, want a change, since it's harming them. As I mentioned, it's striking that even *Business Week*, representing large sectors of the corporate community, wants to go over to a Canadian-style system because even the residual inefficiencies and expenses of the Clinton-style system will also, they assume, be harmful to them.

DB *Vicente Navarro says that a universal and comprehensive health care program is "directly related to the strength of the working class and its political and economic instruments."*

That's certainly true of the Canadian and European experience. Take Canada, which had a system rather like ours up until the mid-1960s. It was changed first in one province, Saskatchewan, where there was a fairly strong labor-based NDP (New Democratic Party) government. It was able to put through a provincial insurance program, driving the insurance companies out of the business. It turned out to be very successful, very effective. It was giving good medical care and reducing costs and much more progressive in payment. That's a crucial fact. It was mimicked by other provinces, also under labor pressure, often through the NDP as an instrument. It's a this kind of umbrella political party with a mildly reformist character and labor backing. Pretty soon it was adopted across Canada nationally.

The history in Europe is pretty much the same. Working-class organizations have been one of the main, but not the only, mechanisms by which people with very limited power and resources can get together to participate in the public arena. That's one of the reasons why unions are so hated by business and elites generally. They're just too democratizing in their character. And Navarro is surely right: The history has been that the strength and organization of labor and its ability to enter into the public arena is certainly related, maybe even decisively related, to an institution of social programs of this kind.

DB *There may be a parallel movement going on in the U.S. today. In California there's a ballot initiative to have single-payer health care.*

There are several states that are toying with it. This is still very much a business-run society. Here business is still playing an inordinate role in determining the kind of system that will evolve. Unless there are significant changes inside the U.S., that is, unless public pressures and organizations mount well beyond what we now see, including labor, the outcome of this will once again be determined by business interests.

DB *I'm not quite clear about how to formulate this question. It has to do with the nature of U.S. society as exemplified in such comments as "Do your own thing," "Go it alone," "Don't tread on me," "the pioneer spirit," all that deeply individualistic stuff. What does that tell you about American society and culture?*

It tells you that the propaganda system is working full-time, because there is no such ideology in the U.S. Business, for example, doesn't believe it. It has always insisted upon a powerful interventionist state to support its interests—still does and always has—back to the origins of American society. There's nothing individualistic about corporations. Those are big conglomerate institutions, essentially totalitarian in character, but hardly individualistic. Within them you're a cog in a big machine. There are few institutions in human society that have such strict hierarchy and top-down control as a business organization. Nothing there about "Don't tread on me." You're being tread on all the time. The point of the ideology is to try to get other people, outside of the sectors of coordinated power, to fail to associate and enter into decision-making in the political arena themselves. The point is to atomize everyone else while leaving powerful sectors integrated and highly organized and of course dominating resources.

That aside, there is another factor. There is a streak of independence and individuality in American culture which I think is a very good thing. This "Don't tread on me" feeling is in many respects a healthy one. It's healthy up to the point where it atomizes and keeps you from working together with other people. So it's got its healthy side and its negative side. It's the negative side that's emphasized naturally in the propaganda and indoctrination.

DB *Have you thought about why the U.S. is such a violent society?*

The U.S. does have many different features than other societies. Part of it is just that it is relatively weak in terms of social and community bonds. So if you travel around Europe, for example, you find that for one thing mobility is simply far lower. People are much more likely to be where they grew up, to be living and working pretty near to where they were. The countries themselves are small by U.S. standards. Moving across borders is much less likely than moving from one place to another in the U.S. But even within a country people tend, I've never seen statistics on this but you see it traveling around, much more than here to be part of ongoing, continuing communities.

Here societies have been very much broken up. Furthermore, communities have simply been dissolved. The forms of organization that do bring people together to work together, like unions, are quite weak in the U.S. The main ones that survive are churches. I think that that has a highly disruptive effect, along with the ideology that you mentioned earlier. The ideal is, get what you can for yourself. That's the ideal that's drummed into people's heads. Bayard Rustin, the civil rights activist, made a point about this back in the early 1960s, when he was asked about why black kids were stealing cars. He said, That's what they're told to do every day on television. They are told all the time that what you're supposed to do is maximize your own consumption any way you can. So they're doing it. Those are the options available to them. They don't have the options that are available to relatively privileged white kids, namely, go to work in a corporate law firm and rip people off that way. So they're ripping people off in ways that are open to them. But they're basically following the ideology that's not only presented but drummed into your head day and night: maximize your own consumption and don't care

281

about anyone else.

DB *And you have the attending media focus on symptoms rather than the causes. Do you know what "smash and grab" is? This is something I discovered last night watching TV news from Chicago. When your car is in traffic or at a stop light, people come along and smash in the window and grab your purse or steal your wallet.*

Right around Boston the same thing is going on. There's a new form. It's called "Good Samaritan robbery." You fake a flat tire on the highway and when somebody stops, jump them, steal their car, beat them up, if they're lucky. If they're unlucky you kill them and take the car off.

There's again a good deal of focus on the symptoms. The causes are deep-seated. For one thing, there are social causes that we've just been barely alluding to, but there are much more immediate causes. One is the increasing polarization of the society that's been going on for the past twenty five years and the marginalization of large sectors of the population who are simply being rendered superfluous. They're superfluous for wealth production, meaning profit production, and hence have no human value, since the basic ideology is that a person's human rights depend on what they can get for themselves in the market system.

Larger and larger sectors of the population are simply excluded and have no form of organization or no viable, constructive way of reacting and therefore pursue the available options, which are often violent. Indeed, those are the ones that are encouraged to a large extent in the popular culture.

DB *It's not just the underclass. A recent Census Bureau report stated that there has been a fifty percent increase in the working poor, that is, people who have jobs and are nonetheles below the poverty level.*

That's part of the Third Worldization of the society. It's not simply unemployment, but also wage reduction. Wages have been either stagnating or declining, actually declining, since the late 1960s. In the Reagan years they declined. Since 1987 real wages have been declining for college-educated people, which was a striking shift. There is supposed to be a recovery going on. There is a kind of recovery going on, that's true. It's at about half the rate of normal postwar recoveries. Job creation during this recovery is less than a third of the rate of preceding postwar recoveries from recession. There have been half a dozen of them.

Furthermore, the jobs themselves are, out of line with any other recovery, low-paying jobs. Wages are not going up. In addition, a huge number of them are temporaries, again out of line with earlier history. This is what's called "increasing flexibility of the labor market." "Flexibility" is like "reform." It's supposed to be a good thing.

Flexibility means insecurity. It means you go to bed at night and don't know if you have a job tomorrow morning. That's called flexibility of the labor market, and any economist can explain that's a good thing for the economy, where by "the economy" now we understand profit-making. We don't mean by "the economy" the way people live. That's good for the economy, and temporary jobs increase flexibility. Low wages also increase job insecurity. They keep inflation low. That's good for people who have money, say, bondholders. So these all contribute to what's called a "healthy economy," meaning one with very high profits. Profits are doing fine. Corporate profits are zooming. But for most of the population, very grim circumstances. And grim circumstances, without much prospect for a future, may lead to constructive social action, but where that's lacking they express themselves in violence.

DB *It's interesting that you should say that. Most of the examples of mass murders are in the workplace. I'm thinking of the various post office killings and fast food restaurants where workers are disgruntled for one reason or another or have been fired or laid off.*

Not only have real wages stagnated or declined, but working conditions have gotten much worse. You can see that just in counting hours of work. Today we happen to be talking on May 2. Yesterday was May 1, which throughout the world has been a working-class holiday, everywhere except in the United States. May Day was initiated in solidarity with American workers who were suffering unusually harsh conditions in their effort to achieve an eight-hour day. This was back in the 1880s. The efficiency of U.S. ideological controls, business controls, is such that this has remained the only country where the day of solidarity with U.S. labor was never even known. U.S. workers finally did, in the 1930s, achieve elementary rights, including the right to an eight-hour day, which had long been achieved elsewhere.

But since then that's been eroded. They've long lost the eight-hour day. Juliet Schor, an economist at Harvard, had an important book on this called *The Overworked American*. It came out a couple of years ago. She studied things like working hours. They have been increasingly steadily. If I remember her figures correctly, by around 1990, the time she was writing, workers had to put in about six weeks extra work a year to maintain something like a 1970 real-wage level.

Along with the increasing hours of work comes increasing harshness of work conditions, increasing insecurity, and reduced ability to protect oneself because of the decline of unions. In the Reagan years, even the minimal government programs for protecting workers against workplace accidents and so on were reduced in the interest of maximizing profits. Furthermore, since the Reaganites regarded the government they ran as basically just a criminal enterprise in the service of the rich, they simply didn't enforce laws on safe working conditions and the like. That again leads to violence. In the absence of constructive options, like union organizing, it leads to violence. It's not very surprising.

A last comment about this May Day story: This morning, May 2, way back on the back pages of the *Boston Globe* there was a little item which said—I was surprised when I saw it, I don't think I've ever seen this here in the U.S.—"May Day Celebration in Boston." So I naturally looked at it. It turned out that there indeed was a May Day celebration, of the usual kind, by immigrant workers—Latin American and Chinese workers—who have recently come here.

They organized to celebrate May Day and to organize for their rights. That's a dramatic example of how efficient business propaganda and indoctrination has been in depriving people of even any awareness of their own rights and history. You have to wait for poor Latino and Chinese workers to have a celebration of a couple hundred people of an international day of solidarity with American workers.

DB *Let's go back to talk a bit more about the health issue. There had been some media attention on AIDS but very little to breast cancer. A half a million women in the U.S. will die in the 1990s from breast cancer. Many men will die from prostate cancer. What are your views on that? Those are not considered political questions, are they?*

If you mean by that there's no vote taken on them, yes, there's no vote taken on them. But obviously all of these things are political questions, if we mean by that questions of policy. You might add to that calculation the number of children who will die or suffer because of extremely poor conditions in infancy and childhood, prenatal and early postnatal.

Take, say, malnutrition. That decreases life span quite considerably. If you count that up in deaths, that outweighs anything you're talking about. I don't think many people in the public health field will question the conclusion that the major contribution to improving health, meaning reducing mortality figures and improving the quality of life, come from simple public health measures, like ensuring people adequate nutrition and safe and healthy conditions of life, water, sewage, and so on.

You'd think in a rich country like this these wouldn't be big issues. But they are for a lot of the population.

Lancet, the British medical journal, the most prestigious medical journal in the world, recently pointed out that forty percent of children in New York City live below the poverty line, meaning suffering conditions of malnutrition and other poor conditions of life which mean very severe health problems all through their lives and very high mortality rates. One of the American medical journals pointed out a couple of years ago that black males in Harlem have about the same mortality rate as people in Bangladesh. That's essentially because of the extreme deterioration of the most elementary public health conditions. That includes social conditions, incidentally.

DB *The government is often fond of declaring war on drugs, war on crime, but there's been no attendant war on breast cancer, for example.*

There is a war on cancer generally. A lot of the biological research is funded with curing cancer as its goal, although not specifically breast cancer.

DB *Some people have linked the increase in breast cancer and prostate cancer to environmental degradation and also to diet, the increase of additives and preservatives. What do you think about that?*

It's presumably some kind of a factor. How big or serious a factor it is I'm not sure.

DB *Are you at all interested in the so-called natural or organic food movement?*

Sure. I think there ought to be concerns about the quality of food. This I would say falls into the question of general public health. It's like having good water and good sewage and making sure that people have enough food and so on. All of these things are in roughly the same category, that is, they have to do not with, say, high-technology medical treatment but with essential conditions of life. These general public health issues, of which eating food without poisons is a part, naturally, are the overwhelming factors in quality of life and mortality, for that matter.

DB *I was at a conference a couple of weeks ago in Washington, D.C. A woman in the audience got up and in addition to attributing all sorts of power to the left, which is total fantasy, she also decried the fact that you are in favor of nuclear power. Does that accurately describe your views?*

No. I don't think anybody's in favor of nuclear power, even business, because it's too expensive. But what I am in favor of is being rational on the topic. Rationality on the topic means recognizing that the question of nuclear power is not a moral one. It's a technical one. You have to ask what the consequences are of nuclear power versus alternatives. I don't think this is true, but imagine that the only alternatives were hydrocarbons and nuclear power. If you had to have one or the other, you have to ask yourself which is more dangerous to the envi-

288

ronment, to human life, to human society? It's not an entirely simple question.

For example, suppose that fusion were a feasible alternative. It could turn out to be non-polluting, in which case it would have advantages. On the other hand, any form of nuclear power has disadvantages. There are problems of radioactive waste storage which are quite serious. Technical problems might be overcome. There are problems of the dangers of how this contributes to nuclear weapons proliferation. Those are negative factors.

On the other hand, there are also potentially positive factors, like lack of pollution. There are other negative factors, like the high degree of centralization of state power, centralized power that's associated with nuclear power. But on the other hand, that's also true of the hydrocarbon industry. The energy corporations are some of the biggest in the world. The Pentagon system is constructed to a significant degree to maintain their power. There is a range of other alternatives, including conservation, decentralized power, options such as solar and so on. They have advantages. But across the board these are problems that have to be thought through.

DB *Let's talk along these lines about the whole notion of economic growth and development. The U.S., with five percent of the world's population, consumes forty percent of the world's resources. You don't have to be a Nobel Prize winner or a genius to figure out what that's leading to.*

For one thing, a lot of that consumption is artificially induced consumption. It's not consumption that has to do with people's real wants. A huge amount of business propaganda, meaning the output of the public relations industry, advertising and so on, is simply an effort to create wants. This has been well understood for a long time, in fact, it goes back to the early days of the Industrial Revolution. There's plenty of consumption, and much of that is artificially induced. People would be probably better off and happier if they didn't have it. Also, the consumption is naturally highly skewed.

Consumption tends to be more by those who have more money, for obvious reasons. So consumption is skewed towards luxury for the wealthy rather than necessities for the poor. That's true not just within the U.S. but on a global scale. That leads to the figures that you describe. The richer countries are the higher consumers by a large measure, but internally to the richer countries, the wealthy are higher consumers by a large measure. And much of that consumption is artificially induced. It has little to do with basic human interests and needs and concerns. It's also in the long term very dangerous. It's healthy for the economy if you measure economic health by profits. If you measure economic health by what it means to people it's very unhealthy, particularly in the long term.

DB *There have been some proposals put forth about something called "sustainable development." There's a social experiment in the Basque region of Spain, in Mondragon. Can you describe that? Have you been there?*

I haven't been there, but I know what you mean.

Mondragon is a basically worker-owned cooperative of a very substantial scale and economically quite successful with many different industries in it, including manufacturing industries of a fairly sophisticated nature. However, remember, it's inserted into a capitalist economy. So it's no more committed to sustainable growth than any other part of the capitalist economy is. Internally it's not worker-controlled. It's manager-controlled. So it has a kind of a mixture of what's sometimes called industrial democracy, that means ownership, at least in principle, by the work force, mixed together with elements of hierarchic domination and control, which means not worker-managed. So it's a mixture. I mentioned before that businesses, say, corporations, are about as close to totalitarian structures, to strict hierarchic structures, as any human institutions are. Something like Mondragon is considerably less so.

Incidentally, before we entirely leave the health-care issue, there's another point that ought to be mentioned. The usual concern is the one that we discussed, namely the fact that all the programs, whether it's from Clinton over to the right, essentially vest power in the hands of huge insurance companies, which means that they will try to micromanage health care to reduce it to the lowest possible level, because naturally they're profit-making. They will also tend away from things like prevention and public health measures, which are not their concern, towards the technical side. It also means that the public has to pay for the enormous inefficiencies involved, such as huge profit, big corporate salaries and other corporate amenities, to big bureaucracy to control in precise detail what doctors and nurses do and don't do. So there are a lot of inefficiencies and inequalities and in my view just immoral elements to it. But that's only one factor.

There's another factor that's rarely discussed. That is that the Clinton program and all others like them are radically regressive. Just ask who pays and how much they pay. In a Canadian-style system, a government insurance system, the costs are distributed as the tax costs are distributed. So to the extent that the tax system is progressive, meaning rich people pay more and in fact pay a higher percentage, which is assumed, correctly, to be the only ethical standard in all the industrial societies, the costs of health care are distributed with heavier costs to the more wealthy.

All the systems being proposed here are radically regressive. They essentially are flat, meaning that a janitor in the corporation and the CEO pay the same amount. That's as if they both paid the same taxes, which is unheard of in any civilized society. That's rarely discussed. If you look at it, it's even worse. It's going to turn out that the janitor will probably pay more. The reason is that the janitor will be living in a poor neighborhood somewhere and the executive will be living in a rich suburb or a downtown highrise, and they will belong to different health groupings. It will turn out the one that the janitor belongs to includes many more poor and high-risk people. The insurance companies will demand higher rates from them than from the executive, who will be from lower-risk wealthier people. So it will turn out that the poor person will probably pay more in the long term. These are just incredible features of any form of social planning. And they're all built into all of these plans. It's very rarely discussed.

DB *Speaking of taxes, there's a new book out by a couple of* Philadelphia Inquirer *reporters called* America: Who Pays the Taxes? *Apparently they are producing evidence in that book which shows that the amount of taxes paid by corporations has dramatically declined in the U.S.*

That's for sure. That's been very striking through the last fifteen years. Actually, the whole tax system is an extremely complex one. People have looked into it for years. Joseph Pechman was one of the leading specialists who pointed out that despite the progressivity that was built into some of the tax system, there are other regressive factors which enter in in all sorts of ways that end up making it very near a fixed percentage.

DB *Let's talk about Richard Nixon briefly. His death generated much fanfare. Henry Kissinger in his eulogy said: "The world is a better place, a safer place because of Richard Nixon." I'm sure he was thinking of Laos, Cambodia and Vietnam. Let's focus on one place that was not mentioned at all in the media hoopla, and that is Chile, and see how it is a "better and safer place." In early September 1970, Salvador Allende was elected President in a democratic election. What were Allende's politics?*

Allende was basically a social democrat, very much of the European character. He would have fit-

293

ted very well into the democratic socialist spectrum in Europe. Chile was a very inegalitarian society. He was calling for redistribution, for help to the poor. He was a doctor, and one of the things he did was to institute a free milk program for half-a-million very poor children to overcome these problems of child malnutrition and deficiency that are the major health issues, as we have been discussing. He called for nationalization of major industries, the major extractive industries, for social regulation, for a policy of international independence, meaning not simply subordination to the U.S., but more of an independent path, programs of that kind, which are not unfamiliar throughout the general social democracy.

DB *Was that a free and democratic election?*

Not entirely, because there were major efforts to disrupt it, mainly by the U.S. That goes way back. For example, in the preceding election, in 1964, in the preparation for that election, which was under Kennedy, and the actual election, which happened to be under Johnson, the U.S. intervened massively to try to prevent Allende from winning. When the Church Committee investigated this years later, it discovered that the per capita expenses for the ultimately winning candidate, the one the U.S. supported, were higher than those of both U.S. candidates, Johnson and Goldwater, in the U.S. elections in the same year. That's a measure of the extent of the U.S. intervention to disrupt the election of 1964.

Similar measures were undertaken in 1970 to try to prevent a free and democratic election. They were very substantial. There were huge amounts of black propaganda about how if Allende won mothers would be sending their children off to Russia to become slaves, and so on. The U.S. threatened to destroy the economy, which it could and in fact did do. So the election was not free and democratic in that sense. There was extensive outside intervention to try to disrupt it.

DB *Nevertheless Allende did win. A few days after his electoral victory, Nixon called in CIA Director Richard Helms, Kissinger, and others for a meeting on Chile. Can you describe what happened?*

That's the meeting of what was called the "40 Committee" that Kissinger chaired. As Helms reported it in his notes, there were two tracks, the soft track and the hard track. The soft track was to "make the economy scream." Those were Nixon's words. The hard line was just to aim for a military coup. These were called track one and track two. Much of this later came out, in part in the Church Committee.

Ambassador Edward Korry, who was a Kennedy-liberal type, was assigned the task of implementing track one, the soft line. Let me quote you his own words as to what track one was: The soft line was to "do all within our power to condemn Chile and the Chileans to utmost deprivation and poverty, a policy designed for a long time to come to accelerate the hard features of a Communist society in Chile." That's the soft line, namely to really make them suffer utmost deprivation and poverty so they'll know from now on they'd better vote the way we tell them. That's the soft Kennedy liberals. The hard line was just to have a military coup.

DB *There was a massive destabilization and disinformation campaign. The CIA planted stories in* El Mercurio *and fomented labor unrest and strikes.*

They really pulled out the stops on this one. Later, when the military coup finally came and the government was overthrown, you had thousands of people being slaughtered, imprisoned, and tortured. Then the U.S. changed its position and gave massive support to the new Pinochet government as a reward for its achievements in reversing Chilean democracy and instituting a murderous terror state of the Brazilian style. So economic aid which had been cancelled immediately began to flow. The U.S. had blocked international aid. That came in. Huge credits were given for wheat. All possible help was given.

The question of torture was brought up to Kissinger by the American Ambassador. Kissinger gave him a sharp lecture, something like, Don't give me any of those political science lectures. We don't care about torture. We care about important things. He also explained what the important things were.

He was concerned, he said, that an Allende success, the success of social democracy in Chile, would be contagious. It would infect southern Europe, like Italy, and lead to the possible success of what was then called Eurocommunism there, meaning the Communist parties were moving in a social democratic direction and hooking up with social democratic parties. Actually, the Kremlin was just as much opposed to that as Kissinger was. So he was afraid that the contagious example of success in Chile under a democratic reformist system would infect places like Italy.

That really tells you what the domino theory is about, very clearly. Even Kissinger, mad as he is, didn't believe that Chilean armies were going to descend on Rome. It wasn't going to be that kind of an influence. The influence would be the demonstration effect of successful economic development, where here the economy doesn't just mean profits for private corporations, but the state of the general population. That's dangerous. If that gets started, it will have a contagious effect. So Kissinger's thinking was quite accurate. Also it's revealing. In those comments he revealed the basic story of U.S. foreign policy for decades.

DB *You see that pattern repeat itself in Nicaragua in the 1980s, the threat of a good example.*

Everywhere. The same was true in Vietnam, in Cuba. It was true of Guatemala, of Greece. Always. That's the basic story: The threat that there will be a contagious effect of successful development.

DB *Kissinger also said, again speaking about Chile, that "I don't see why we should have to stand by and let a country go Communist due to the irresponsibility of its own people."*

This is the *Economist* line, that we should make sure that policy is insulated from politics. If people are irresponsible, they should just be cut out of the system. Kissinger is just an extreme example of what

Jefferson called an "aristocrat," with utter contempt for democracy and complete dedication to service to power.

DB *I'm also reminded of Seymour Hersh's description of Kissinger sitting in the Oval Office while Nixon was ranting and raving about Jews, making very anti-Semitic remarks, and he was just sitting there, saying nothing.*

He was also sitting there while even worse things were being said about blacks, in fact, he was participating in them. The racism of the Nixon administration was appalling. When Nixon gave Kissinger instructions as to how to write his first State of the Union address, according to people there, he said, "Put something in it for the jigs." Kissinger apparently nodded approvingly or quietly. Jigs being blacks.

DB *What about the role of the CIA in a democratic society? Is that an oxymoron?*

You could imagine that a democratic society would have an organization that carries out intelligence gathering functions. But that's a very minor part of what the CIA does. The CIA is mainly a branch of the executive to carry out secret and usually illegal activities that the executive branch wants. It wants them to be kept secret because it knows that the public won't accept them. So it's highly undemocratic even domestically. The activities that it carries out are quite commonly efforts to undermine democracy, as the Chilean case through the

1960s into the early 1970s demonstrates with great clarity. It's by far not the only one. Although we talk about Nixon and Kissinger, similar policies were being carried out by Kennedy and Johnson in the earlier Chilean election.

DB *Is the CIA an instrument of state policy or does it formulate policy?*

You can't be certain. My own view is that the CIA is very much under the control of executive power. I've studied those records fairly extensively in many cases, and there are very rare examples when the CIA undertook initiatives on its own. It often looks as though it's undertaking initiatives on its own, but that's because the executive wants to preserve deniability. The executive branch, say, Kennedy, doesn't want to have documents lying around saying, I told you to murder Lumumba. That's Eisenhower in that case. Or, I told you to overthrow the government of Brazil. They don't want such documents around. Or I wanted you to assassinate Castro. Or whoever it may be. The executive would like to be protected from such exposure. As a result, they try to follow policies of plausible deniability, which means that messages are given to the CIA to do things but without a paper trail, without a record. When the story comes out later it looks as if the CIA is doing things on their own. But if you really trace it through, I think this almost never happens.

DB *Let's stay, in Henry Stimson's words, in "our little region over here which has never bothered anyone," Latin America and the Caribbean. Let's move* *from Chile in the 1960s and 1970s to Haiti in the 1990s. Jean-Bertrand Aristide is elected President in December 1990 in what has been widely described as a free and democratic election. I think he got 67% of the vote. Seven months after taking office he is overthrown in a coup d'état. Do you see any connections there in U.S. policy?*

When Aristide won it was a big surprise. He was swept into power by a network of popular grass roots organizations, what was called *Lavalas*, the flood, which outside observers just weren't aware of. They don't pay attention to what happens among poor people. There had been very extensive and very successful organizing. Out of nowhere came this massive network of organized grass roots popular organizations and managed to sweep their candidate into power. The U.S. expected that its own candidate, a former World Bank official named Marc Bazin, would win the election. He had all the resources and support. It looked like a shoe-in. The U.S. was willing to support a democratic election, figuring that its candidate would easily win. He lost. He got fourteen percent of the vote, and Aristide got about 67%. The only question in anybody's mind at that time should have been, how is the U.S. going to get rid of him, for very much the reasons that Kissinger explained in the case of Chile. That is so uniform and invariant that the basic question was, What will be the method for getting rid of this disaster?

The disaster became even worse in the first months of Aristide's office. During those seven months there were amazing developments. Haiti, of course, is an extremely impoverished country, with

awful conditions. Aristide was nevertheless beginning to get places. He was able to reduce corruption
extensively, to trim a highly bloated state bureaucracy, winning a lot of international praise for this, even
from the international lending institutions, the IMF
and the World Bank, who were offering him loans
and preferential terms because they liked what he
was doing. He was getting independent support outside the U.S. Furthermore, he cut back on drug traf-
ficking. The flow of refugees to the U.S. virtually
stopped. Atrocities were reduced to way below what
they had been or would become. They were very
slight. There was a considerable degree of popular
engagement in what was going on, although the con-
tradictions were already beginning to show up. There
were constraints on what he could do, external constraints.

All of this made the democratic election even
more unfavorable and unacceptable from the point of
view of U.S. policy, and indeed the U.S. moved at
once to try to undermine it through what were naturally called "democracy-enhancing programs." The
U.S., which had never cared at all about centralization of executive power when its own favored dictators were there, all of a sudden became involved in
trying to set up alternative institutions that would
undermine executive power in the interests of
greater democracy. A number of those groups, which
were alleged to be human rights and labor groups,
survived the coup and became the governing author-
ities after the coup. This went on for a couple of
months. On September 30, 1991 the coup came. The
Organization of American States declared an embargo. The U.S. joined it but with obvious reluctance.

The Bush administration was really dragging its feet. It was perfectly obvious. The government focused attention on alleged atrocities or undemocratic activities of Aristide, downplaying the major atrocities that were taking place right then, and the media went along.

While people were getting slaughtered in the streets of Port-au-Prince, the media were concentrating on alleged human rights abuses under the Aristide government, the usual pattern. We're familiar with it. Refugees started fleeing again because the situation was deteriorating so rapidly. The Bush administration blocked them, instituted in effect a blockade to send them back. Within a couple of months, in early February (the embargo was instituted in October), the Bush administration had already undermined the embargo by instituting an exception, namely, that U.S.-owned companies would be permitted to ignore the embargo. The *New York Times* called that "fine-tuning" the embargo to improve the restoration of democracy. The fine-tuning meant that U.S. companies could continue to proceed without any concern for the embargo.

Meanwhile, the U.S., which is known to be able to exert pressure when it feels like it, found no way to influence anyone else to observe the embargo, including the Dominican Republic next door. The whole thing was mostly a farce. Pretty soon Marc Bazin, the U.S. candidate, was in power as Prime Minister, with the ruling generals behind him. That year, 1992, U.S. trade with Haiti continued not very far below the norm despite the so-called embargo.

During the 1992 campaign Clinton bitterly attacked the Bush administration for its inhuman policy of returning refugees to this torture chamber, which is incidentally not only inhuman but also in flat violation of the Universal Declaration of Human Rights, which we claim to uphold. He announced that he was going to really change all this stuff. His first act as elected President, even before he took office, was to make the Bush blockade even harsher. He imposed even harsher measures to force fleeing refugees back into this hellhole. Ever since then it's simply been a matter of seeing what kind of finessing will be carried out to ensure that the popularly elected government doesn't come back into office. It only has another year and a half to run, so they've more or less won that game. Meanwhile the terror increases. The atrocities increase. The popular organizations are getting decimated. People are suffering.

U.S. trade meanwhile continues and in fact went up by about 50% under Clinton under the so-called embargo. In fact, Haiti, which is a starving island, is exporting food to the U.S., fruit and nuts, under the Clinton administration. This went up by a factor of about thirty-five under Clinton as compared with Bush. Baseballs are coming along nicely. This means women are working in U.S.-owned factories where, if they meet their quota, they get ten cents an hour. Since they don't usually meet their quota, their wages go down to something like five cents an hour. They don't last in it very long. Softballs in the U.S. are advertised as being unusually good because they're hand-dipped into whatever it is that makes them hang together properly. They're hand dipped by Haitian women into toxic substances with obvious effect. The work conditions are indescribable.

All of this continues, in fact has increased,

under Clinton. Meanwhile, the conditions for forcibly returning refugees have gotten much harsher. The terror and the torture have increased. The U.S. tried for a long time to get Aristide to "broaden his government in the interests of democracy." Broaden the government is a phrase which means throw out the two-thirds of the population that voted for you. They're the wrong kind of people. And bring in what are called "moderate" elements of the business community, those who don't think you just ought to slaughter everybody and cut them to pieces and cut their faces off and leave them in ditches. Those are the extremists. The moderates think you ought to have them working in your assembly plants for fourteen cents an hour under conditions of the kind I described. Those are the moderates. So bring them in and give them power and then we'll have a real democracy. But unfortunately, Aristide, being kind of backward and disruptive and the whole series of bad words, has not been willing to go along with that. Therefore the U.S. has failed in its efforts to broaden the government and restore the democratic system.

This policy has gotten so cynical and outrageous that Clinton has lost almost all major domestic support on it. Even the mainstream press is denouncing him at this point. So there will have to be some cosmetic changes made. But unless there's an awful lot of popular pressure, these policies will continue in one way or another, and pretty soon we'll have the moderates in power. Then they'll even be able to run a democratic election, if people are sufficiently intimidated, popular organizations are sufficiently destroyed, and people get it beaten into their heads that either you accept the rule of those with the guns and the gold-plated Cadillacs or else you suffer in unrelieved misery. Once people understand that, you can have a democratic election and it will all come out the right way. Everybody will cheer.

DB *In this period of Aristide's exile, he has been asked to make concessions to the junta, to Cédras and François.*

And the right-wing business community.

DB *This is kind of curious. For the victim, the aggrieved party, to make concessions to his victimizer.*

It's perfectly understandable. The U.S. was strongly opposed to the Aristide government. It had entirely the wrong base of support and power. What he is supposed to do is to cede power to those who count. The U.S. has no particular interest in Cédras and François, but it does have a lot of interest in the sectors of the business world that are linked to American corporations. I mean the people who are the local owners or managers of those textile and baseball-producing plants. Those who are linked up with U.S. agribusiness. Those are the people who are supposed to be in power everywhere. When they're not in power it's not democratic and we therefore have to make concessions to bring them into power.

DB *Let's say Aristide is "restored." But given the destruction of popular organization and the devastation of civil society, what are his and the country's* *prospects?*

Some of the closest observation of this has been done by Human Rights Watch, the Americas Watch branch of it. Back over a year ago they came out with a good report in which they described what was going on. They gave their own answer to that question, which I thought was plausible. They said that things are reaching the point (this is over a year ago) that even if Aristide were restored, the lively, vibrant civil society based on grass-roots organizations that had brought him to power would have been so decimated that it's unlikely that he would have the popular support to do anything anyway. I don't know if that's true or not. Nobody knows, any more than anyone knew how powerful those groups were in the first place. Human beings have reserves of courage that are often hard to imagine. But I think that's the plan. The idea is to try to decimate the organizations, to intimidate people sufficiently that it won't matter if you have democratic elections.

There was an interesting conference run by the Jesuits in El Salvador. Its final report came out in January of this year. They discussed questions of this kind. This is several months before the Salvadoran elections. They were talking about the buildup to the elections. They did discuss, as a lot of people did, the ongoing terror which was substantial and which was plainly designed to keep up front in people's minds that you better vote the right way or else. But they also pointed out something else which is much more important. That had to do with the long-term effects of terror. And they've had plenty of experience with this. The long-term effects of terror, they said, are simply to "domesticate people's aspirations" and to reduce their aspirations to those of the powerful and the privileged. Terror instills into people's minds the idea that there is no alternative. Drive out any hope. Domesticate aspirations. Subordinate yourself to the powerful. Once that achievement has been reached, perhaps by massive and horrifying terror, as in El Salvador, after that you can run democratic elections without too much fear.

DB *The U.S. refugee policy is in stark contrast. You mentioned it briefly. Cuban refugees are considered political and are accepted immediately into the U.S., while Haitian refugees are termed economic and are refused entry.*

That's determined by ESP, since they never check with them. In fact, if you look at the records, people who are being refused asylum suffer enormous persecution. Just a couple of weeks ago there were two interesting leaks from the Immigration and Naturalization Service, INS. One is a Haitian desk officer who was discovered by Dennis Bernstein at KPFA, who interviewed him. He had been working in the Port-au-Prince embassy. He described how they were not even making the most perfunctory efforts to check the credentials of people who were applying for political asylum because they don't want them. At about the same time there was a leak of a document from Cuba, from the U.S. interests section in Havana, which checks asylum, complaining about the fact that they can't find genuine political asylum cases. The people who are claiming asylum can't

307

really claim serious persecutions by international or even U.S. standards. At most they claim various kinds of harassment that wouldn't qualify them. They're worried about this. So here are the two cases, side by side. I should mention that the U.S. Justice Department has just made a slight change in U.S. law which makes the violation of international law and the Universal Declaration of Human Rights even more grotesque. It has just determined that Haitian refugees who reach U.S. territorial waters, by some miracle, can also be shipped back. That's never been allowed before. I doubt that any other industrial country allows that.

DB *Do you have a few more minutes?*

I'm afraid I have another appointment. They are probably trying to get on the line right now.

DB *OK. Let's wind it up. Thanks a lot. Talk to you soon.*

Index

A

Achbar, Mark, 161, 241
Adams, Gerry, 171
Adams, John Quincy, 87
Aetna Life Insurance, 194
Africa debt service, 220
Africa Watch, 73-74
Aidid, Mohammad Farah, 74
air-traffic controllers' strike, 29
airline industry, 269
Albert, Mike, 170
Allende, Salvador, 187, 293-296
Alperovitz, Gar, 35-36, 37
Alternative Radio, 173, 187
America: Who Pays the Taxes, 293
American Steelworkers Union, 33
Americas Watch, 221, 306
Amin, Samir, 108
Amnesty International, 133, 176
Apple, R.W., 197
Arab League, 61-62
Aristide, Jean-Bertrand, 300-302, 304, 305, 306
aristocrats and democrats, 243-245, 298
Arkan (Zeljko Raznjatovic), 81
Asia, East and capitalism, 19-20
Asia Pacific Summit, 232, 240
Asia,environment vs. economy, 190-191

B

Bacques, James: *Other Losses*, 224
Bakunin, Mikhail, 244
Barbie, Klaus, 226-227
Barre, Siad, 69-70, 74
Bazin, Marc, 300, 302
Beloff, Nora, 79
Bengal, India, 85-86
Bernard, Elaine, 191, 192, 195
Bernstein, Dennis, 307
biotechnology and patents, 10-11
biotechnology industry, 39
birth control and education, 54

Black male incarceration, 21-22
Boeing Aerospace Co., 240, 269
Bolivian economy, 50-52
Boston City Hospital, 52-53
Boston Globe acquisition, 147-148, 150-151
Boston Globe and Vietnam, 154-155
Boulder Daily Camera, 183-184
Boutrous-Ghali, Boutrous, 75
Boyer, Paul: *When Time Shall Be No More*, 262
Bradley Foundation, 264
Brazil, 7, 180, 181, 186
breast cancer, 286-287
Bretton Woods, 5, 6, 13, 19, 204
Burnham, William Dean, 263
Bush, George
  intervention policy, 65
  Iran-Contra pardons, 81-82
  Japan visit, 16-17
  jobs=profits, 107-108
  and Saddam Hussein, 61-62
  and Somalia, 71, 75-76
business. *see* corporations

C

California educational system, 40
Cambodian refugees, 223-224
Cambridge, MA, killing of student in, 100
camel and scorpion story, 94-95
Camp David negotiations, 135-136
Canada, employment in, 15-16, 49
Canada-U.S. free-trade agreement, 15-16, 45
Canadian Health Care System, 15, 16, 192, 276, 278
"Canadian-Style" health care. *see also* health care system, U.S.; insurance companies and health care; single payer program, Canadian style
"Canadian-style" health care, 114-115

cancer research, 286-287
capital, internationalization of, 12-13
capital, unregulated financial, 204
capital and growth rate, 182-183
capital flight, 20
capital punishment, 176
capitalism, crisis of, 19-20, 68
capitalism and environment, 25-26
capitalist systems, 23-25, 37
Carnegie, Andrew, 33-34, 99
Carothers, Thomas, 234-235
Caterpillar Inc., 29, 34
Cédras, Raoul, 305
Central America, 151
Central American solidarity movement, 157-158
Chetniks, 78-79
Chiapas rebellion, 209-210, 213-214
Chicago underground tunnels, 31
Chile, 52, 186, 293-297
China, 91, 232
Chomsky, Noam
  boxing anecdote, 99-100
  Chiapas article, 213
  Chronicles of Dissent, 200
  death threats, 142-144
  Letters from Lexington, 169
  mail, 160, 161-162, 173
  Manufacturing Consent, 223
  New York Times, 141-142
  origin of name, 170-171
  Philadelphia A's, 270-271
  Political Economy of Human Rights, 225
  Rethinking Camelot, 59
  Senate Foreign Relations Committee, 141
  Turning the Tide, 189-190
  Wall Street Journal fantasy, 28-29
  Year 501, 59, 61
Church Committee (U.S. Senate), 294, 295
CIA (Central Intelligence Agency), 231-

232, 296, 298-299
Clark, Miss, 270-271
class and race, 105, 109-110
classical intervention, 64-65
Clinton, Bill
  CEO of corporate America, 116-117
  Haiti policy, 302-304
  pro-business, 196-197
  social initiative, 215
Clinton administration
  NAFTA and GATT, 48
  pro-Israeli bias, 129-130
coca exports, 51
Codevilla, Angelo, 92
colonialism, settler, 172
colonialism and racism, 93
communications system, democratic, 251
competition and cooperation, 98-99
competitive ethic, 98-99
computer networks, 148
Congressional Trade Act (1947), 46
conspiracy theories, 162-163
consumption, artifically induced, 290
cooperation and competition, 98-99
corporate mercantilism, 12, 49
corporations, 245, 246, 280
  Adam Smith's views, 249
  beneficial effects of, 197
  fascist structures, 123
  government intervention, 268-270
  as monopolies, 119
  power flow, 237-238
  taxes paid by, 293
  U.S. based, 36-37
crime, increase in, 179
crime and violence, 281-282, 284
crime bill, U.S., 175, 214-215
Croatia, 79

D

Daimler-Benz Ag., 217-218

Index

de Dias Parra, Juan, 179-180
de Haan, Jacob, 140
de Waal, Alex, 74
debt crisis and Third World, 167, 220
democracy, definition of, 234-235
democracy, formal, 242-246
democracy, industrial, 291
democracy and family structure, 249-251
democracy and media, 251
democracy assistance project, 234
democrats and aristocrats, 243-245
deportations, 131, 133
deregulation, 103
Dewey, John, 245-246, 247
drug epidemic, 51, 221-222
drug trade, 198-199
Duff, Peggy, 225-226

E

East Asia and capitalism, 19-20
Eastern Airlines and unions, 268
Eatwell, John, 183
economics, enterprise, 106-107
economics, entrepreneurial, 267
economics, neo-classical, 49
economics, rational, 26-28
Economist (London), 27, 277
economy, global, 47-48, 167, 203-205
education, public, 128
Egypt, 163-166
eight-hour work day, 284-285
electronic technology, 148
embargo on Haiti, 301-302
enterprise economics, 106-107
environment and capitalism, 25-26
environmental crises, 55
Environmental News Network, 15
environmental protection, 48
Environmental Protection Agency standards, 45
Europe, 56, 58, 90-91

European Community, 9, 47, 56-57
exports=intrafirm transfers, 236

F

fair-trade practices, 17
family structure and democracy, 249-251
Farah, Douglas, 151
fascist tendencies in U.S., 236-237
Ferguson, Thomas, 235-236
Financial Times (London), 36, 117, 168, 186-187, 191, 203, 204
Fischer, Louis, 83
food, economy of, 50
Ford Motor Co., 216, 238
Foreign Relations Committee (U.S. Senate), 141
Foxman, Abraham, 137, 138
François, Joseph Michel, 305
Fraser, Doug, 30
free-market system, 8, 49, 102-103, 167-168, 268
free-trade, 239-240
free-trade agreement,Canada-U.S., 15-16, 45
Friedman, Thomas, 63
From the Sea (White Paper), 72
Frum, David, 141, 142
Fulbright, J. William, 141
fundamentalism, Islamic, 134, 263
fundamentalism in U.S., 125-127
fundamentalist media, 126-127
fundamentalist society, 262, 263

G

Galbraith, James, 212
Gandhi, Mahatma, 82-84
GATT
  benefits, 184
  economic structure, 9-11
  and environment, 45-46
  free trade agreement, 238-239
  and job losses, 15

311

and managed trade, 12
  resistence to, 209
  secret decisions, 46, 47, 209
Gehlen, Reinhard, 227-228
General Agreement on Tariffs and
  Trade. *see* GATT
General Motors, 36, 43-44, 219
Germany, 57-58
global warming, 54, 188-189
Golden, Tim, 210
Gore-Perot television debate, 208
government as enemy, 177-178
grace, paradox of, 97
Great Britain and International
  Monetary Fund, 8
Greider, William, 42
Grenada intervention, U.S., 76-77
growth rates and capital, 182-183
gun control, 176-177, 178, 199-200
Gypsies, 58

H

Haan, Jacob de, 140
Ha'aretz (Israel), 131
Haiti, 300-308
Hamas, 134, 135
Hattori, Yoshihiro, 169
health care system, U.S., 114-115, 194,
  274-278, 291, 292. *see also* Canadian-
  style health care; single-payer pro-
  gram, Canadian style
Helms, Richard, 295
Herman, Edward, 159-160, 223, 225
Herman, Edward: *Demonstration
  Elections*, 115
Hersh, Seymour, 298
Hersi, Mohammed, 74
Himmelstein, David, 276
Hoagland, Eric, 154
Homestead, Pa. strike, 33, 34, 99
Honduras and Miskitos Indians, 221-
  222

human nature, 95-98
human rights, U.S. aid and, 159-160
human rights in China, 232-233
Human Rights Watch, 306
humanitarian assistance, United States,
  72-73
Humboldt, Wilhelm von, 247
Hume, David, 112, 127
Hussein, Saddam, 61-64

I

India, 84-89
Indian Removal Act, 77. *see also* Native
  Americans
industrial policy, 37-38, 39
Indyk, Martin, 129
information, access to, 156-158
information highway, 252, 259-260
insurance companies, threats from U.S.,
  15
insurance companies and health care,
  115, 275, 291, 292
intellectual community, 163-165, 244
intellectual property rights, 10
International Monetary Fund, 5, 6-8, 9,
  50, 51, 301
Internet communications, 254, 261
intervention, classical, 64-65
intervention, humanitarian, 77
intifada, 134, 138, 140
investment theory of politics, 235-236
investors and investment decisions, 121-
  123
Iran-Contra pardons, 81-82
Iraq, bombing of, 61
Iraqi Kurds vs. Turkish Kurds, 89-90
Ireland, 93, 171-173, 220
Islamic fundamentalism, 134, 263
Islamic movement, 165-166
Israel, 62, 129-139
Italy and resistance, 230-231

Index

J

Jackson, Jesse, 16
Jakobson, Roman, 170
Japan, 17, 18-19, 24, 43
Jay, John, 247
Jefferson, Thomas, 111, 243-245, 247
Jews and collective suicide, 83-84
jobs=profits, 17, 107-108
Jones, Mother, 34
journalism. *see* media headings
Joyce, Michael, 264

K

Kennan, George, 231
Kennedy, John F., 60, 64-65, 196, 197
Kenya, 70
Kerry, John F., 223
Keynes, John Maynard, 5
The Killing Fields (film), 224
Kirkpatrick, Jeane, 221
Kissinger, Henry, 293, 295, 296-297, 298
knowledge as a commodity, 155-156
Knox, Henry, 87
Kofsky, Frank, 269
Kolko, Gabriel: *Politics of War*, 232
Kondratieff cycles (economics), 199
Korry, Edward, 295
Krugman, Paul, 216
Kurds, 63, 89-90

L

Labor Advisory Committee, 46, 47
labor and NAFTA, 207-208
labor-based party, 191-192
Labor Committee Intelligence Service, 144
labor market, flexible, 239-240
labor unions. *see* unions
Lake, Anthony, 233-234
Lancet (British), 105, 287
LaRouche, Lyndon, 142-143
Lasswell, Harold, 244
Latin America, 7, 20, 50-52, 180-181. *see*
also names of individual countries
Lebanon, Palestinian deportees in, 131
left, the (U.S.), 120-121, 163, 164-165, 256
Lewis, Anthony, 179, 181, 182, 184, 192, 193, 194
liberalism, classical, 247, 248
Liberty (U.S. ship), 62
Lippmann, Walter, 243, 245
lobbying, corporate and labor, 193-194
Lombard League (Italy), 59
Long, Huey, 124
Lorenzo, Frank, 268
Los Angeles, South Central, 213-214

M

MacNeil-Lehrer News Hour, 257-258
Mahdi, Ali, 74
malnutrition clinic, Boston, 52-53
managed competition, 275
managed trade, 12, 17, 49
Mandate for Change, 106, 118, 266-267
Manufacturing Consent (film), 161, 241
maquiladora, 43
marijuana, criminalization of, 198
Markusen, Ann: *Dismantling the Cold
War Economy*, 41
May Day, 284, 285-286
Mazzocchi, Tony, 191, 192, 195
McChesney, Bob: *Telecommunications,
Mass Media and Democracy*, 251, 252
McClintock, Michael: *Instruments of
Statecraft*, 228
media, 177-178
media, fundamentalist, 126-127
media and democracy, 251
media and information transfer, 156-157
media and scholarship balance, 150-155
media ownership, 148
Menchu, Rigoberta, 92-93
Mexico
  economic miracle, 44
  effects of NAFTA, 44-45, 185-186

intrafirm transfers, 238
NAFTA opposition, 210-211, 212
unions, 44, 215-216
Milam, Lorenzo, 254-255
military spending, 39
Miskitos Indians, 221-222
Mondale, Walter, 30-31
Mondragon, Spain, 290-291
Morgan (Mohammed Hersi), 74
Mother Jones, 34
multinational firms, 13

N

NAFTA
consequences, 44-46, 102, 184-186
free trade agreement, 238-239
labor contributions, 193
labor tactics, 207-208
and low wages, 216
media coverage, 207-209, 210
pro-active critiques, 211-213
resistance to, 206
secret decisions, 46-47
Nash, Nathaniel, 187
Nasser, Gamal Abdel, 166
Nasser, Sylvia, 26
National Bureau of Standards and
Technology, 270
National Caucus of Labor Committees,
142-143
National Public Radio, 256-257
National Security Council Report, 231
Native Americans, extermination of, 35,
77-78, 87
natural food movement, 288
natural sciences, 150, 152
Navarro, Vicente, 105, 275, 278, 279
Nazi war criminals in U.S., 226-228, 229
Nehru, Jawaharlal : *The Discovery of
India*, 87
New Deal period, 236
New York Times, 33, 153, 302

acquisiton, *Boston Globe*, 150-151
Chile elections, 186, 191
on environment, 25-26
on labor, 34-35
and Mexico, 210
and NAFTA, 184-185, 193, 194
paradox of 1992, 103
quoting Chomsky, 141-142
U.S. fiscal policy, 30
New York Times Magazine, 52
Nicaragua, 219, 221
Niebuhr, Reinhold, 96-97
Nixon, Richard, 7, 82, 293, 295, 298
no-fly zone, 64, 65
non-violence philosophy, 82-83
North Africans in Spain, 58-59
North American Free Trade Agreement.
see NAFTA
nuclear power, 288-289

O

Omaar, Rakiya, 73
Operation Mop-Up, 143
Operation Paper Clip, 226
Operation Restore Hope, 69
organic food movement, 288
Organization of American States, 301
organize, call to, 112-114, 149, 189-190,
195, 242
Orwell, George, 82, 84

P

paradox of grace, 97
patents and biotechnology, 10-11
Pechman, Joseph, 293
Pentagon and Somalia, 70
Pentagon system, 38, 41, 71, 269, 270,
289
Peretz, Martin, 141
Perkins, Frances, 34
Perot, Ross, 57, 117, 206-207, 208, 210,
212
Pinochet, Augusto, 296

Index

PLO (Palestine Liberation Organization), 136
Poland, 277
policy or politics, 277, 297
political arena, public, 264-266
politics, investment theory of, 235-236
politics or policy, 277, 297
population, control of, 127-128
population limitation, 53-54
Powell, Colin, 70
POWs, American, 223, 224
POWs, British treatment of, 225-226
POWs, U.S. treatment of, 224-225
Presley, Elvis (stamp), 116
prison labor in China, 233
prisoners dilemma (game theory), 113
prisons, United States, 22
production, internationalization of, 204-205
Progressive Policy Institute: *Mandate for Change*, 106, 118
property rights vs. working rights, 46, 47
prostate cancer, 286-287
public arena of politics, 264-266
Public Broadcasting System, 254, 256-257
public health issues, 286-288, 291
public radio, 252-254

Q

Qaddafi, Muammar, 62

R

rabble defined, 242
Rabin, Itzhak, 137-139
race and class, 105, 109-110
race and racism, 93-96, 135
radio, control of, 251-256
Raskin, Marc, 144
rational/irrational market policies, 26-28
Rauff, Walter, 227

Raznjatovic, Zeljko, 81
Reagan, Ronald, 17, 29, 30-31, 221
reforms, UNESCO study on, 219-220
refugees, Cuban, 307-308
refugees, Haitian, 302-304
religious attitudes, American, 125-126, 262-263
Republican convention (1992), 124
resistance movement, anti-fascist, 229-230
"restless many," 111-112
retraining programs, U.S., 217
right-to-work laws, 16
Rishmawi, Mona, 132
Romero, Federico, 230
Russell, Bertrand, 144-145
Rustin, Bayard, 281-282

S

Sachs, Jeffrey, 50
Sadat, Anwar, 166
Sagan, Carl, 55
Sahnoun, Mohammed, 75
El Salvador elections, 306-307
Schanberg, Sidney, 222-224
Schlesinger, Arthur, 60
scholarship and media balance, 150-155
Schor, Juliet:*The Overworked American*, 285
Schoultz, Lars, 160
Schwarzkopf, Norman, 63
Science (journal), 188
sciences, 150-152, 156
scorpion and camel story, 94-95
Second Amendment, 176-177
Security Council resolutions (U.N.), 130-131
security zone, 135-137
Serbia, 79-81
settler colonialism, 172
Shahak, Israel, 247
Shamir, Yitzhak, 140

Sharon, Ariel, 138-139

Shiites, 63

Simon, Bob, 61

Simpson, Chris: *Blowback*, 226

single-payer health care, California, 279

single-payer program, Canadian style, 274-276, 292. *see also* Canadian Health Care System; health care system, U.S.; insurance companies and health care

Skidelsky, Robert, 236-237

Smith, Adam, 86, 109, 111, 123-124, 127, 248-249

Snow, C.P., 152

social conditioning, 100-101

social contract, 205, 206

social contract, Europe, 43

social control, U.S., 22-23

social policy, U.S., 175-176

Solarz, Steven, 133-134

Solow, Bob, 41

Somalia, 38, 69, 70, 73-76, 92

South Central Los Angeles, 213-214

South Lebanon Army, 136-137

Soviet Union and Security Council, 68

Spain, 58-59

sports, role of, 128, 258-261

Stark (U.S. ship)

state industrial policy, 71

Stimson, Henry, 299

Stockman, David, 42

Summers, Lawrence, 26, 27

Supreme Court appointments, 118-119

sustainable development, 290-291

T

technology, communications, 254

technology, interactive, 259-261

telecommunications, 14, 204

television, commercialized, 253, 255, 256

Thatcher, Margaret, 205-206

Third World

  capital loans, 7, 8, 103

  development, 5

  economics, 10

  and imperialism, 85, 92

  model, 101-102, 103

  rational market policies, 26-28

Third World Resurgence (Malaysia), 209

Thompson, E.P.: *The Making of the English Working Class*, 264

trade, centrally managed, 49

Trevelyan, Charles, 85

tribalism, 55-57

Turkish Kurds vs. Iraqi Kurds, 89-90

U

Umm Qasr, 67

UNESCO study on reforms, 219-220

unions, 185-186

  health care provision, 191-192

  Homestead strike, 33-34

  Mexican, 44, 215-216

  and social contracts, 43

  U.S. workforce, 29-30

United Auto Workers, 29, 30, 34

United Nations, 65-69

United States

  aid and human rights, 159-160

  class and race, 57, 105-106, 108-109, 121

  debt, 42, 119-120, 121

  defense expenditures, 11

  economy, 38-39, 71

  foreign policy, 297

  and GATT, 9-10

  health care system, 114-115, 194, 274-278

  hunger in, 52-53

  international trade, 14

  intervention policy, 72-73

  mid-east policy, 63-64

  political parties, 117-118

  race. *see* class and race

  refugee policy, 302-304, 307-308

Index

resource consumption rate, 289-290
social breakdown, 168-169
social control, 21-23
society and culture, 279-281
state industrial policy, 37-38, 39
Third Worldization, 101-102, 283
trade deficit, 14
and United Nations, 66, 67, 130, 132
Universal Declaration of Human Rights, 303, 308
U.S.-Israeli alliance, 129-130
Ustasha, 78-79

V

Vietnam and media, 155
violence, European culture of, 90-91
violence and crime, 281-282, 284
Volkswagon Co., 216, 219
von Humboldt, Wilhelm, 247

W

Waal, Alex de, 74
wages and working conditions, U.S., 206, 217-218, 283-284
Wall Street Journal, 40, 41, 54, 92, 121, 196
war criminals, 81
Washington Institute for Near East Studies, 129
Washington Post, 151, 153, 159, 213
Weizman, Chaim, 134
Whalen, J.A.: *Appeal to Reason*, 119
Wicker, Tom, 256
Wilson, Woodrow, and Haiti, 64
Wintonick, Peter, 161, 241
Woolhandler, Steffie, 276
work conditions, 285
workers, skilled, 40-41
working poor, 283
working rights vs. property rights, 46, 47
World Bank, 301
  accountability, 9
  Latin America study, 180

market economy, 50
  pollution plans, 25-28
  Third World programs, 5-6, 8
World Court, 132
World Policy Review, 212
Worldwatch, 53

XY

Yaseen, Sheikh, 134
Yeltsin, Boris, 197-198
Yugoslavia, 78

Z

Zionist movement, 139-140

Tapes Available

Since its inception Alternative Radio has made a special effort to record and archive Noam Chomsky's lectures and interviews. For a complete listing of AR's Chomsky holdings, request a catalogue:

Alternative Radio, P.O. Box 551, Boulder, Colorado 80306 TEL 1-800-444-1977 ar@orci.com
www.freespeech.org/alternativeradio

"U.S. Human Rights Policy: Rhetoric & Practice", May 10, 1998, Two tapes, $24.

"Activist Victories," May 10, 1998, $24.

"The Multilateral Agreement on Investment," March 6, 1998, $12.

"Understanding Ourselves," November 3, 1997, $12.

"Hope Springs Eternal," November 12, 1997. Three tapes, $36.

"Social Change: From the '60s to the '90s," with Kathleen Cleaver, October 16, 1997. Two tapes, $24.

"An Inquiry into Global Capitalism," October 3, 1997, $12.

"The U.S. and Israel Strategic Alliance," September 24, 1997. Two tapes, $24.

"The Culture of Terrorism," March 3, 1997. Two tapes, $24.

"The Triumph of the Market," March 4, 1997. Two tapes, $24.

"The Cold War and the University," with Howard Zinn, February 20, 1997, $12.

"Propaganda and Control of the Public Mind," February 7, 1997. Two tapes, $24.

"The Myth of the Free Market," April 13, 1996, $12.

Special Offer

$185 for the entire package of twenty-one tapes. Price includes shipping for the U.S. only. Please add $10 for all other countries. Prepaid orders only. Visa and MasterCard accepted. Phone orders call 1-800-444-1977.